lonely planet

AUSTRALIA

Sarah Reid, Andrew Bain, Rosamund Brennan,
Emmylou Dzubiel, Charles Rawlings-Way, Steve Waters

Meet our writers

BENNY MARTY/SHUTTERSTOCK

Andrew Bain

Andrew is a travel writer who was drawn to Tasmania almost 20 years ago by the siren call of its outdoor opportunities.

Rosamund Brennan

@rosamundbrennan

Based in Fremantle, Western Australia, Rosamund is a freelance journalist focusing on travel, culture and society. If there's a story buried in the bush, hidden in the archives, or carved into an ancient rockface, she will gladly find it.

Emmylou Dzubiel

@emmylou.marie

Emmylou is a Perth-based writer who finds her flow state when hiking serene landscapes, developing recipes and sharing languages.

Charles Rawlings-Way

@crawlingsway

Chares is an ordinary swimmer but loves beaches – even just for a moody stroll on a rainy afternoon. He was born in Devon, grew up in Hobart, and is back in Hobart again after 25 years of adventures elsewhere.

Previous spread Manly Beach (p66), Sydney

CKTRAVELS.COM/SHUTTERSTOCK

Torres Strait
Thursday Island
Cape York
PAPUA NEW GUINEA
SOLOMON ISLANDS
Nhulunbuy
Arnhem Land
Weipa
Groote Eylandt
Cape York Peninsula
CORAL SEA
Gulf of Carpentaria
Great Barrier Reef
Cooktown
Port Douglas
Cairns
Normanton
Innisfail
Ingham
Townsville
Charters Towers
Mt Isa
Cloncurry
Bowen
Airlie Beach
Whitsunday Islands
SOUTH PACIFIC OCEAN
Flinders River
Mackay
Winton
Longreach
Barcaldine
Rockhampton
Gladstone
QUEENSLAND
Great Dividing Range
Simpson Desert
Birdsville
Bundaberg
K'gari
Hervey Bay
Charleville
Lake Eyre North
Noosa Heads
Maroochydore
Brisbane & Coastal Queensland 134
Toowoomba
Brisbane
St George
Surfers Paradise
Byron Bay
Lake Torrens
Bourke
Flinders Ranges
Grafton
Broken Hill
Darling River
Port Augusta
Tamworth
Coffs Harbour
NEW SOUTH WALES
Nyngan
Whyalla
Port Macquarie
Dubbo
Eyre Peninsula
Port Stephens
Lord Howe Island
Bathurst
Mildura
Newcastle
Adelaide
Port Lincoln
Hay
Sydney
Wagga Wagga
Goulburn
Sydney & Coastal New South Wales 44
Murray Bridge
Swan Hill
Wollongong
Murray River
CANBERRA
Kangaroo Island
Horsham
Batemans Bay
Albury
VICTORIA
Mt Gambier
Ballarat
Melbourne
Warrnambool
Geelong
Melbourne & Victoria 96
TASMAN SEA
King Island
Bass Strait
Flinders Island
Devonport
Launceston
Tasmania 184
Queenstown
TASMANIA
Hobart

Feast on fresh seasonal seafood paired with sophisticated local wines. Live ancient stories told through Aboriginal art. Meet an iconic Australian animal – or a few. Traverse the crimson outback. Sip barista-made coffee while exploring laneway street art. Find a treasure at a local market. Take the road trip of a lifetime. Have a remote beach all to yourself. Marvel at the biodiversity of blockbuster marine ecosystems. Journey beyond where the paved road ends.

This is Australia.

TURN THE PAGE AND START PLANNING YOUR NEXT BEST TRIP →

INDONESIA
SAVU SEA
TIMOR SEA
Melville Island
Cobourg Peninsula
Bathurst Island
Darwin
Jabiru
Kakadu National Park
Cape Londonderry
Joseph Bonaparte Gulf
Victoria River
Katherine
Mataranka
Wyndham
Kununurra
Cape Leveque
The Kimberley
Daly Waters
INDIAN OCEAN
Derby
Fitzroy Crossing
Fitzroy River
Broome
Halls Creek
Darwin & the Northern Territory 278
Tennant Creek
NORTHERN TERRITORY
Port Hedland
Karratha
The Pilbara
North West Cape
MacDonnell Ranges
Exmouth
Gibson Desert
Alice Springs
Newman
Ningaloo Reef
Little Sandy Desert
Yulara
Uluru-Kata Tjuta National Park
Carnarvon
Shark Bay
WESTERN AUSTRALIA
Great Victoria Desert
Marla
Mt Magnet
SOUTH AUSTRALIA
Coober Pedy
Geraldton
Nullarbor Plain
Perth & Western Australia 234
Kalgoorlie - Boulder
Eucla
Ceduna
Norseman
Great Australian Bight
Perth
Fremantle
Wagin
Bunbury
Esperance
Margaret River
Albany
Adelaide & South Australia 212
SOUTHERN OCEAN
0 500 km
0 250 miles

Kangaroos, Northern Territory

Sarah Reid

@sarahreidtravels

Sarah is a Byron Bay–based travel journalist and positive-impact travel advocate. She's a big fan of exploring Australia – even her own backyard – with Indigenous guides.

Steve Waters

Steve has been travelling, hiking, volunteering in, working in, and writing about northern Western Australia for over 15 years.

Contents

CHAMELEONSEYE/SHUTTERSTOCK

Snorkelling, Great Barrier Reef (p176)

Acknowledgement of Country

Lonely Planet would like to acknowledge all First Nations people throughout this country, who have nurtured and maintained the land since time immemorial. This guide was written on, and is written about, the lands of many diverse nations.

We recognise the unique and ongoing connection that Aboriginal peoples have to land and waters and thank them for their efforts to preserve them. We pay our respects to Elders past and present and extend this respect to any Aboriginal or Torres Strait Islander people who may be reading this guide.

We also recognise the ongoing efforts of Aboriginal peoples for reconciliation, justice, and social, cultural and economic self-determination. Sovereignty was never ceded. Australia always was, and always will be, Aboriginal land.

Cultural Sensitivity Warning

Aboriginal and Torres Strait Islander readers are advised that this guide may contain names and images of people who have since passed away.

The Great Barrier Reef has more than 600 coral species.

There are more than 35 ocean pools in Sydney, carved out of the rock face.

Humpback whales travel up to 10,000km on their annual migration from Antarctica to the East Coast.

AQUATIC ESCAPADES

With over 10,000 beaches across the country, the Australian coastline was made for fun in, on and around the water. From snorkelling in the Great Barrier Reef to surfing the legendary point breaks of NSW, chasing waterfalls in coastal forests and watching whales frolic along the coast, the region is ripe for aquatic pleasures. Get ready to dive in!

Left Diving, Great Barrier Reef (p176)
Right Humpback whale, Queensland
Below Stingray, Hamelin Bay (p258)

→ WHALE WATCHING

May to November is peak whale-watching season across the east and west coasts of Australia, as pods of whales travel to warmer waters to mate and calve.

UWE BERGWITZ/SHUTTERSTOCK

★ GREAT BARRIER BEAUTY

Australia's coastline is littered with shipwrecks. Great snorkelling spots include the *Omeo* shipwreck just off Perth's coast.

▸ Learn more about the *Omeo* shipwreck on p249

RIGHT: YVES DEHOUCK/SHUTTERSTOCK; LEFT: JEFF HUNTER/GETTY IMAGES

↑ AN ARRAY OF RAYS

Home to smooth stingrays, black stingrays and eagle rays, WA's Hamelin Bay is the place to go if you love rays.

▸ For more on Hamelin Bay see p258

Best Experiences on Water

Marvel at the sheer size of the Great Barrier Reef as fish surround you. (p176)

Swim alongside whale sharks in WA's Ningaloo Marine Park. (p266)

Dive with grey nurse sharks at NSW's South West Rocks. (p78)

Cruise the islands of the Whitsundays on a barefoot charter. (p166)

Roll out your towel on Sydney's blockbuster beaches. (p64)

About 25% of Australia's fresh produce is grown in Bundaberg, Queensland.

Seventy million oysters are produced annually in New South Wales.

There are more than 2000 cafes and coffee shops in Melbourne.

GOING GOURMET

From the farm-fresh produce of Bundaberg to the plump oysters of the New South Wales coast and the fine wines of Margaret River, Australia is an epicurean delight. Discover lauded regional restaurants redefining modern Australian fine dining, kick back in cool cafes offering much more than avo on toast, feast on fresh seafood straight off the trawlers and explore the vibrant multicultural culinary scenes of the capital cities.

Left Seafood, Rockingham, Western Australia
Right Bush tucker (p152)
Below Oysters

→ BUSH TUCKER

Look out for Kakadu plum, Tasmanian pepperberry and saltbush on restaurant menus, and join an Indigenous tour to learn about traditional uses for native plants.

JACKSON STOCK PHOTOGRAPHY/SHUTTERSTOCK

★ STARS & HATS

The Michelin guide has not begun to review Australian venues, so there are no star-rated eateries here (yet). The homegrown chef's-hat system delivers restaurant ratings.

RIGHT: JONATHON STOKES/LONELY PLANET; LEFT: RONAN O'CONNELL/LONELY PLANET

↑ ZERO-FOOD-MILE TREATS

From buckets of berries to trays of oysters, many producers sell fresh food directly from their farms; look out for signs and roadside stalls.

Best Food Experiences

Dine from dawn to dusk in Queensland at the Gold Coast's cafes, restaurants and bars. (p140)

Experience eclectic cuisine in Sydney's Chinatown. (p54)

Savour fresh seafood at markets and restaurants in Leederville, WA. (p242)

Find the perfect brew in one of Melbourne's laneway cafes. (p102)

FILEDIMAGE/SHUTTERSTOCK

CRAFT DRINKS & WINE

Home to around 65 wine-growing regions, Australia promises that a great glass of local wine is never far away. Craft breweries are even more abundant, along with an ever-expanding network of distilleries, most with cellar doors. From old-world classics to bold new styles, the Australian drinks industry is one to savour. Cheers!

Best Wine & Spirits Experiences

Take your pick from more than 200 wineries in WA's Margaret River. (p254)

Sip your way along Tasmania's Tamar Valley wine region. (p206)

Sample premium gin in SA's McLaren Vale. (p222)

Find a new favourite cocktail in Sydney's best bars. (p56)

Savour coastal chardonnay at wineries in Victoria's Mornington Peninsula. (pictured; p117)

ISLAND TIME

Dotted along the Australian coastline are hundreds of islands with a remarkable diversity of attractions, from dazzling coral reefs to Indigenous culture, luxury glamping to colonial history. Many of these stunning islands are easily visited on day trips from the coast, while others tempt you to stay a while.

LEFT: ALEXANDRE.ROSA/SHUTTERSTOCK; BOTTOM: JOAO INACIO/GETTY IMAGES

→ BREATHTAKING BEACHES

Some of Australia's most stunning beaches can be found on islands, such as the pure white sands of Whitehaven Beach in the Whitsundays.

▶ See p168 for more on the Whitsundays

Best Island Experiences

Marvel at the brilliant blue inland lakes of K'gari, off Queensland. (p162)

Sail around the idyllic tropical islands of Queensland's Whitsundays. (p168)

Explore Tasmania's convict history on Maria Island. (p204)

Get back to nature on South Australia's Kangaroo Island. (p226)

Cycle between ice-blue beaches on WA's Rottnest Island. (p250)

★ SETTLE IN

Many Australian islands have bargain camping. In Queensland, you can camp on a number of Great Barrier Reef islands for just $7.50 per person per night.

Above K'gari (p162), Queensland
Left Whitehaven Beach, Whitsundays (p166), Queensland

ABORIGINAL ART

From ancient rock art to modern centres where you can talk to artists and see work in progress, Aboriginal art offers intriguing insights into the world's oldest living cultures.

LEFT: INGEHOGENBIJL/SHUTTERSTOCK; BOTTOM: NIGEL JARVIS/SHUTTERSTOCK

→ A MODERN PRACTICE

Aboriginal artists continue to reinvigorate traditional practices, using time-honoured techniques to create modern works and increasingly employing light and sound.

Best Aboriginal Art Experiences

Admire ancient rock art galore in the NT's Kakadu National Park. (p286)

See William Barak's seminal *Ceremony* at Melbourne's Ian Potter Centre. (p113)

Buy a treasure at Cairns Indigenous Art Fair. (p161)

Tour the excellent Aboriginal art centres and galleries of Alice Springs. (p288)

Marvel at ancient hand stencils in Mulka's Cave in WA. (p273)

★ ART AS CULTURE

While there's no word in Aboriginal languages for 'art', in Aboriginal cultures visual imagery has always connected past, present and future, and linked people to their homelands.

Above Mulka's Cave (p273), Western Australia
Left Ian Potter Australian Art Centre

OUTBACK EXPLORERS

Stunning expanses of secluded land await you in the Australian outback, boasting some of the most beautiful landforms you'll see anywhere. From unbelievably clear night skies to great gorges and epic monoliths rising from the seemingly endless desert, the outback is full of possibilities.

LEFT: CHAMELEONSEYE/SHUTTERSTOCK; BOTTOM: PICS BY NICK/SHUTTERSTOCK

→ SOME LIKE IT HOT

The Australian outback can be significantly hotter than major cities. Some towns see regular runs of 40°C days over summer, with minimal rainfall.

Best Outback Experiences

Go underground in the unique SA town of Coober Pedy. (p230)

See huge crocodiles up close in the NT's Kakadu National Park. (p286)

Find a surreal 'breaking wave' in the WA outback. (p270)

Follow the 4WD trails of Queensland's Cape Tribulation. (p174)

Watch Aboriginal stories come to life with modern technology at Uluṟu. (p289)

★ WIDE RANGING

About 81% of Australia is broadly defined as rangelands – what most Australians know as the outback.

Above Coober Pedy (p230), South Australia
Left Campervan in the outback

CAIRNS & TROPICAL NORTH QUEENSLAND Trip Builder

TAKE YOUR PICK OF MUST-SEES AND HIDDEN GEMS

Cairns is an unmissable stop on any east coast traveller's itinerary, but the fun doesn't end at this buzzy gateway to the Great Barrier Reef and the Daintree Rainforest. There are oodles of attractions all the way along this lush stretch of coastline.

Trip Notes

Hub towns Cairns, Port Douglas, Townsville

How long Allow two weeks

Getting around Hire a car at Cairns Airport, or book a tour; many tours include hotel transfers.

Tips The humidity is lower during the June-to-October dry season, and stinger suits aren't required for marine activities, making this time ideal for outdoor exploration. Visit at the beginning or end of the season to avoid the bulk of the crowds.

Cooktown

Embark on a road trip to historic Cooktown via the storied 4WD-only Bloomfield Track, or via the longer, sealed inland route, which takes roughly the same amount of time.

4½hr from Cairns

Port Douglas

Relax poolside at one of the holiday town's many resorts, enjoy long walks (and maybe a swim) at fabulous Four Mile Beach and make the most of the easy access to the Daintree Rainforest's Mossman Gorge.

1hr from Cairns

Atherton Tablelands

Chase waterfalls, swim in crater lakes, spot quirky wildlife and explore an incredible outdoor museum in the refreshingly cool hills above Cairns.

1½hr from Cairns

Cape Tribulation

Immerse yourself on a day (or longer) trip to 'Cape Trib', where the rainforest meets the Great Barrier Reef.

2½hr from Cairns

Great Barrier Reef

Sign up for an outer-reef day trip for the best snorkelling and diving in the iconic marine park, or enjoy the reef for longer on an overnight experience.

1½hr from Cairns or Port Douglas

Cairns

Sultry Cairns has been upgraded with flash hotels and a hip bar scene, making the multicultural seaside city a fantastic base for reef and rainforest excursions.

2¼hr from Brisbane

Cassowary Coast

Discover hidden beaches, kick back at relaxed pubs, and look out for the formidable feathered namesake of this laid-back coastal region between Cairns and Townsville.

1½hr from Townsville

Townsville

Go koala spotting on Magnetic Island, take an Aboriginal tour in Townsville, and sign up for a day trip to snorkel or dive the Museum of Underwater Art at John Brewer Reef.

4½hr from Cairns

SYDNEY & COASTAL NEW SOUTH WALES

BEACHES | FOOD | HISTORY

RESEARCHED BY PHILLIP TANG AND SARAH REID

salesforce

SYDNEY & COASTAL NSW
Trip Builder

Dine, drink and beach to your heart's content in cosmopolitan Sydney, with the endlessly captivating harbour as a backdrop and national parks surrounding the city. Then head up the coast to uncover happening regional food scenes.

QUEENSLAND

NEW SOUTH WALES

Moree

Narrabri

Catch a drag show at heritage-listed cultural icon, the **Imperial Erskineville** (p53)
6mins from Central Station

Dubbo

Orange

Get a taste of the South Coast's rugged beauty on a bushwalk in **Royal National Park** (p72)
1hr from Sydney

0 200 km
0 100 miles

PREVIOUS PAGE: ELIAS BITAR/SHUTTERSTOCK
FROM LEFT: ALEX YOUROUKELIS/SHUTTERSTOCK, MARISA ESTIVILL/SHUTTERSTOCK, CAMCP/SHUTTERSTOCK, AQUARIUS TRAVELLER/SHUTTERSTOCK, HYSERB/SHUTTERSTOCK

they come alive with a tour, but you can easily wander around yourself, time-jumping with lunch in a modern-day cafe or shopping at the outdoor market. Architecture highlights are the sandstone splendour of Sydney Observatory, the brick warehouses of Campbell's Stores, and Sergeant Major's Row of terrace houses.

Archaeological digs have discovered the remains of households, and there are a number of museum sites to visit here, the main one being the **Big Dig Archaeology Education Centre**. Tucked away down a laneway, **The Rocks Discovery Museum** digs deep into the area's history on an artefact-rich tour. Sensitive attention is given to the Gadigal people, and there are interesting tales of early colonial characters.

First Contact

James Cook's monument-marked landing place is on the southern side of the park in **Kurnell**. The Kurnell Visitor Centre conveys the impact of European arrival on the local Aboriginal people, and has information on the surrounding wetlands and Cook's life and expeditions.

Further out west, several interesting historic houses date from the very earliest days of colonisation. Parramatta was founded with First Fleet convict labour when Sydney Cove proved to be lousy for growing veggies.

Left Hammocks, Hyde Park Barracks (p59)
Below The Rocks Discovery Museum

CREATURES
of Sydney

03

01

02

04

05

06

01 Ibis
Sydney's 'bin chicken' fossicks for food scraps in park bins and is drawn to tourists snacking at Circular Quay.

02 Silver gull
Loves screeching 'kwarwh' and fighting other seagulls for chips at the beach.

03 Laughing kookaburra
The bird emblem of NSW. If you don't hear them in Centennial Park, any other national park is a safe bet.

04 Australian magpie
Swoops from trees at joggers, cyclists and jumpy tourists in September (and around) to protect its chicks.

05 Sulphur-crested cockatoo
So rowdy, so Sydney, this parrot rules from Mrs Macquarie's Point to the outer suburbs, where cockatoo gangs have learnt to open garbage bins.

06 Rainbow lorikeet
This parrot flocks for sunset orchestras wherever there are grevillea, bottlebrush, banksia or eucalypt trees – so: everywhere in Sydney.

07 Flying fox
Look up for another Hyde Park and Centennial Park nightly visitor

07

08

09

10

11

13

12

as this bat, silhouetted against the sky like a superhero, seeks eucalyptus pollen.

08 Huntsman spider
After summer downpours, this fist-sized visitor dries off on bedroom walls looking deadly – but it's not. Its bite does hurt, however.

09 Sydney funnel-web spider
The world's second-most-venomous spider adores Sydney gardens after rain. There have been no deaths since an antivenin was devised in 1981.

10 Eastern water dragon
Even lizards love Sydney's water and sun, especially in Lane Cove National Park and the bush around Parsley Bay.

11 Lace monitor (goanna)
See this giant, gentle lizard sunbathing along the Manly Scenic Walkway.

12 Brushtail possum
Catch the possum's retro-reflective eyes at night as it scurries around Hyde Park between its homes in Moreton Bay fig and eucalyptus trees.

13 Brush-turkey
Wanders leafy North Shore suburbs scratching up million-dollar gardens, breaking off only to fight (the males, that is).

01 PODDUBNAYA_ART/SHUTTERSTOCK, **02** ARLIFTATOZ2205/SHUTTERSTOCK, **03** ANITAPOL/SHUTTERSTOCK, **04** PURPLEPAPERCAT/SHUTTERSTOCK, **05** SUTTHIPHONG CHANDAENG/SHUTTERSTOCK, **06** ERIC ISSELEE/SHUTTERSTOCK, **07** VOLODYMYR BURDIAK/SHUTTERSTOCK, **08** SABZA/SHUTTERSTOCK, **09** PAUL LOOYEN/SHUTTERSTOCK, **10** BENNY MARTY/SHUTTERSTOCK, **11** PAUL LOOYEN/SHUTTERSTOCK, **12** LILIYA BUTENKO/SHUTTERSTOCK, **13** RUSS JENKINS/SHUTTERSTOCK

06 Let's BEACH

BEACHES | NATURE | SURFING

Nowhere else in the world does the city kiss the sea so spectacularly. Sydneysiders are blessed with over 100 beaches, each with its own personality. Hidden strands favour sunbathing with a book, and some stretches of dramatic water are known only to surfers.

FRANCESCA PIANZOLA/SHUTTERSTOCK

How to

Getting here and around The eastern beaches can be reached from the city centre by bus. For the north, take a ferry from Circular Quay to Manly.

When to go Sunny weekdays can be quieter, especially in the mornings. Cloudy days see fewer crowds and more locals and surfers.

Surf safety Sydney's lifeguards and volunteer surf lifesavers watch over certain stretches of major beaches, marked with red-and-yellow flags, where it's safest to swim.

Social Swimming

Clovelly Beach is all concrete, so you can laze back and have a drink or jump straight off the platform into the water. Afterwards, there's a good bowlo (lawn bowls club) uphill for a drink and a game with friends. Plus **Clovelly Bowling & Recreation Club** has the best views over the coast of any bowlo in the world.

Quiet Swimming

Mahon Pool near Maroubra is calm and less busy than most beaches, but with dramatic surf at its edges. At **Little Bay Beach**, south of Malabar, you can't even see any buildings, just the beautiful flat water and outcrops for snorkelling. It's very quiet, with mostly local swimmers. Quiet **Hermit Bay Beach**, at the end of Nielsen Park's walking trails, faces the distant Sydney Harbour Bridge. It's ideal for

AI YOSHI/GETTY IMAGES

Top left Little Bay Beach
Left Mahon Pool

reading a book on the soft wheat grass under shady trees. You don't even need to touch the sand; you can launch off a little rock wall into the water. **Shelly Beach** in Manly is protected from wild weather. There are no southerly winds, so you can take in the serenity.

Ocean Pools

If you have young kids or shark paranoia – or the surf just doesn't excite you – you can chill out at one of Sydney's approximately 35 artificial ocean pools, located up and down the coast and inside the harbour. Most are free. Some, like Mahon Pool and **Bronte Bogey Hole**, are what are known as bogey holes: natural-looking rock pools where you can safely splash about and snorkel, even while the surf surges in. Calm **McIver's Ladies Baths** (also known as Coogee Women's Baths) is open only to women and children; **Fairlight Beach Rock Pool** is similarly quiet and family-friendly. Others, like **Maccallum Pool** and the famous

Surfing for Beginners

The most important thing at the beginning is just to get out there. Your paddling won't get stronger unless you're in the water all the time. Sydney beaches can get crowded, but don't let that deter you. Focus on getting your own waves.

Stay away from Bondi – it's so busy. **Manly** is relaxed and best for starting out. It can be quite protected, unlike Bondi and Maroubra, whose aggressive waves can dump you. **South Cronulla** is a long, more isolated beach with loads of space to find your own stretch.

Lucy Small,
surfer and activist
@saltwaterpilgrim

Nude Beach

Lady Bay Beach is Australia's oldest nudist beach. It's not just for ladies – gay men, straight couples and international visitors have sought solace in the calm, blue waters in their birthday suit for decades. Shrug off your clothing and the distant city, sheltered by Lady Bay's two rocky natural piers.

MARK KRIEDEMANN/GETTY IMAGES

Bondi Icebergs, resemble swimming pools. The ocean pools normally close one day a week so the seaweed can be cleaned out.

Walking & Snorkelling

The most famous beachside walk is the spectacular 6km **Bondi to Coogee Coastal Walk**, but there are plenty of trails (sydneycoastal councils.com.au/projects/walking-coastal -sydney), with some of the most surprising ones around the harbour. The **Harbour Bridge to Spit Bridge** walk and the **Spit Bridge to Manly** walk are excellent stretches. Or do the 80km **Bondi to Manly** (bonditomanly. com) stretch over a few days. One of the best **snorkelling** spots is **Gordons Bay**, where an underwater nature trail has been set up, or at **Shelly Beach**, next to Manly.

Whale Watching

Each year, more than 50,000 humpback and southern right whales pass along Sydney's coast between May and November as they migrate between Antarctica and the warmer waters of the Pacific. It's easy to spot their spouts from the cliffs – grab a perch at Waverley Cemetery and keep an eye out for breaches and spouts.

RIGHT: NATA9M/SHUTTERSTOCK; LEFT: ISABELLA MOORE/LONELY PLANET

Left Manly Beach
Above top Lady Bay Beach
Above Bondi to Coogee Coastal Walk

07 Blue Mountains MAGIC

VINTAGE | CULTURE | VIEWS

A high-society retreat in the 1800s, the Blue Mountains region has style in spades. Explore culture, relax among heritage-listed buildings or drink an artisanal cocktail in an atmospheric bar. After you've recharged your batteries indoors, venture out into the area's glorious natural bounty.

ALEXANDRE ROSA/SHUTTERSTOCK

How to

Getting here Trains on the Blue Mountains line leave regularly from Sydney's Central Station. The gateway town of Glenbrook is about an hour by car along the Great Western Hwy from Sydney.

When to go March and April, with light crowds, is a great time to hike. Avoid hot, busy December to February.

Call ahead Some shops and restaurants are closed on Monday, and local businesses close early on the weekend.

DAVID COLEMAN/HAVE CAMERA WILL TRAVEL/ ALAMY STOCK PHOTO

Indoor Pursuits

Champagne Charlie's cocktail bar in Katoomba's historic Carrington Hotel (1883) transports you to a bygone era of glitz, glamour and free-flowing sparkling wine. Take a seat under the stained-glass dome and choose from a menu of traditional and modern cocktails, an extensive range of wines, and beer from the Carrington's own Katoomba Brewing Company.

Drawing its inspiration from Shanghai teahouses, the Hydro Majestic hotel's **Salon du Thé** encompasses the building's former Billiards Room and Cats Alley ladies' lounge. Have an afternoon pot of tea after walking in the gardens, or try one of the unique, tea-inspired cocktails before dining at the hotel's Wintergarden restaurant.

GEOFF DUDE/FLICKR/CC BY-NC-ND 2.0 DEED

Salacious Australian Art

The historic house of renowned Australian artist and author Norman Lindsay now showcases his numerous paintings (many of them considered scandalous at the time), sculptures, etchings, and illustrations from his children's novel *The Magic Pudding*. Expect lush gardens, unique art and a view into Lindsay's bohemian life.

Top left View of the Three Sisters (p70)
Left Salon du Thé, Hydro Majestic
Above Champagne Charlie's

Vintage Shopping

Hunt for treasure in this popular antiquing destination. Run by veteran art and antiques dealer Steven Archer, the **Katoomba Antique Centre** also contains a small camera museum. Vinyl enthusiasts shouldn't miss the nearby **Velvet Fog Record Bar**, with a wide range of rare albums. **MacArthur's Arcade** has everything from china to furniture to vintage clothing. Downstairs is **Mr Pickwick's Fine Old Books**, home to 60,000 vintage and secondhand volumes, and across the road in the old post office is the **Katoomba Vintage Emporium**.

Vintage-clothing enthusiasts will love **Leura Vintage**, and **Hazelbrook Cottage Antique Centre** offers a rustic collection of furniture and period Australiana.

Outdoor Delights

Hiking in Blackheath is almost synonymous with the Grand Canyon walk, but there are

Hiking the Blue Mountains

Prince Henry Cliff Walk
Connecting Katoomba and Leura, this moderate hike passes the famed Three Sisters with views of Ruined Castle and three waterfalls. The track follows the base of the cliffs that make up Katoomba and Leura, allowing you to view the Jamison Valley from the ground floor.

Grand Cliff Top Walk
Designed to be walked over two days, this newer 19km trail hugs the spectacular cliffs between Wentworth Falls and Katoomba, with surreal views of valleys, sandstone peaks and waterfalls on the way.

For significant hikes, fill out a trip intention form, and borrow a personal locator beacon from a tourist-information centre or police station.

LEAH-ANNE THOMPSON/SHUTTERSTOCK

CHAMELEONSEYE/SHUTTERSTOCK

Far left Prince Henry Cliff Walk
Left Grose Valley
Below Red Hands Cave

many easier and less crowded walks that don't skimp on beautiful views of the **Grose Valley**. The 1.8km **Fairfax Heritage Walking Track** is entirely wheelchair accessible. Visit in spring to see the waratahs and vibrant wildflowers in full bloom.

The whimsical name, relatively short distance and swimming hole at the end make the 1km **Jellybean Track** a favourite with families during the sunny months. An 8km loop track takes you to **Red Hands Cave**. View axe-carving grooves and the vibrant hand-stencil gallery created by the local Dharug people. The stencils in the Red Hands Cave are between 500 and 1600 years old and are some of the best hand-stencil art in Sydney and its surrounds.

Pies & Sweets

Every Australian town has a pie shop that you absolutely must try, and Blackheath is no different. The **Bakehouse on Wentworth** is a local and tourist favourite, with unforgettable pies. This is a great place to fuel up before heading off on a hike.

A staple in many children's trips to the Blue Mountains, the **Candy Store Leura** has walls lined with boiled lollies and chocolates ranging from Australian classics to modern and imported sweets.

MARC ANDERSON/ALAMY STOCK PHOTO

08 Traverse the LAND & SEA

VIEWS | WALKING | OUTDOORS

Situated within **Royal National Park**, the 26km Coast Track stretches between Bundeena and Otford. Cross clifftops, explore coastal heathland and take a dip in the Pacific. Hike the whole track over two days, or visit the sites as short day walks.

TRAVELLING.ABOUT/SHUTTERSTOCK

Trip Notes

Stay hydrated Be sure to carry sufficient water or water-treatment options, as there is no access to drinking water on the walk.

Check the weather Some sections are steep and exposed, so it is not advised to hike during heavy rain or high winds.

Bring proper gear Waterproof shoes are a must, as you will be walking across creeks and beaches.

Track Ecology & Views

The track moves through rocky clifftops, beach and coastal heathland. In springtime, the salty sea air gives way to honeyed blossoms from the abundant native flora. After the summer fire season, the lower levels of bushland regenerate quickly, demonstrating the perseverance of the Australian landscape. With elevations of over 1300 metres above sea level, the views to the sea are awe-inspiring.

01 Centring on the relationship between the Dharawal people and the orca, the **Jibbon rock carvings** were made at least 1000 years ago.

02 The **Jibbon shell midden**, a pile of shells and animal bones discarded at least 3000 years ago, indicates what the Dharawal ate before colonisation.

03 Perched upon a rock shelf, the pure-white sandstone **Wedding Cake Rock** has deep cracks separating it from the rest of the cliff face.

04 Secluded **Wattamolla Beach** is sheltered by mountains and has a waterfall. It's perfect for a swim before you continue walking.

05 Visit the perfectly circular **Figure Eight Pools** at low tide. At other times, the rock pools are submerged and potentially dangerous.

FROM TOP: DESTINATIONS JOURNEY/SHUTTERSTOCK, THE ESCAPE OF MALEE/SHUTTERSTOCK

09 NOSHING in Newcastle

FINE DINING | HIP BARS | EAT STREETS

Once a gritty industrial city, today's Newcastle – affectionately known as 'Newy' – has transformed into one of Australia's most happening dining destinations. With an ever-increasing array of cool cafes, top-notch restaurants and buzzy bars, and the Hunter Valley wine region right on its doorstep, it's the kind of place where you'll want to arrive hungry – and thirsty.

ALEX JACK PHOTOGRAPHY

How to

Getting around Cruise between eateries on an e-bike for just $2 per 10 minutes or $10 per day courtesy of Newcastle's Bykko scheme.

When to go April is Newcastle Food Month, with oodles of culinary events, masterclasses, 'plate date' deals and more.

While you're here Fully reopened in 2026, the reimagined **Newcastle Art Gallery** holds one of Australia's most significant collections, with works by Australian masters and more. The gallery's Hilliers cafe adds to the town's food offer.

FORT WHISKEY PTY LTD

Top left Dish, Momo
Bottom left Coal & Cedar

Cool Cafes

This relaxed seaside city was made for cafe culture. For ocean views with your smoked-salmon bagel, head to **Merewether Surfhouse**, or tuck into scrambled eggs with macadamia pesto at **Estabar**, opposite Newcastle's main beach. In the city centre, **Momo** serves an innovative all-vegan menu (though cow's milk is available for coffees), while **Mockingbird** in Hamilton is the place to go when you're in the mood to pair your morning coffee with something more adventurous than avo toast – red velvet pancakes with Persian candy floss, perhaps?

Top Tables

Newcastle's fine-dining scene is on the up, with produce-driven **Flotilla**, Italian-influenced **Humbug** and French-inspired **Bistro Penny** all bagging a coveted 'hat' in the SMH Good Food Guide 2026 Awards. Relaxed Humbug serves terrific pastas – perfect for a special night out that won't break the bank.

Eat Streets

Newcastle has birthed several 'eat streets' packed with restaurants and bars. Among the best known is **Darby St** in Cooks Hill, just south of the city centre, where you'll find more than 20 restaurants, bars and cafes along a 400m stretch between Queen and Bull Sts. In Hamilton, west of the city centre, **Beaumont St** offers antique shopping by day, and a thriving bar and restaurant scene by night. Right in the city, **King St** and **Hunter St** are also packed with drinking and dining options.

Bar Hopping

Coal & Cedar Cocktails are mixed with flair at this hard-to-find New York–style speakeasy.

Koutetsu The quirky vibe of this West End bar hints at its former life as a pawn shop.

Grain Store With a rotating selection of 21 craft beers on tap, the warehouse-turned-bar is a top spot for a pint and a burger.

Customs House Hotel Drink in the history of this watering hole, which has a great beer garden.

King Street This three-level live music venue with several bars was enlarged and renovated in 2023.

10 Perfect Port Stephens WEEKENDS

GREAT BEACHES | SCENIC WALKS | ICONIC WILDLIFE

Just 2½ hours north of Sydney, Port Stephens offers the ultimate nature hit with its beaches, coastal walks, wildlife encounters and massive sand dunes surrounding an immense natural harbour. It always feels like the weekend here, where seafood rules local menus.

JUNHAOLU/GETTY IMAGES

Dolphins & Whales

Port Stephens is famous for its bottlenose dolphins (pictured). Humpback whales join the party in winter, making it a great time to book a cetacean-watching cruise. You can also opt to 'join the pod' with Dolphin Swim Australia, which holds a permit from NSW Parks to operate responsible wild-dolphin swims.

Trip Notes

Getting around There's a good local bus network, including services to Newcastle.

When to go October to April for wild dolphin swims; late May to early November for whale watching.

Seafood Try Little Nel, Little Beach Boathouse, Rick Stein at Bannisters, and Sandpipers, or grab a tray of fresh oysters at Holberts Oyster Supplies.

Local tipples A winery, distillery and brewery can all be found at B.Farm, overlooking the vines.

01 Get your bearings – and enjoy incredible views – atop Tomaree Head (161m), reached via the invigorating **Tomaree Head Summit Walk** (2.2km return). A side trail leads to WWII gun emplacements.

02 Cool off with a dip at **Zenith Beach**, below Tomaree Head, arguably the most dramatic of the 26 beautiful beaches to choose from in Port Stephens.

03 Contribute to the rehabilitation and conservation of an Aussie icon by visiting the **Port Stephens Koala Sanctuary**. There's also glamping accommodation.

04 Experience the famous shifting seaside dunes of **Worimi Conservation Lands** on a quad-bike tour with Aboriginal-owned Sand Dune Adventures.

05 Stake out a top spot to watch the sunset – ideally over a drink at waterside bar-restaurant the Deck – at **Soldiers Point**, located on a peninsula jutting into the Karuah River.

IAN WOOLCOCK/SHUTTERSTOCK, 365 FOCUS PHOTOGRAPHY/SHUTTERSTOCK

11 DIVE INTO the North Coast

SHARK DIVING | SNORKELLING | MARINE WONDERS

The Great Barrier Reef isn't the only great place to go scuba diving in Australia. North Coast NSW is one of the best places in the world to dive with critically endangered grey nurse sharks, a large, placid species that aggregates in several spots along the coast at different periods throughout the year. Here's where to see them.

How to

When to go The water temperature can dip below 20°C on the North Coast in winter, but there's no bad time of year to go diving (just bad weather). All operators rent wetsuits.

Qualification Some shark dive spots are suitable for open-water divers, while others require advanced open-water certification. Check with your operator.

Snorkelling There's great snorkelling at many dive sites; some operators allow snorkellers to join trips at a reduced cost.

Nguthungulli Julian Rocks Temperate and tropical waters meet at this rocky outcrop off Byron Bay, attracting more than 1000 marine species, including over 530 species of fish. Grey nurse sharks (which grow up to 3.6m long) aggregate here from June to November, but as soon as they leave another major attraction arrives: beautifully patterned (and similarly docile) leopard sharks until May, along with manta rays. Bottom-dwelling wobbegong sharks can be seen year-round.

South West Rocks Running 125m right through Fish Rock, which lies 2km off South West Rocks on the Mid-North Coast, Fish Rock Cave offers year-round grey-nurse sightings, along with a plethora of other marine life, from moray eels to friendly blue groupers. In the summer months, grey nurse sharks rest in the azure cave entrance, presenting an incredible photographic opportunity. While Nitrox certification isn't essential, it's recommended for this dive.

Other Great North Coast Dives

Cook Island Green turtles are the main attraction at this relatively shallow dive site just off Tweed Heads.

North Solitary Island Colourful anemones carpet the sea floor in this section of the Solitary Islands Marine Park.

South Solitary Island This shallow dive site off Coffs Harbour is great for learning, and there's plenty of temperate marine life, similar to Byron Bay's.

Port Stephens A popular dive site off Port Stephens is the Looking Glass at Broughton Island, a narrow trench where grey nurse sharks aggregate.

David Robinson, *shark ecologist, founder of the Cape Byron Leopard Shark Project and owner of Sundive Byron Bay @sundivebyronbay*

Forster and Seal Rocks On the Barrington Coast, Forster and nearby Seal Rocks are home to more than a dozen dive sites. Many of these are also visited by grey nurse sharks year-round. Top picks include the Pinnacle, a deeper dive off Forster (where the dive operators are located), and Big Rock at Seal Rocks, which is surrounded by several gutters patrolled by graceful grey nurse sharks.

FDURAND/SHUTTERSTOCK

RUGLIG/SHUTTERSTOCK

Above Grey nurse shark
Left Green turtle

12 Gondwana Hikes GALORE

FOREST | ADVENTURE | WATERFALLS

Comprising more than 30 national parks and reserves between southeast Queensland and Newcastle, the UNESCO-listed Gondwana Rainforests of Australia holds the world's most extensive areas of subtropical rainforest. Get your Gondwana fix on these great hikes near the coast in the NSW section.

ALEX CIMBAL/SHUTTERSTOCK

How to

Getting around You'll need your own car to access most Gondwana parks.

When to go Hiking is excellent year-round, though the risk of dehydration and heat stroke increases in summer.

Safety Always tell someone where you're going and when you plan to return, and pack adequate water and gear.

Parks pass Visiting several NSW national parks with parking fees? It may be cheaper to purchase an annual multi-parks pass ($65; nationalparks.nsw.gov.au).

MICHELLE HOLIHAN/SHUTTERSTOCK

Minyon Falls Loop, Nightcap National Park

Distance 13km
Duration Three to four hours

Just 45 minutes west of Byron Bay, this hike takes you from the top of Minyon Falls to the base of the magnificent waterfall, some 100m below. Tracing the Nightcap escarpment, the track begins in wet sclerophyll forest before descending into a cooler subtropical wonderland as the rainforest canopy closes in towards the bottom of the valley. Enjoy a dip in the natural waterfall pool before hiking up the other side of the escarpment for front-on views of the falls from the Minyon Grass Picnic Area before walking back to the trailhead along the road (1km).

JACKSCOTT/SHUTTERSTOCK

Bushfires

More than 50% of the Gondwana Rainforests burned during Australia's 2019–20 bushfires, and the habitats of rare and threatened flora and fauna suffered catastrophic damage. Nearly all affected tourism infrastructure has since reopened, though, and the rainforest continues to recover with the assistance of governments, Aboriginal groups, scientists and local communities.

Top left Minyon Falls **Left** Nightcap National Park **Above** Kookaburra

Iluka Rainforest Walking Track, Iluka Nature Reserve

Distance 5.2km return
Duration One to three hours

In Iluka Nature Reserve near Yamba, the Iluka Rainforest Walking Track offers an easy stroll through lush coastal forest to Iluka Bluff in neighbouring Bundjalung National Park. Look out for the brightly coloured noisy pitta, and listen for the sharp crack of the whipbird. The Bluff is a great spot for a picnic lunch and a swim (or snorkel) before heading back the same way, with great whale watching from June to early October.

Crystal Shower Falls Walk, Dorrigo National Park

Distance 3.2km return
Duration 90 minutes

Mist-shrouded rainforest towers above you on this short but stunning walk in Dorrigo National Park, an hour's drive west of Coffs

Quirky Gondwana Wildlife

Alberts lyrebird Look for this shy bird scratching for soil-dwelling invertebrates. In winter and early spring you might hear the male's unique call mimicking sounds he's heard over the years, or see him do his magnificent tail fan dance.

Red-legged pademelon If you're still and quiet, you can see these small macropods feeding on fruit and leaves in the early morning and late afternoon.

Land mullet The largest member of the skink family is often mistaken for a snake.

Lamington crayfish Usually a bright turquoise, this large freshwater crayfish is typically seen in rainforest creeks above 300m.

Wendy Bithell, *ecotour guide and founder of Vision Walks Eco-Tours, which operates on Bundjalung Country in northern NSW @visionwalks*

CHARLIE BLACKER/SHUTTERSTOCK

Far left Red-legged pademelon
Left New England National Park
Below Lamington crayfish

Harbour via the Waterfall Way scenic drive. The trail takes you behind the fairy-tale Crystal Shower Falls, and a suspension bridge carries you across the valley in front of the falls for Insta-worthy views. Return the same way or extend the walk by looping back via Tristania Falls on the Wonga Walk, which adds 2.2km to the journey. Don't miss the Skywalk Lookout next to the Rainforest Centre on your way out, nor the charming hinterland town of Bellingen on the drive back to the coast.

Cascades Track, New England National Park

Distance 5.7km loop
Duration Three hours

An hour southwest of Dorrigo National Park, New England National Park hugs the Great Escarpment, some 1500m above sea level. A highlight is the Cascades Track, which takes you past vivid green moss-covered boulders, flourishing ferns and gushing cascades. Look out for unusual fungi and the velvet worm, a living fossil that looks like a velvety caterpillar. This rough track has short, steep hills that could be challenging for small children.

RIGHT: ANDYWAK/SHUTTERSTOCK; LEFT: HAL BERAL/GETTY IMAGES

The Byron Bay Experience

PARADISE REDEFINED

Between its eye-watering property prices and trending eateries, today's Byron Bay is a bit different from the sleepy coastal idyll 'discovered' by surfers in the 1950s, with hippies hot on their sandy heels. Scratch Byron's highly Instagrammable surface, however, and you'll discover a destination that still has plenty of substance.

RENATOK/SHUTTERSTOCK

'Cheer up, slow down, chill out', reads the welcome sign at the northern entrance to Byron Bay. The middle part of this mantra is easy enough to master, as you'll likely find yourself in a queue of traffic by the time you see it.

Such are the trade-offs of the ever-increasing popularity of this iconic Northern Rivers beach town, which now receives more than 2.2 million visitors per year – that's around 183 tourists for each of its 10,900-odd residents. But dramatic headlines describing Byron as a 'paradise lost' only tell one side of the story.

An important meeting place for Bundjalung nation clans for more than 22,000 years, this genetically blessed corner of NSW – known as Gabanbaa to the local Arakwal people – changed forever when European colonists arrived in the late 1800s. First cedar-getters and farmers set about felling a 75,000-hectare swathe of tropical lowland rainforest stretching from Byron to Lismore known as the Big Scrub; only 1% of this still stands today. Then sand-mining operations turned Byron's exquisite coastline into a barren wasteland. More extractive industries followed, with the Byron Bay township of the 1950s and 1960s described in local historical records as 'reeking from the stench' of local piggery, abattoir and whaling factories.

It wasn't until these industries had all wound down by the early 1980s that Byron (originally named Cavvanba, an Anglicised version of Gabanbaa) began to transform back into a version of the paradise maintained by the Arakwal, who secured a historic Indigenous Land Use Agreement in 2001 that led to the formation of Arakwal National Park. Industrial workers transitioned to jobs in the service indus-

Left Surfers, Byron Bay
Centre Cape Byron Lighthouse
Right Cafe, Byron Bay

CONSTANTIN STANCIU/SHUTTERSTOCK

AMPUEROLEONARDO/GETTY IMAGES

try, including tourism, while proposed developments that risked compromising the regeneration of Byron's natural environment – or the lifestyles of its new wave of alternative, eco-conscious locals – were passionately resisted.

Byron Today

It is extraordinary that today's Byron is still a low-rise beach town in a gorgeous natural setting with a strong community spirit, despite the increasing pressures of housing (un)affordability, climate change and urban development. And while locals may complain about how busy, expensive and pretentious their home has become, many will concede that Byron's popularity has its benefits, the town now boasting one of Australia's finest regional dining scenes, a packed calendar of cultural events and a booming sustainable-fashion industry. Dotted with lauded restaurants and independent boutiques of their own, hinterland villages such as Bangalow and Federal, as well as nearby beach towns including Brunswick Heads and Lennox Head, have also become destinations in their own right.

> An important meeting place for Bundjalung nation clans for more than 22,000 years, this corner of NSW – known as Gabanbaa to the local Arakwal people – changed forever when European colonists arrived.

Sure, reality-TV stars might now outnumber surfers at the Beach Hotel. And the days of scoring Byron's famous waves to yourself are long gone. But it's impossible to deny that the Bay is still a special place.

How to 'Do' Byron

While it may seem more responsible to stay away from destinations struggling with overtourism, planning an eco-conscious visit that supports the local community is often a more sustainable choice.

In Byron, this means avoiding unhosted holiday rentals outside the town centre, which are a major contributor to Byron's housing crisis, and supporting locally owned businesses committed to sustainable operations, so your money benefits the community as well as the environment. It means treading gently on the fragile ecosystem, and respecting local culture and laws. These small gestures protect Byron's natural beauty and individual character.

13 Eat the TWEED

GOURMET PRODUCE | CRAFT DRINKS | COUNTRY DRIVES

At NSW's north-eastern tip, the Tweed region's rich volcanic soils brim with fresh produce, which travels just metres to the plates of the region's ever-increasing array of restaurants. Home to one of the Tweed's top tables (Paper Daisy), the Hamptons-meets-NSW-coast Halcyon House hotel makes a fine base to explore the exciting local food and drinks scene between beach swims.

ARTUR BEGEL/SHUTTERSTOCK

How to

Getting around Navigating the Tweed's winding hinterland roads in a hire car is all part of the experience.

When to go Here you can top off a great meal with a swim in the sea year-round.

Burringbar This tiny hinterland village has a cheesemaker, a natural wine shop and bar, and a huge antiques store.

Festival Indulge in bespoke food experiences at the Savour the Tweed festival in October or November.

EARTH BEER COMPANY

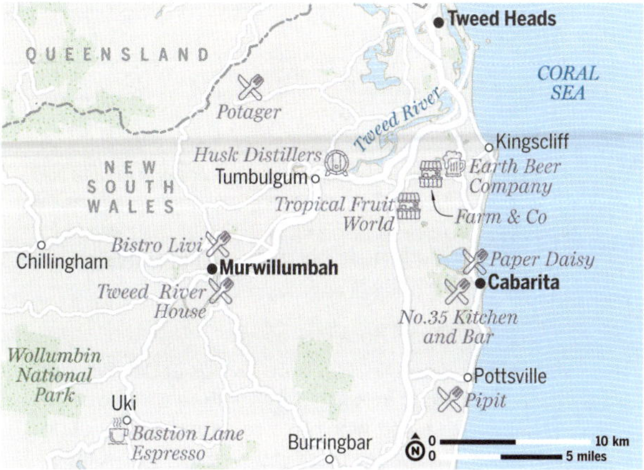

Top left Oysters
Bottom left Earth Beer Company

Top tables Heads began to turn in Sydney when **Paper Daisy** opened in 2015 with its creative Mod Oz dishes. Then in 2019, Paper Daisy chef Ben Devlin moved on to open **Pipit**, his own coastal fine diner in nearby Pottsville, to acclaim. Notable openings since have included 'Italian-ish' Cabarita restaurant **No.35 Kitchen and Bar**, Mod Oz/French Murwillumbah restaurant **Tweed River House**, and small European-inspired restaurant **Bistro Livi** – also in Murwillumbah – which was awarded the prestigious Good Food Guide Regional Restaurant of the Year for 2024. Deeper in the hinterland, longstanding local favourite **Potager** features produce from its own kitchen gardens on its hearty lunch menu.

Drinks Coffee shops don't get much more atmospheric than **Bastion Lane Espresso**, set in a historic Uki post office. In Tumbulgum, **Husk Distillers** offers tours and tastings of its iconic Ink Gin and agricole rums made with local sugar-cane juice. On an avocado farm in Cudgen, **Earth Beer Company** serves its eco-conscious craft brews in a lovingly restored packing shed.

Farm Gates Shop for farm-fresh produce at **Farm & Co** or come for breakfast or lunch overlooking the organic farm in Cudgen. Five minutes down the road, **Tropical Fruit World** has a stall brimming with everything from dragon fruit to mangoes. There's a cafe here too, and family-friendly tractor farm tours.

Did Someone Say Oysters?

In the Tweed you're never far away from fresh seafood, and at the **Oyster Shed** in Tweed Heads you can feast on oysters that have been farmed right in front of you. Another fun way to sample local seafood is on a tour with **Catch a Crab**, run by the same company. Trap live crabs, go 'pumping' for yabbies and learn about the region's working oyster farms on a 2½-hour boat tour on the Tweed River. Spanner crabs, mud crabs and sand crabs are all found there at various times of the year.

Listings

BEST OF THE REST

Sydney Dining Hit List

Catalina $$$

The seafood is so fresh that you could go fishing out the window at this Rose Bay classic. The inventive, varied set menu makes any special occasion sparkle.

Ester $$$

Well-sourced Australian seafood prepared with global influences in Chippendale. Don't miss the blood-sausage sandwich or the excellent vegan set menu.

LuMi Dining $$$

Totally delicious blends of Italian and Japanese influences. Tasting menus are a tour de force. In the city.

Margaret $$$

Top chef Neil Perry's Double Bay restaurant is known for its steak, but the raw entrees and wood-fire-grilled fish are also excellent.

Bathers' Pavilion $$$

The modern French-Australian seasonal menu at Balmoral Beach focuses on produce from small local providers, with plenty of seafood.

Neptune's Grotto $$$

A moody underground restaurant near Circular Quay offering spins on traditional Italian.

First Nations Sydney

Guringai Aboriginal Tours

This Aboriginal-owned and operated tour company offers excellent insights into the cultural heritage of beautiful Ku-ring-gai Chase National Park on its three-hour Basin Track Tour.

Red Hands Cave

Heading deeper into Ku-ring-gai Chase National Park, the Resolute picnic area has faint Aboriginal handprints in ochre at Red Hands Cave. Then, the Resolute Track heads past an Aboriginal engraving site.

Bondi Rock Engravings

Aboriginal rock engravings at Ben Buckler Point in North Bondi feature a whale and a turtle, with two shields and an eel not far away. See more in the nearby golf course.

Whale Watching Sydney

Learn about the importance of whales in Aboriginal cultures on a three-hour whale-watching trip between mid-May and November.

Blak Markets

Sydney's roaming Blak Markets are a great place to purchase Indigenous artworks and handicrafts. It is a popular meeting place for Sydney's Indigenous community, with smoking ceremonies and musical performances.

WONGYMARK1/SHUTTERSTOCK

Humpback whale

Sydney Drinking Dens

Eau-de-Vie $$$

Hidden away, but worth tracking down for its cocktail wizardry when you've had enough of the endless sunshine.

Lazybones Lounge $$

Head out of the city centre and discover the mellow vibes and live music at this low-lit Marrickville star that will take you as you are.

Uncle Ming's Bar $$

A dark Chinese cave of cinema fantasies lives in this small bar secreted in a basement by a shirt shop. It's an atmospheric spot to delve into the cocktail or dumpling menu.

Free Fun in Sydney

Art Gallery of NSW

One of Sydney's best museums, especially after its large-scale renovation. There are regular concerts, screenings and children's activities, and free guided tours.

Chau Chak Wing Museum

This University of Sydney museum exhibits Indigenous cultural objects and Australian, European and Asian art. The Mummy Room keeps kids amused with a 2500-year-old Egyptian mummified cat.

White Rabbit

Cutting-edge Chinese art (works produced since 2000) that is edgy, funny, sexy and idiosyncratic. Among Sydney's best contemporary art galleries.

Green Spaces & Beaches

Wandering the city's parks, gardens and national parks (though there's a vehicle fee) is gratis, and rolling out your towel on the sand is an Australian staple.

MIN JING/SHUTTERSTOCK

Art Gallery of NSW

Sydney Harbour

You can walk over that other great icon, the Sydney Harbour Bridge, and wander through Luna Park (there's a charge for rides).

Historical Buildings

Many of Sydney's most beautiful old buildings are free to enter, including the Customs House, the Mint, St Mary's Cathedral, the State Library and the GPO. For political entertainment, visit Parliament House on sitting days.

Architectural Gems

Window-shoppers should peruse the exquisite Queen Victoria Building and the Strand Arcade. For more modern architectural thrills, check out Central Park and the nearby Dr Chau Chak Wing Building.

Best Bakeries & Cafes

Reuben Hills $$

The star is the fantastic single-origin coffee, roasted on the premises in Surry Hills, but the stellar fried chicken, tacos and *baleadas* (Honduran tortillas) are worthy too.

Black Star Pastry $

Gourmet pies and delicious sweets, including its social-media star, watermelon cake. Stores in the CBD, Newtown and beyond.

Grounds of the City $$

You won't notice the crowds of the QVB inside this Parisian-style cafe. An oasis of vintage decor and excellent coffee, this is a reinvigorating pit stop on any city-centre adventure.

Bourke Street Bakery $

A Surry Hills institution, with additional outlets also in Barangaroo, North Sydney, Marrickville and beyond.

Fredo Pies $

In the small village of Frederickton, just off the Pacific Hwy north of Kempsey, this pie shop is an institution for East Coast road trippers. The 25-plus options include a crocodile pie.

Hilltop Store $$

Housed in a restored general store in Sawtell, this charming Coffs Coast cafe is known for its simple but refined breakfast and lunch menus, with coffee by Single O.

Supply Coffee $

A micro-roastery, espresso bar and licensed cafe in Coffs Harbour's jetty precinct, Supply is a top spot for coffee, breakfast (from 6.30am) or lunch, with creative menu options including a blue-spanner-crab omelette.

Bruns Bakery $

Huge, busy Bruns Bakery in Brunswick Heads does a roaring trade in pies, pastries, bread, cakes and more. It has a similarly excellent sister bakery in Suffolk Park, Byron Bay.

Cubby Bakehouse $

Opposite the Tweed River at Chinderah, the bakery-cafe has earned a cult following for its French baguettes.

Bread Social $

Stop into this buzzy Tweed Heads bakery for a custard tart before you cross the Queensland border.

Shop Australia in Sydney

RM Williams

Everything you need for the fair-dinkum jackaroo or jillaroo look.

Strand Hatters

Complete your Crocodile Dundee ensemble with an Akubra hat.

Aboriginal & Pacific Islander Art

Represents community-based Aboriginal and Pacific Islander art from a gallery in Waterloo.

Australian Wine Centre

Stock up on the top Aussie drops.

Gannon House Gallery

Inspiring selection of Aboriginal art in the Rocks, purchased directly from artists.

Ken Done Gallery

Browse joyful art featuring Australian landscapes and icons, and don't miss the gift shop.

Opal Minded

Opal aficionados love this jewellery shop.

Regional Art Galleries

Tweed Regional Gallery & Margaret Olley Art Centre

The key draw of this lauded gallery, perched above the Tweed River, is the recreated studio

ALEXI ROSENFELD/GETTY IMAGES

Bourke Street Bakery

of the late Margaret Olley, Australia's celebrated painter of still lifes and interiors.

Lismore Regional Gallery

Inland from Byron Bay, Lismore has a flourishing arts scene. After touring the gallery, which features contemporary works in all disciplines, seek out the vibrant street-art gallery nearby.

Yarrila Arts & Museum

A highlight at this Coffs Harbour arts complex, opened in 2023, is the Robert & Janice Hunter Collection featuring the works of 33 Aboriginal artists from Central Australia, the Kimberley and Arnhem Land.

Glasshouse Regional Gallery

The striking Port Macquarie arts hub showcases up to 25 exhibitions per year featuring contemporary, Indigenous, historical, traditional, design and sculptural artworks, along with artist talks and workshops.

Wollongong Art Gallery

Sets the standard for regional art museums, with an impressive collection of modern Aboriginal art.

Bundanon

World-class contemporary art exhibitions made possible by artist Arthur Boyd's gift of his Illaroo property.

South Coast Detour

Black Cockatoo $$

Follow the cool kids to this hidden bar on a night out in youthful Wollongong.

Cupitt's Estate $$

Uncover one of Australia's most underrated wine regions in the Shoalhaven region. Cupitt's has a winery, craft brewery, fromagerie and restaurant.

SASANAN TRAKANSUEBKUL/SHUTTERSTOCK

Bodalla Dairy Shed

Green Patch Beach

One of the loveliest beaches in gorgeous Jervis Bay, with mint-green waters.

Pebbly Beach

Docile kangaroos frequent this beach in Murramarang National Park, with nary a pebble in sight.

Oyster Shed on Wray Street $

Oysters are the essential South Coast seafood. Slurp them down by the Clyde River in Batemans Bay.

Bodalla Dairy Shed $

Get a taste of the South Coast's dairying history at this micro-dairy, which bottles all its milk in-house.

Barunguba Montague Island

Snorkel with wild fur seals around this culturally significant island off the coast of Narooma.

Central Tilba

This heritage-listed former gold-mining town is a prime example of early colonial architecture.

Eden Killer Whale Museum

Learn about the area's whaling history and local Aboriginal connections to whales at this fascinating museum.

By Caoimhe Hanrahan-Lawrence
Caoimhe is a Wiradjuri writer from rural New South Wales, currently living in Sydney on Wangal-Eora land.

Australia's First Nations Peoples

CUSTODIANS OF EARTH'S OLDEST CONTINUOUS CULTURES

Indigenous Australian cultures date back at least 65,000 years. Prior to European invasion in 1788, there were approximately 300 distinct language groups and 500 dialects. Now, Aboriginal and Torres Strait Islander peoples make up only 3.8% of the population. Most live in urban areas, though some maintain traditional lifestyles in remote areas.

Left Budj Bim Cultural Landscape (p129)
Centre Quandongs
Right Protests against the Australia Day date

HOLLI/SHUTTERSTOCK

Walking the Dreaming

Aboriginal cultures and spirituality revolve around Dreaming and Dreamtime. The Dreamtime tells us about how things came to be. It details the creation of the natural world – rivers, mountains, plants, animals, and everything in between.

The Dreaming explains why things are the way they are, such as the birth of the first platypus, how the echidna got her spines, and the meanings of certain constellations. The Dreaming is always occurring, without a defined beginning or end. It tells us about how we should behave, about our culture and families, and about living from and respecting the land.

Dreamtime and Dreaming stories differ across nations, though some nations share the same or similar stories. These stories have been passed down through oral storytelling, dance and art, and now many stories have also been written down.

An important part of the Dreaming is that Aboriginal peoples are the custodians, not the owners, of the land they live on. Instead, the relationship between the land and the people is a reciprocal one, where we care for the land because it cares for us.

Many of these Dreaming stories are connected to Songlines, which are paths walked by the spirits in the Dreamtime. Songlines serve many purposes, such as preserving history, detailing agricultural practices and mapping the land.

DALLASETTA/SHUTTERSTOCK

ANDREW BAIN/ALAMY

Living off the Land

For many years it was assumed that Indigenous peoples were hunter-gatherer societies prior to invasion. However, Aboriginal testimonies and recent historical research indicate that Indigenous societies employed complex aquaculture and agriculture practices. Structures such as weirs and dams still exist, and agricultural techniques and knowledges are being revived and passed on.

> Dreamtime and Dreaming stories differ across nations, though some nations share the same or similar stories. These have been passed down through oral storytelling, dance and art.

Many Aboriginal and Torres Strait communities recognise different seasons from those in the Western calendar. These seasons usually align with the area's weather patterns or relate to the local flora and fauna. The Wurundjeri people of Victoria recognise seven seasons, such as Biderap, which is sunny and dry, and Warin, when the wombat and the moth are by the creek. Understanding the Indigenous calendar in the area you are visiting may help you better prepare for the specific weather of the region. Knowing when to dress for the hot and windy, the wet and windy, or the cool and dry can make a big difference to your enjoyment of your travels.

Bush tucker (food) and bush medicine are still used today. Some bush tucker, such as pepperberry, quandong and Davidson's plum, is used in fusion cooking and can be found in restaurants.

ⓘ The Difficult Date

The date 26 January, when the First Fleet of colonisers arrived at Sydney Cove in 1788, officially became Australia Day in 1994. For Aboriginal and Torres Strait Islander peoples, 26 January is a more sombre occasion, marking the beginning of invasion, seizure of the land and erosion of culture. It is referred to as the Day of Mourning, Survival Day or Invasion Day. For many Indigenous people and their supporters, Invasion Day is a day of remembrance and resistance rather than celebration. The issue is contentious in Australia, and calls to keep or change the date occur every year.

Countries, Clans & Cousins

Individual clans exist within Aboriginal nations. Clans within the same language group usually speak dialects that are mutually intelligible. Within these clans are individual families, though Aboriginal families integrate the extended family more than most Western societies do. In some communities it is common to refer to your mother's sister as Mum rather than Aunty, and to call your first cousins your brother- or sister-cousins. Some people may use 'cousin' to refer to anyone within their clan, skin group or language group. 'Cuz' is also a term of affection among Aboriginal people even if they are from completely different nations.

Family and community ties are vital to Aboriginal cultures. Your family tells you who you are and where you come from. Many nations identify family ties by plant and animal totems.

Family and community ties are vital to Aboriginal cultures. Your family tells you who you are and where you come from. Many nations identify family ties by plant and animal totems. It is common to have your personal totem plus three further totems indicating your nation, your clan and your family ties. Sadly, much of this information has been lost, and it is a difficult journey for some people to find their family totems.

Aboriginal People Today

Across Australia, it is estimated that approximately 150 Aboriginal and Torres Strait Islander languages are still spoken and there are continuing efforts to revive languages among Indigenous communities. It is now possible to listen to music, watch TV shows or take classes in a number of Indigenous languages. Aboriginal words are also present in the Australian vernacular. Animals such as koalas, dingos, barramundi and galahs derive their names from Aboriginal languages, as do billabongs and boogie boards.

Similarly, Aboriginal words from different communities have spread through Australian Aboriginal English, the dialect of English spoken by many Aboriginal people across the country.

Around 62% of Indigenous Australians live on the east coast. This may surprise some visitors to Australia who think that they do not see many Aboriginal people in the region. Others are confused when a light-skinned person identifies as Aboriginal. It is widely accepted among Aboriginal communities that percentage of Aboriginality has little

RICHARD T. NOWITZ/GETTY IMAGES

CHAMELEONSEYE/SHUTTERSTOCK

LISA MAREE WILLIAMS/GETTY IMAGES

JAMES D. MORGAN/GETTY IMAGES

bearing on identity and involvement in the community. People with light skin and blonde hair can proudly identify as Blak or Blackfullas. A common metaphor used by First Nations communities is that of a cup of tea: no matter how much milk you put in the cup, no matter how pale it becomes, it's still tea.

This also means that a lot of Aboriginal people live off Country, meaning that they live on the land of another nation.

Since 1975 the first Sunday of July has marked the beginning of NAIDOC Week, which is dedicated to celebrating Aboriginal cultures, histories and perseverance. Communities, cities, schools and other institutions hold events that celebrate and build awareness about the rich and diverse Aboriginal cultures in Australia today.

Sorry Day (26 May) commemorates the formal apology from the Australian Government in 2008 for its role in the Stolen Generations. From 1910 to the 1970s, Aboriginal children were forcibly removed from their families to integrate them into white society. Aboriginal people today still feel the effects of this policy through loss of culture, family ties and language.

Signs of Respect

An Acknowledgement of Country and a Welcome to Country are important statements that identify and thank the custodians of the land on which an event takes place. Anyone, Aboriginal or not, can give an Acknowledgement. Welcomes can only be given by Elders from that country, or a member of the community who has been given permission by their Elders.

Elders and cultural teachers are usually referred to with 'Aunty' or 'Uncle' before their first name, in the same way that respect is conferred by the use of 'Sir' or 'Ma'am'. This recognises the knowledge and experience that our Elders hold.

Far left Making a boomerang
Left Aboriginal items made from wood, bone and shell
Above left Koomurri dancers celebrating NAIDOC Week
Above right Australian and Aboriginal flags

MELBOURNE & VICTORIA

CULTURE | HISTORY | FEASTING

RESEARCHED BY CRISTIAN BONETTO, TRENT HOLDEN AND SARAH REID

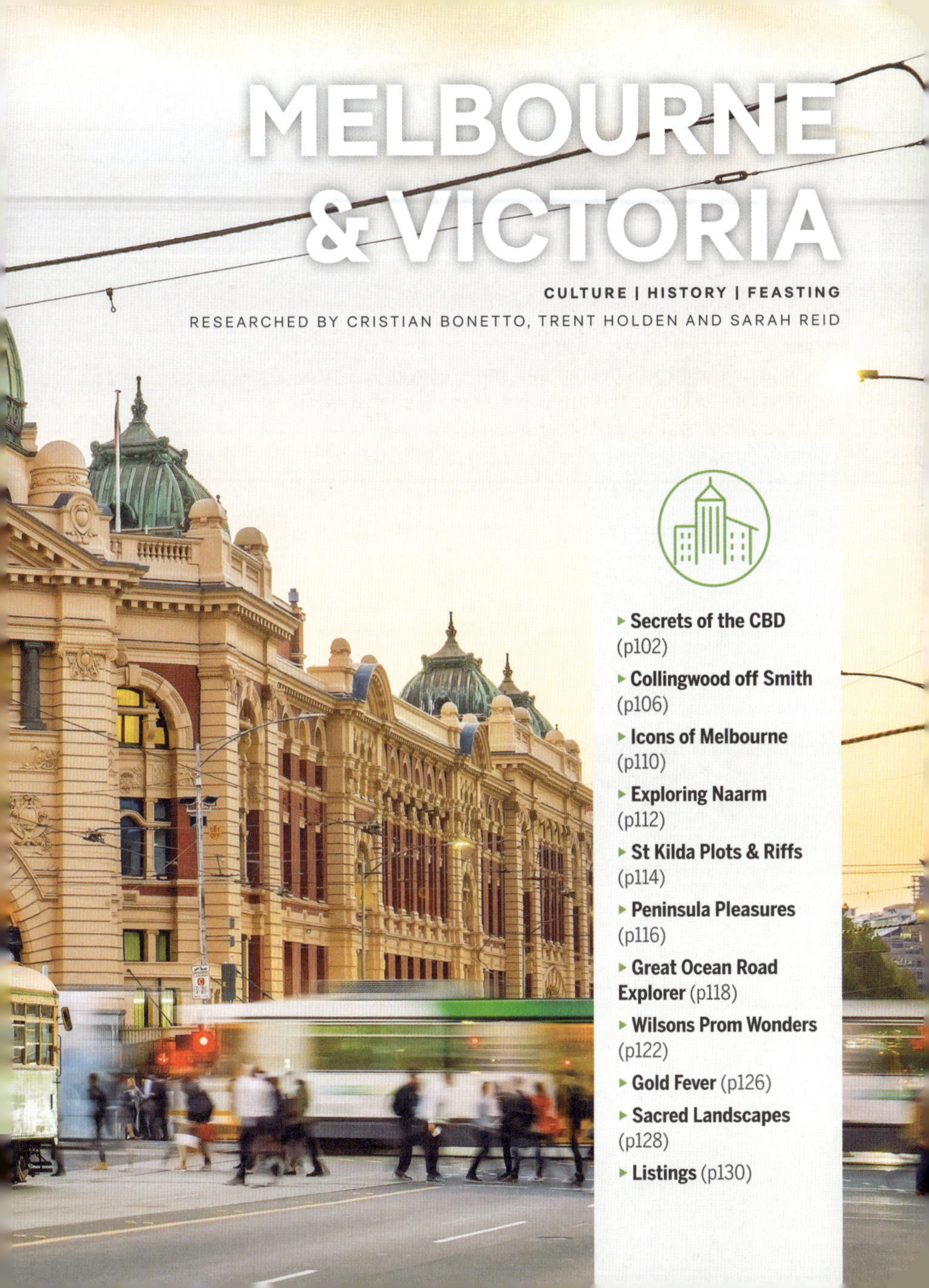

MELBOURNE & VICTORIA
Trip Builder

Forget blockbuster beaches and endless sunshine: Melbourne's beauty is deeper and more complex. This is Australia's most cultured metropolis, an electrifying mix of art, design, dining, architecture and cultures. Wild coastlines, wineries and a treasure trove of historical attractions await those who venture beyond.

PREVIOUS PAGE: F11PHOTO/SHUTTERSTOCK
FROM LEFT: FILEDIMAGE/SHUTTERSTOCK, PAUL HARDING 00/SHUTTERSTOCK

Enlargement
PARKVILLE
FITZROY
COLLINGWOOD
Yarra Bend Park
Studley Park
KEW
CARLTON
Be moved at the **Bunjilaka Aboriginal Cultural Centre** (p112)
15min from Melbourne CBD
Interact with Melbourne creatives at **Collingwood Yards** (p107)
20min from Melbourne CBD
Fitzroy Gardens
MELBOURNE
EAST MELBOURNE
Stumble upon studios and offbeat shops in the **Nicholas Building** (p104)
10min from Melbourne
Royal Botanic Gardens
Kings Domain
SOUTHBANK
Seek street art, negronis and killer eats in Melbourne's **laneways** (p102)
5min from Melbourne CBD
Royal Botanic Gardens
SOUTH MELBOURNE
PORT MELBOURNE
SOUTH YARRA
Fawkner Park
ALBERT PARK
Albert Park Lake
PRAHRAN
Albert Park
MIDDLE PARK
Catch a play, gig or cult flick in **St Kilda** (p114)
30min from Melbourne CBD
ST KILDA WEST
Hobsons Bay
ST KILDA
0 2 km
0 1 miles
Yarram
Inverloch
Corner Inlet
Wilsons Promontory National Park
Bass Strait
TASMAN SEA
0 100 km
0 50 miles

Practicalities

SHUANG LI/SHUTTERSTOCK

ARRIVING

Melbourne Airport Frequent SkyBus services (pictured) reach Southern Cross Station in central Melbourne, with additional services to Docklands, Southbank and St Kilda. Tickets purchased online are usually cheaper; a one-way/return adult ticket to Southern Cross Station costs from $24.90/41.70. A taxi to the city costs from around $70. Journey time is around 25 minutes for both.

Avalon Airport SkyBus also runs between Avalon Airport and Southern Cross Station. A one-way/return adult ticket costs from $28/52.90.

HOW MUCH FOR A

Piccolo (coffee) $5

Wood-fired pizza $28

Northcote Social Club gig $20–55

WHEN TO GO

DEC–FEB
Hot days and cool changes, music festivals, outdoor cinema and Grand Slam tennis.

MAR–MAY
Mild weather, golden foliage and the Melbourne Food & Wine Festival.

JUN–AUG
Chilly days made for museums, blockbuster NGV exhibitions, AFL matches and cosy pubs.

SEP–NOV
Footy-finals fever, Melbourne Cup fashion, temperamental weather.

GETTING AROUND

Trams, trains and buses Melbourne's iconic trams criss-cross the (walkable) city centre and extend into the suburbs. V/Line trains and buses service regional Victoria.

Tickets and passes Trams, trains and buses use electronic myki cards, available from train stations, some city tram stops, 7-Eleven stores and by using Google Pay on Android smartphones. A two-hour adult fare is $5.70, capped at $11.40 for the day ($8 on weekends and public holidays). A Free Tram Zone covers central Melbourne.

Driving Handy for day trips to regions surrounding Melbourne, including the Mornington Peninsula and destinations beyond.

EATING & DRINKING

Beyond Melbourne's celeb-chef restaurants is a wealth of affordable eateries serving authentic global cuisines. Hit Chinatown and Swanston St (city centre) for East Asian, Carlton for Italian, Brunswick and Coburg for Middle Eastern, North Richmond for Vietnamese, Footscray (pictured top right) for Vietnamese and Ethiopian, and, further out, Oakleigh for Greek.

The Melbourne region claims some outstanding gin distilleries, including Four Pillars, voted 'World's Best' several years running. Other makers worth sniffing out include Melbourne Gin Company and Brogan's Way.

Must-try Asian
Lee Ho Fook (p103)

Best wine bar
Marion (p131)

TOP: SHUANG L / SHUTTERSTOCK
BOTTOM: BROGAN'S WAY

CONNECT & FIND YOUR WAY

Wi-fi Free hot spots in central Melbourne include Bourke St Mall, Queen Victoria Market and Melbourne Museum; select VicFreeWiFi. Free wi-fi is common at libraries, museums, cafes and apartment rentals.

Navigation Melbourne's largely grid-style road system makes navigation straightforward. If driving, consider that some narrower inner-city streets are one way.

WHERE TO STAY

Book well ahead if your trip coincides with major events such as the Australian Open (January), Formula 1 Grand Prix (March) and Melbourne Cup (November).

Neighbourhood	Pro/Con
City Centre (CBD) and Southbank	World-class cultural sights, shopping, dining and entertainment. Noisy.
Carlton, Fitzroy and Collingwood	Victorian-era architecture, vibrant dining, arts and nightlife, interesting shops.
Brunswick and Northcote	Further out but Melbourne's hipster heartland. Great bars and live-music venues.
St Kilda	Cosmopolitan beachside neighbourhood. Seedy in parts.
Regional Victoria	Holiday apartments on the Great Ocean Road, chalets in the Victorian Alps and great national-park campsites across the state await.

FOUR SEASONS IN ONE DAY

The weather in Melbourne and areas beyond is infamously erratic. Bring layers of clothes you can peel off or slip on as required throughout the day.

MONEY

Halftix (halftixmelbourne.com) offers discounted theatre tickets, including to blockbuster musicals and Melbourne Theatre Company productions. Also check out todaytix.com.

Seek out Melbourne happy-hour deals on foot; liquor laws restrict overt online promotion.

14 Secrets of THE CBD

CREATIVITY | ARCHITECTURE | FOOD

Melbourne's CBD (Central Business District) holds its cards close to its chest. Here, laneways and unassuming doors lead to impeccably curated galleries and shops, architectural wonders, and rooftop drinks with sucker-punch views. Lace up your coolest kicks and seek out the city's finest assets.

JAKE RODEN

How to

Getting around The CBD is relatively compact and best explored on foot. Free city trams are a handy backup.

When to go Some shops don't open before 11am and some office buildings are closed on weekends, so consider exploring on a weekday afternoon. Note that some businesses close for several weeks in January.

Melbourne Street Tours Three-hour explorations of the city's dynamic street-art scene, as well as street-art workshops. Book online.

TONKA

Down the Laneways

Degraves St, Centre Pl, Hardware La and graffiti-drenched Hosier La may be the CBD's most Insta-famous laneways, but other alleyways harbour exceptional finds. On Warburton La, **Myrtle Wine Bar** celebrates locally sourced ingredients and Aussie wines, while nondescript Watson Pl harbours **Craft Victoria**, a gallery-store championing local makers. Relics from an infamous slum punctuate Casselden Pl, where a 19th-century brothel (the only single-storey house left in the CBD) is now **Little Lon Distilling Co**, an intimate cocktail bar offering gin masterclasses. Excellent eateries and bars dot Crossley and Liverpool Sts, while gritty Duckboard La claims Steen Jones' soaring 'Melbourne' mural, exceptional Chinese eatery **Lee Ho Fook** and new-school Indian **Tonka** (order the *pani puri* – filled, deep-fried flatbread shells).

PARKER BLAIN

Suburban House Museums

While the National Gallery of Victoria is a must for culture vultures, consider booking a guided tour of **Lyon Housemuseum** or **Justin Art House Museum (JAHM)**. Located in suburbia, both showcase private collections of contemporary art, exhibited in the collectors' covetable homes.

Top left Little Lon Distilling Co
Left Lee Ho Fook
Above Tonka

Vertical Villages

Step out of the laneways and into Melbourne's 'vertical villages': early-20th-century buildings stacked floor upon floor with independent galleries, eateries, bars and more. Legendary artist and muse Vali Myers had her studio in Swanston St's **Nicholas Building**, where subway-tiled corridors lead to one-off enterprises peddling everything from local millinery to vintage Manolo Blahnik slingbacks. Directly above the building's leadlight arcade, Flinders Lane Gallery showcases the work of Australian artists. You could spend all afternoon and evening in art-nouveau **Curtin House**, shopping for niche streetwear at unisex PAM, leafing through design tomes at Metropolis Bookstore, or downing cocktails and jungle curry at Cookie. Hit the rooftop bar for skyscraper views (and seasonal rooftop cinema), and always check the line-up at The Toff (anything from experimental DJs to hipster Balkan duos). The Toff's Orient Express–style private booths are hot property; book ahead to secure one. On Lonsdale St, one-time cigarette factory Pacific

Design Delights

The **Capitol** is a spectacular art-deco theatre. Designed by Marion Mahony Griffin and Walter Burley Griffin, it has a flamboyantly geometric ceiling and hosts interesting cultural events. In **Guildford Lane**, residents and businesses have populated their doorstops and balconies with potted plants, turning the street into a little oasis. At the rear of NGV International, the magical **Grollo Equiset Garden** hosts the gallery's annual Architecture Commission and comes alive over the summer months. Lastly, floating, open-air bar **Ponyfish Island** is perfect for watching boats motor by.

Simone LeAmon, *designer and former advocate and former Curator of Contemporary Design and Architecture at the National Gallery of Victoria @simoneleamon*

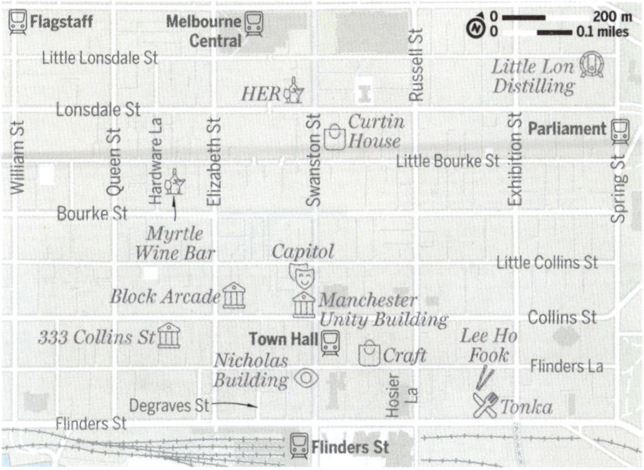

Left Capitol theatre
Below 333 Collins St

House is now **HER**, a four-level culinary destination whose offerings include a rooftop bar and a music room inspired by Japanese listening bars.

Hidden Wonders of Collins Street

On prestigious Collins St, architectural highlights often lie hidden in plain sight. Take **333 Collins St**, a Gotham-esque 1990s office building built over a spectacular domed banking chamber from the 1890s. Across the street, the ornate exterior of the **ANZ Bank** (1883–87) hints at the Venetian-inspired opulence inside. After fawning over the banking hall's 23-carat gold-leaf detailing, head through the doors at the rear to reach the stained-glass Cathedral Room. At mosaicked **Block Arcade** (1893), many miss Phillip Goatcher's allegorical ceiling painting (1907) in the L'Occitane store. On the north-east corner of Collins and Swanston Sts, the **Manchester Unity Building** (1932) houses Victoria's first escalator and restored lifts adorned with elegant Queensland maple. Head up the escalator to peek at what was once a glamorous art-deco shopping arcade; press the buzzer to enter and head along the arcade to exit to the lifts. Monthly building tours (manchesterunitybuilding.com.au) include access to the rooftop and boardroom, the latter an internationally renowned art-deco masterpiece; the afternoon 'Wine and Cheese Tour' is best.

RIGHT: FILEDIMAGE/SHUTTERSTOCK; LEFT: ALEX CIMBAL/SHUTTERSTOCK

15 Collingwood off SMITH

CREATIVITY | COFFEE | BEER

Once infamous for sooty factories and toothless footy-club supporters, gentrifying Collingwood fizzes with dynamic creativity and enterprise. Veer east of its of-the-moment dining-and-retail strip, Smith St, to discover sky-scraping street art, heritage-listed quirks, and some bloody good beer and coffee to boot.

How to

Getting here From the CBD it's a 15- to 20-minute ride on tram 86.

When to go Later in the week is best, with Saturday afternoons especially good for a buzzy, neighbourhood vibe.

Classic dives Hazy Collingwood memories are made rocking out at indie-music pub the Tote or queer club the Peel (aka 'the Squeal').

Going Japanese Brunch on *tamagoyaki* (Japanese omelette) at factory-turned-cafe-store CIBI or book a traditional Japanese bathing experience at Ofuroya.

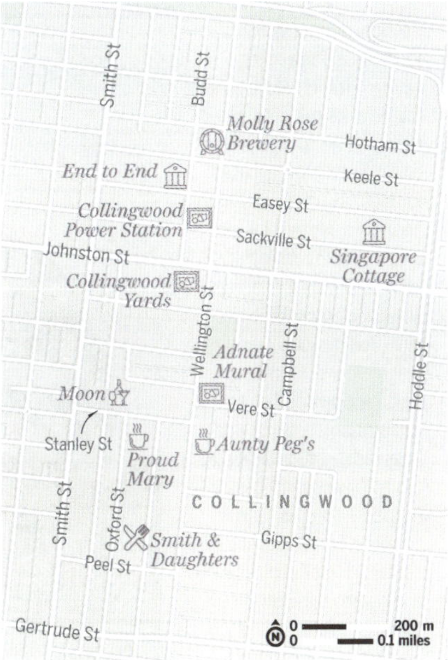

Doing the Yards

A 6500-sq-metre precinct of galleries and studios, community radio stations, one-off shops, bars and some of Australia's leading artist-run initiatives, **Collingwood Yards** is a hotbed of cultural collaborations. Before heading in (try to visit Thursday to Saturday), resident artist Emily Floyd recommends checking the Bus Projects (busprojects.org.au), Westspace (westspace.org.au), Liquid Architecture (liquidarchitecture.org.au) and Agency Projects (agencyprojects.org) websites for current exhibitions, talks and performances. Artist markets are sometimes held in the courtyard, itself flanked by Social Studio, selling fashion, design and accessories by Indigenous and culturally diverse creatives; check out its atelier upstairs.

Top left and left Entrances to Collingwood Yards

Art on the Streets

Collingwood's gritty streets are nectar for street artists. Local public-housing tenants feature in **Adnate's 20-storey mural** (corner of Wellington and Vere Sts). Stand further south on Wellington St to fully appreciate the tallest mural in the southern hemisphere. Adnate's work also features at **Collingwood Power Substation** (corner of Budd and Sackville Sts), alongside fellow Melbourne-based Rone. Budd St and the alleyways off it are always pimped with eye-popping works, and you'll find large-scale jaw-droppers on the side wall of nearby **46 Easey St**. Collingwood also claims one of the world's few surviving murals by American pop artist Keith Haring, painted on the side of what is now **Collingwood Yards'** Johnston St Building.

Architectural Curiosities

Down narrow Waterloo Rd lies the heritage-listed relics of the former **Yorkshire Brewery**. Among them is a polychromatic brick brew

Living History

Collingwood Yards was formerly a trade college where I studied. I love finding traces of its material history. Outside my studio there's a beautiful blackboard used for teaching carpentry. In the courtyard, **Hope St Radio** (hopestradio.community) hosts convivial gatherings; all are welcome. Yálla-birr-ang (Collingwood) has a rich history of First Peoples creative practice. For a sonic exploration, I recommend local radio station **3CR** (3cr.org.au). I've been listening to it for as long as I can remember. Favourite podcasts centring First Peoples' voices and community-led struggle include *Yarra Elders Precious Memories* and *Thursday Breakfast Interviews.*

Emily Floyd, *artist working in sculpture and public installation*
@emilyfloyd0

Carn the Pies!

Australian Rules Football (AFL) is Melbourne's unofficial religion and Collingwood's 'Magpies (The Pies)' one of its most colourful teams. While the professional team plays home games at the MCG (mcg.org.au), its spiritual home **Victoria Park** hosts Collingwood's women's team (collingwoodfc.com.au/teams/aflw); catch them January to late March/early April.

tower, designed in the Second Empire style and Melbourne's tallest building between 1867 and 1888. If the timber abode at 136 Sackville St looks dropped straight out of vintage Asia, that's because it is. Dubbed the **Singapore Cottage**, it's a rare example of the prefabricated abodes commonly imported to Melbourne during the 1850s gold rush. Nearby, daredevil modern engineering underscores concrete office block **End to End** (48 Easey St). Designed by Collingwood's provocative ITN Architects, the building is wildly crowned by three decommissioned train carriages. One of the carriages is home to top-notch burger bar **Easey's**.

From Brunch to Brew

South of Johnston St, brunch creatively at **Proud Mary Coffee**, whose sibling **Aunty Peg's** is practically a 'cellar door' for speciality coffee (served only black); check its socials for community cupping sessions. Rock 'n' roll chef Shannon Martinez is behind plant-based restaurant **Smith & Daughters** and the more casual **Smith & Deli**, while intimate wine bar **Moon** has a rocking selection of niche vino by the glass. North of Johnston St, **Acoffee** makes flawless lattes. A few doors down, locals kick back with IPAs and ales at craft brewery the **Mill**. For an impromptu beer crawl, roll onto **Molly Rose Brewery** to slurp Nic Sandry's out-of-the-box brews.

Left End to End
Above top Victoria Park
Above Acoffee

ICONS
of Melbourne

02

01

04

07

03

05

06

01 Flinders Street Station Clocks
When Melburnians say 'Meet me under the clocks', they mean the row of timekeepers at Flinders Street Station.

02 W-class Trams
Melbourne's tram network is the world's largest and its historic W-class trams the most iconic. Ride one on the City Circle line.

03 Aqua Profonda
Fitzroy swimming pool's endearingly misspelt Italian translation of 'deep water' is a legacy of the postwar immigration that transformed Melbourne.

04 Weeping Woman
Mysteriously stolen from the NGV in 1986, Picasso's *Weeping Woman* was found safe and sound in a train-station locker.

05 Melbourne Cricket Ground
Immortalised in Paul Kelly's song 'Leaps and Bounds', the 'G' is the cathedral in which footy-mad Melburnians worship their gods.

06 Skipping Girl
North Richmond's Skipping Girl (Little Audrey) began life advertising vinegar in 1936. Today she's the city's sweetheart.

07 Pellegrini's
It's still 1954 at this CBD

08

09

11

10

12

13

espresso bar, a bastion of Italo-Melburnian life and forefather of the city's coffee culture.

08 Brighton Bathing Boxes
Brighton beach's Victorian-era bathing boxes are hot property. In 2019, No 15 sold for a cool $340,000.

09 St Kilda Pier Kiosk
St Kilda Pier's Edwardian pavilion is an architectural phoenix, rising from the ashes after burning down in 2003.

10 American Doughnut Kitchen
A trip to the Queen Victoria Market isn't complete without doughnuts from this 1950 food van.

11 National Gallery of Victoria (NGV) Water Wall
Memories are made running your fingers along this trickling wall.

12 Royal Exhibition Building
This UNESCO World Heritage–listed show-off features a dome inspired by the Duomo in Florence.

13 Vault
Opinion was divided when Ron Robertson-Swann's sculpture was unveiled in 1980. Moved twice, it now calls Southbank home.

01 BOYLOSO/SHUTTERSTOCK, **02** LEONARD ZHUKOVSKY/SHUTTERSTOCK, **03** ASHTON 29/FLICKR/CC BY-SA 4.0, **04** BENJAMIN CRONE/SHUTTERSTOCK, **05** FILEDIMAGE/SHUTTERSTOCK, **06** DUNCAN CUNNINGHAM-REID/FLICKR/CC BY 2.0 DEED, **07** NILS VERSEMANN/SHUTTERSTOCK, **08** F11PHOTO/SHUTTERSTOCK, **09** SERGUEI LEVYKIN/SHUTTERSTOCK, **10** ICKEDA/SHUTTERSTOCK, **11** 365 FOCUS PHOTOGRAPHY/SHUTTERSTOCK, **12** CORNFIELD/SHUTTERSTOCK, **13** ROB DEUTSCHER/FLICKR/CC BY 2.0 DEED

16 Exploring NAARM

HISTORY | CULTURE | NATURE

Melbourne's birthday cake may still be shy of 200 candles, but the land on which the city stands has sustained the Wurundjeri and Boon Wurrung people of the Kulin nation for at least 40,000 years. To its Traditional Custodians, Melbourne is Naarm, and the city's bounty of Aboriginal art, stories and knowledge offers a deep connection to place as moving as it is enlightening.

JON AUGIER/MUSEUMS VICTORIA

How to

Getting around Federation Sq faces Flinders Street Station. Melbourne Museum and the Royal Botanic Gardens are within walking distance of the CBD. Trams reach both.

When to go Aboriginal Melbourne can be experienced all year.

Barak Building Looking north up Swanston St from the Shrine of Remembrance, you'll notice a 31-storey, black-and-white building embedded with the face of Wurundjeri-willam artist, diplomat and *ngurungaeta* (clan leader) William Barak (1824–1903).

KIRAKIRAANG/SHUTTERSTOCK

Journey through time The evocative Bunjilaka Aboriginal Cultural Centre at **Melbourne Museum** explores many facets of Victoria's oldest living cultures. Learn about the art of possum-skin cloaks and the ingenuity of Budj Bim's ancient aquaculture system, listen to traditional songs of mourning, and reflect on Victoria's frontier wars. From the galleries, the easily missed Milarri Garden Walk is a beautiful spot for quiet contemplation.

Important art On Federation Sq, explore works by Victorian Indigenous artists at the National Gallery of Australia's **Ian Potter Centre**. According to Myles Russell-Cook, the NGV's former senior curator of Indigenous art, key works include William Barak's *Ceremony* (1898), Maree Clark's *Ritual and Ceremony* (2012), Destiny Deacon's *BLAK* (2020) and Brook Andrew's *Sexy and dangerous* (1996; printed 2005).

A walk in the park As eucalyptus-scented smoke billows from the *tarnuk* (wooden dish), Kulin nation ancestors are acknowledged and you are welcomed to Country. The sacred *tanderrum* ceremony forms part of the Royal Botanic Gardens' **Aboriginal Heritage Walk** (rbg.vic.gov.au). Tours lead visitors through Naarm's foremost public gardens to learn about local Aboriginal culture and knowledge, from the city's six seasons to medicinal bush tucker. Book online.

Top left Melbourne Museum
Bottom left Ian Potter Centre

Culture Hub

A visit to the **Koorie Heritage Trust** on Federation Sq is a must for any itinerary, offering a unique insight into Indigenous culture. Immerse yourself in our exhibitions from Victorian First Nations artists, and experience one of the largest collections of Koorie art and artefacts on permanent display. Our Aboriginal Walking Tours are led by First Nation guides and help you gain an understanding of how Melbourne's city centre has changed over time and the significance of the Birrarung (Yarra River) to the local Kulin peoples. Our shop supports local artists and craftspeople and all products sold are authentic and unique.

Tom Mosby,
CEO of the Koorie Heritage Trust
@koorie_heritage_trust_inc

17 ST KILDA
Plots & Riffs

CULTURE | HERITAGE | COCKTAILS

Postwar Jewish enclave, red-light district, punk-rocker hub, artists' muse: bayside St Kilda has always been an eclectic bohemian at heart. While property prices may be stratospheric, there's still magic on these streets, at rock-and-roll joints, independent theatres and a Golden Age picture palace. Catch a gig, play or double feature, and let that old St Kilda energy sparkle.

GREG BALFOUR EVANS/ALAMY STOCK PHOTO

How to

Getting here From the CBD, trams 16 and 96 reach St Kilda (around 30 minutes). For Red Stitch and the Astor, catch a Sandringham-line train to Windsor.

When to go Year-round, but summer in St Kilda is festive.

Classic hangouts Generations of artists have brunched, slurped coffee and scribbled down ideas at Galleon Cafe, eaten Polish cheesecake at Monarch Cakes and dined Italian-style at Cicciolina; the latter has an easily missed back bar.

PAULHARDINGOO/SHUTTERSTOCK

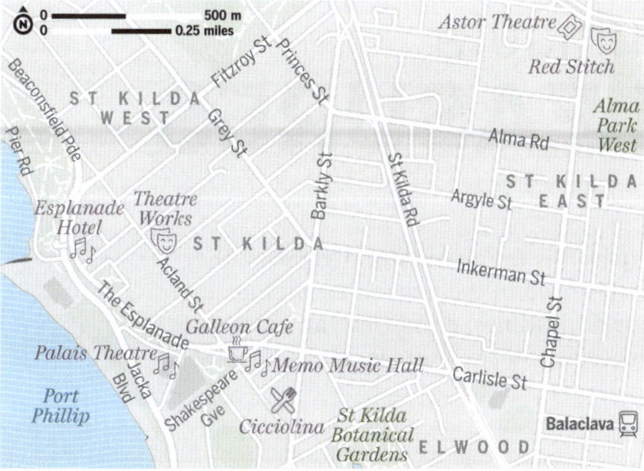

Top left Esplanade Hotel
Bottom left Palais Theatre

Cult films in a deco landmark At night there's something deliciously noir about the softly lit lobby at the **Astor**, car lights gleaming on a rainy Chapel St outside. It might be those elegant curves, the intimate bar named after the hotel in *The Shining*, or the tinkering bell of resident feline Duke (named after John Wayne). In business since 1936, this grand old cinema has a brilliant programme of cult classics and double bills, best viewed with a choc-top ice-cream from the bar.

Homegrown drama Watching someone unravel is intense, especially when they're within touching distance. There are only 81 seats in the converted church hall used by **Red Stitch**, and the ensemble's productions of contemporary theatre are intelligent and powerful. These include world premieres of new Australian works, developed exclusively with the company. **Theatre Works** is another platform for diverse local voices. Hankering for a contemporary circus work exploring Australia's socio-political landscape? You'll probably see it here.

Music at the Memo Some of the biggest names in rock, jazz, blues and electronica have played historic St Kilda venues like the **Palais** and the **Esplanade**, while the summertime St Kilda Festival – a showcase for local acts – draws massive crowds. For a more in-the-know experience, catch an act at **Memo Music Hall**, a 1920s dance hall now hosting Aussie rock and jazz legends, contemporary singer-songwriters and cabaret.

A Ghost at the Espy

Everyone who's anyone in Australian music has rocked St Kilda's **Esplanade Hotel**. Singer-songwriter Paul Kelly recorded tracks in its legendary Gershwin Room, while late Daddy Cool guitarist Ross Hannaford held a long-running residency in the front bar. Built as a seaside hotel in 1878, its guests reputedly include Mark Twain and Sarah Bernhardt. Legend has it the French actress checked in with 12 pets. These days, the Espy's best-kept secret is the Ghost of Alfred Felton, a top-floor cocktail lounge named for the art collector and philanthropist who kept rooms here until his death in 1904.

18 Peninsula PLEASURES

BEACHES | SPAS | WINE

As good for a day trip as it is for an indulgent getaway, the Mornington Peninsula is well versed in the finer things in life, offering both wild and genteel coastlines, mind-clearing hikes and spas, stellar restaurants, wineries and sculpture gardens.

NATALIA VOSTRIKOVA/ SHUTTERSTOCK

Trip Notes

Getting here Hire your own car to properly explore the peninsula, a 70- to 90-minute drive south of central Melbourne.

When to go Mid-December to late January is peak season, with crowds and high prices; February to mid-March offers beach weather with thinner crowds.

Dining Book notable restaurants at least a month ahead, especially if visiting in summer and on weekends; some places only open later in the week.

Top Picks

Torello Farm stocks great local produce like Cape Schanck olive oil, Main Ridge olives and sourdough bread from Mary Mother Bakes. Excellent small winery **Avani** has biodynamic estate syrah and pop-up restaurants in summer. For an interesting walk, head right of **Flinders Pier** (pictured right), past the yacht club and around the cliff.

Brigitte Hafner, *chef and owner of Tedesca Osteria @tedesca72*

01 Hike the wild coast from Cape Schanck to **Bushrangers Bay** (5.2km return). If the tide is low and the weather warm, soak in the rock pools at the eastern end of the bay.

02 Drop into sleepy **Flinders** for coffee and a quick gallery hop. Duck into Manyung Gallery for Australian painting and sculpture, and Cook Street Collective for art and craft from local makers.

03 Quaff elegant local pinot noir and chardonnay at **Pt Leo Estate** and roam the winery's bay-facing sculpture garden, featuring large-scale contemporary pieces by renowned artists such as Jaume Plensa and Kaws.

04 Reserve a long, decadent lunch (or Saturday dinner) at **Tedesca Osteria**, set in a restored farmhouse and praised for its beautiful wood-fired cooking, locavore produce and progressive wine list.

05 Hop between healing mineral pools at **Peninsula Hot Springs** (pictured left), set among native tea trees. For a more luxe vibe, opt for neighbouring **Alba Thermal Springs & Spa**. Book both in advance.

FILEDIMAGE/SHUTTERSTOCK

19 Great Ocean Road EXPLORER

BEACHES | WILDLIFE | GOURMET

Stretching from Torquay to Allansford, the Great Ocean Road is Australia's most fabled coastal drive, a 240km route where bracing southern waters meet luxuriant forests, emerald fields and salty beach towns. Stay a while and let its secrets, legends and flavours bewitch you.

HON CHUNG HAM/ALAMY STOCK PHOTO

How to

Getting here The route's eastern gateway is Torquay, 103km southwest of Melbourne via the M1. Rent your own wheels for maximum freedom.

When to go February and March are warm, with fewer crowds than December and January. Winter is whale-watching season.

Go west Drive from the east for the best views and easy access to lookouts.

Accommodation Book well ahead in summer, at Easter and in school-holiday periods, especially in Lorne, Anglesea and Apollo Bay.

MICHAEL XIAOS/SHUTTERSTOCK

Forest Secrets

Much of the Great Ocean Road lies within **Great Otway National Park**, which sprawls from Torquay to Princetown and north through the Otway Ranges in a sweep of rugged beaches, lush fern gullies and towering mountain ash. While some of its highlights are well known – koala spotting in Kennett River, hiking to Hopetoun Falls (especially beautiful in late winter and spring), wandering through the rainforest canopy at **Otway Fly Treetop Adventures** – others are less familiar. Few know that just outside Forrest, tranquil **Lake Elizabeth** is one of the best places in Australia to spot platypuses, particularly when canoeing with local experts **Otway Eco Tours** (platypustours.net.au). Another mysterious local creature is the fungus gnat larva (native glow-worm), which inhabits particularly cool, wet sections of the

YMGERMAN/SHUTTERSTOCK

Making Waves

At the eastern edge of the Great Ocean Road lies legendary surf spot **Bells Beach**. Head there early in the morning to watch pros ride its world-famous right-hand breaks, at their peak in autumn and winter. Inspired? **Go Ride a Wave** (gorideawave.com.au) runs lessons along the Great Ocean Road.

Top left Otway Fly Treetop Adventures
Left Great Ocean Road
Above Koala, Great Otway National Park

rainforest. As darkness falls, wrap up warm and take a walk along the **Maits Rest Trail** (800m) near Cape Otway or **Madsens Track Nature Walk** (1.5km) at Melba Gully (west of Lavers Hill). Eyes adjusted to the darkness, you will see them, their delicate blue-green threads glowing ethereally in the dark.

Apostles, Shipwrecks & Treasure

Rising out of savage, shipwrecking waters, the **Twelve Apostles** make for a grand finale at the western end of the Great Ocean Road. The monumental limestone stacks are especially spectacular juxtaposed against the setting sun, shortly after which little penguins begin waddling out of the ocean on their way home (bring binoculars). Further west, **Loch Ard Gorge** is where the sole two survivors of the *Loch Ard* – a British iron clipper wrecked nearby in 1878 – swam to safety. Washed-up cargo included the Loch Ard Peacock, a life-size majolica sculpture bound for Melbourne's

Where Whalers Once Slumbered

While many wrap up their Great Ocean Road drive at the Twelve Apostles, it's worth continuing west to spend a night or two in the old whaling town of **Port Fairy**. There's a haunting quality to the place, its pine-graced streets flanked by snug cottages and stoic stone inns fit for a period coastal drama. Consider slumbering at impeccable **Drift House** and make a dinner reservation at cosy **Merrijig Kitchen**, located in Victoria's oldest inn. If you're visiting during the popular Port Fairy Folk Festival in March, note that accommodation can book out a year ahead; plan accordingly.

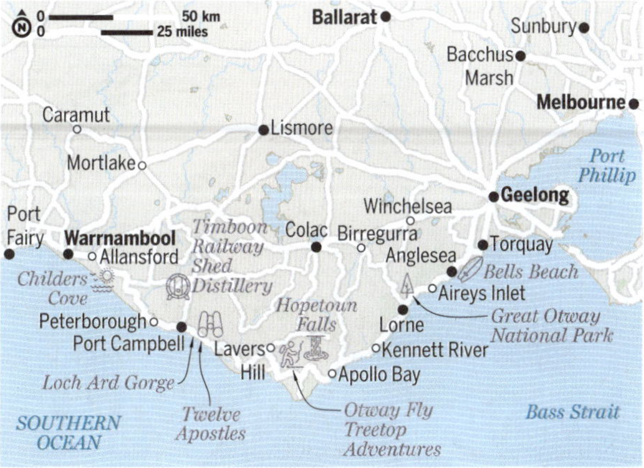

Great Exhibition of 1880. Valued at over $4 million, the exquisite Minton piece is now on display at Warrnambool's **Flagstaff Hill Maritime Museum**. Further west still lies **Childers Cove**, a beautiful, solitary beach that's one of the Great Ocean Road's best-kept secrets.

Savour the Region

Don't just see the Great Ocean Road; taste it. Feast on next-level fish and chips at **Fish by Moonlite** in Anglesea and sip native-botanicals gin at Torquay's **Great Ocean Road Gin**. Down by Apollo Bay's harbour, **Apollo Bay Fishermen's Co-op** both sells and cooks off-the-boat local fish and southern rock lobsters, caught sustainably by local skipper 'Frosty' and his crew. Inland from the Twelve Apostles, Josh Walker crafts elegant single-malt whisky at his **Timboon Railway Shed Distillery**, which also stocks local artisanal comestibles. North of the Otway Ranges, in sleepy Birregurra, you'll need to book a few months ahead for a table at Dan Hunter's internationally acclaimed farmhouse restaurant **Brae**, where extraordinary tasting menus might include a guided walk through the produce garden.

Left Port Fairy
Below Childers Cove

20 Wilsons Prom WONDERS

WALKS | WILDERNESS | BEACHES

Turquoise waters and bone-white sands meet pristine bushland at Wilsons Promontory (affectionately known in Victoria as 'the Prom'). A very popular place for hiking and camping, this is one of Australia's most spectacular swathes of coastal wilderness.

JORDISTOCK/SHUTTERSTOCK

Skull Rock

Emerging from the sea like a villain's lair in an Indiana Jones film is the remote and enigmatic island known as Skull Rock. This monolith used to be off-limits to tourists, but thanks to **Wanderer Adventures**, you can cruise close to its 130m-wide cave. Getting here is half the fun: cool amphibious boats pick you up from the sands of Norman Beach for a memorable 2½-hour tour of the Prom's unique coastal wilderness. This is Victoria's largest marine protected area, so you'll pass islands home to seals, penguins and muttonbirds. Keep an eye out for bottlenose dolphins and, from May to October, southern right whales.

Southern Prom Circuit

One of the best ways to experience the Prom is to lace your boots and set out on a long walk through part of its vast wilderness. Hikes

WILSONS PROMONTORY CRUISES

How to

Getting here and around Tidal River is 224km southeast of Melbourne. You'll need your own vehicle, as there's no public transport. Otherwise, **Hike & Seek** (hikeandseek.com.au) runs day tours.

When to go August to November is ideal, with spring wildflowers, whale watching, temperate weather and lighter crowds.

Wildlife From inquisitive wombats at your camp site to kangaroos and emus along the **Prom Wildlife Walk** (2.3km return), this is a destination rich in native fauna.

Top left Skull Rock
Left Bottlenose dolphin

last anywhere from 30 minutes to a week, and there are all kinds of trails depending on your time and energy. Stretching over 36km, the **Southern Prom Circuit** is the park's signature trek, a three-day, two-night camping adventure showcasing the Prom's stunning biodiversity. The route takes in eucalypt-scented forests, fern gullies and mountaintop lookouts before concluding at blissful white-sand beaches where you can camp overlooking calm azure waters.

Big Drift

Though there's no shortage of golden beaches across Wilsons Prom, there's nothing else quite as monumental as the sands found at the Big Drift. These spectacular inland dunes rise from the encroaching woodland in a surreal and unexpected sight: it feels as though you've landed on another planet as you wander across the evocative landscape, admiring views over the expansive Vereker range bushland and the distant ocean. For

Best Hikes

Sealers Cove Along the walk you'll see multiple forest types and ecosystems, and you'll get to visit Sealers Cove (one of Australia's best beaches!). Approximately five hours return.

Mt Oberon Lookout This is an unmissable, world-class panorama overlooking Wilsons Prom. The best time to visit is at sunset. Approximately 2½ hours return.

Beach trifecta Starting at Tidal River campground, you can walk to Squeaky Beach, Picnic Bay and Whisky Bay via coastal walking tracks and beaches. Approximately three hours return, but you'll want to spend longer on the beach!

Bill Gurnett, *former Parks Victoria ranger and co-owner of Gurneys Cider @gurneyscidery*

Wilsons Prom Lightstation

You can sleep in a 19th-century cottage at mainland Australia's most southerly lighthouse. Mind you, you'll earn your rest: to get here you must walk 20km (one way) through the Prom's beautiful hinterland. Climb to the top of the windswept beacon for views over Bass Strait.

the best photos, come at sunrise or sunset, when the sands glow rose gold. If you're into stargazing, come back at night to witness a spectacular galactic light show. Sandboarding is also a thing here, so if you've got an old boogie board, bring it along to surf the Big Drift's sandy swells.

Walks from Tidal River

If you're not sold on a multiday wilderness hike, you'll be happy to learn that many of the Prom's iconic attractions are only a short stroll from the park's headquarters at Tidal River. If you have time for just one walk, make it the trip up **Mt Oberon**. At the summit you'll be treated to all-encompassing, life-affirming vistas across the entire national park. A beach walk is also a good choice. The most well known of these is the walk to the aptly named **Squeaky Beach**, which makes sounds like a dog toy as you stroll across its powdery quartz sands. Equally spectacular is nearby **Whisky Bay**, with its chalky white sands, sparkling aquamarine waters and photogenic lichen-splattered boulders.

Left View from Mt Oberon
Above top Wilsons Prom Lightstation
Above Squeaky Beach

21 Gold FEVER

AUSTRALIAN HISTORY | ARCHITECTURE | FAMILY FUN

Ballarat was the world's richest alluvial goldfield during its peak in 1852 and 1853, and it shows through its towering Victorian-era architecture. Here you step back into the gold-rush era at a number of excellent attractions – as well as the townscape itself – then get a taste of modern Ballarat, which is gaining distinction for dining.

PAUL HARDING/SHUTTERSTOCK

How to

Getting there The town is 115km northwest of Melbourne. It takes about 90 minutes to get there by car or train.

When to go Come at any time of year; the mild days in spring and autumn are ideal for outdoor exploration.

Meal break Armstrong St North is considered the city's 'feast street'. Modern Vietnamese joint **Saigon Allée** makes a good banh mi at lunch. On Mair St, **Aunty Jacks** is a multilevel industrial brewpub with a menu of hearty favourites.

PAUL HARDING/SHUTTERSTOCK

Top and bottom left Sovereign Hill

Return to the Gold Rush

The 'living museum' of **Sovereign Hill** is a recreated pioneer town set during the height of the city's gold rush. Walk among in-character townsfolk and see the blacksmith at work, musket-firing by a state trooper and a gold pour demonstration. Go down Red Hill Mine for a 12-minute self-guided tour that tells the story of the Welcome Nugget, a huge 69kg gold nugget found in 1858. Try your hand at gold panning by the creek; you can keep any gold you find.

Three to four hours is the recommended minimum time to explore the 30,000-sq-metre town.

An Uprising Remembered

The **Eureka Centre**, at what is believed to be the site of the Eureka Rebellion, takes visitors through the differing perspectives of the insurgency and, notably, houses the original Eureka flag. It is regarded as the 'birthplace of Australian democracy', as the incident resulted in an official inquiry into the administration of the goldfields; this led to the abolition of the controversial monthly gold license and the start of other democratic reforms, such as voting rights for miners. There's hours of reading for inquiring minds via the central touchscreens, though the wall-mounted signboards and the centre's guidebook (received upon entry) give a sufficient summary.

Around 1½ hours is ample for most visitors to take in the centre and the surrounding **Eureka Stockade Memorial Park**, which contains containing several monuments of remembrance.

Discover Gold After Dark

Visit Sovereign Hill at night with a separate ticket for **AURA**, an immersive experience that tells the story of gold from its creation and how it shaped Ballarat through an outstanding 90-minute sound-and-light show. Visitors begin in an indoor 3D theatre, then ride through the site in an open-air vehicle for further multi-sensory storytelling at outdoor and semi-outdoor theatre spaces. Be sure to dress for evening weather. Up to five wheelchair users per session can be accommodated in this fully accessible experience, with vehicle access via lift.

22 SACRED Landscapes

ROCK ART | ABORIGINAL AQUACULTURE | GUIDED TOURS

Among Victoria's many significant cultural landscapes are two blockbusters in the state's west. The volcanic landscape of Budj Bim is home to Australia's oldest and most extensive Aboriginal aquaculture system, while the hilly wilderness of the Grampians contains 80% of the state's Aboriginal rock art. Both sites offer intriguing insights into the ingenuity and spirituality of the world's oldest surviving cultures.

ANDREW BAIN/ALAMY

How to

Getting there From Melbourne, Budj Bim National Park is 330km west and Grampians (Gariwerd) National Park is 260km northwest. The two parks are about 90km apart.

When to go Both parks are open year-round. Mild days in spring and autumn are ideal for exploring.

Camping There's a campground at Lake Surprise in Budj Bim National Park and 12 vehicle-based campgrounds in Grampians (Gariwerd) National Park (parks.vic.gov.au).

LITTLE ADVENTURES/SHUTTERSTOCK

Budj Bim

Spanning nearly 100 sq km and predating the Pyramids, the UNESCO World Heritage–listed **Budj Bim Cultural Landscape** features sophisticated aquaculture systems built by the Gunditjmara people over 6600 years ago, using lava flows to create channels, weirs, and dams to trap and harvest *kooyang* (eels) and fish.

Begin your visit at the Gunditjmara-run **Tae Rak Aquaculture Centre** (9am-4pm Wed-Sun) on the shores of Tae Rak (Lake Condah), about 30 minutes from the main entrance to Budj Bim National Park, which has a bush tucker cafe and tour desk.

It's possible to see some of the aquaculture sites yourself but, while information boards are helpful, learning about the site's history and cultural significance from a Gunditjmara guide is more meaningful. Tours ($89 to $199) range from a two-hour wetland tour to a full-day cultural walk.

Grampians

Home to the Jardwadjali and Djab Wurrung peoples for at least 22,000 years, the ancient sandstone landscape of the **Grampians (Gariwerd) National Park** is pivotal to their Dreaming. Rising from the plains of western Victoria, this unique environment, covering about 1700 sq km, has also provided an important source of food and shelter for Aboriginal groups for generations. Its rocky overhangs are a canvas for about 200 pieces of rock art. Among the national park's many walking trails are a handful of short walks that take you to artworks open to the public.

Top left Tae Rak Aquaculture Centre
Bottom left Gulgurn Manja Shelter

Grampians Rock Art Sites

At the northern end of Grampians National Park, the **Gulgurn Manja Shelter** displays handprints and emu tracks, and the **Ngamadjidj Shelter** is painted with white figures.

In the park further south, the **Billimina Shelter** is decorated with 2500 motifs. They include 55 human stick figures, as well as hundreds of vertical lines thought to have been used to count events in retelling stories or to record the number of days spent at a place. Nearby is the **Manja Shelter**, which features some of Victoria's best examples of hand stencils.

At **Bunjil's Shelter** in the Black Range Scenic Reserve near Stawell, you can see a depiction of the Creation spirit Bunjil and his two dingoes.

Listings

BEST OF THE REST

Old Masters, Mod Mavericks

NGV International

While the NGV's Australian collection occupies the Ian Potter Centre at Federation Sq, its international works are housed in its behemoth St Kilda Rd building, home to the world's largest stained-glass ceiling and Tiepolo's epic *Banquet of Cleopatra*.

ACMI

Federation Sq's high-tech museum of screen culture in all its forms: film, TV, video art, even video games. Dig deep at exhibitions, screenings, talks and themed festivals.

Heide Museum of Modern Art

In a bucolic setting in suburban Bulleen, the former home of art patrons John and Sunday Reed is renowned for its modernist architecture and modern Australian art.

Buxton Contemporary

Weird, wonderful and thought-provoking shows of contemporary Australian art in Southbank, featuring the private collection of Michael Buxton.

Melbourne Tales

State Library Victoria

One of the world's great libraries, with breathtaking heritage spaces and free galleries showcasing everything from early Melbourne paintings to bushranger Ned Kelly's armour.

Melbourne Museum

In the UNESCO World Heritage–listed Carlton Gardens, this sprawling natural- and cultural-history museum delves into the city's extraordinary backstory from refreshing perspectives.

Immigration Museum

A dynamic museum exploring identity, diversity and stories from one of the world's most multicultural societies. Suitably set in Melbourne's beautifully restored Old Customs House.

Rockin' Melbourne Nights

Corner Hotel

Everyone from Ben Harper to the Dandy Warhols has played this rambunctious Richmond pub. Catch an up-and-comer or certified music legend.

Northcote Social Club

In hipster heartland Northcote, NSC is a great pub for emerging singer-songwriters and bands, both local and touring.

Northcote Theatre

Another on-point Northcote venue, set in a restored, heritage-listed cinema dating from 1912. Bonus points for the on-site trattoria, wine bar and rooftop bar.

Cherry

Noel Gallagher once offered to buy this CBD dive bar – testament to its X factor. It's a

RICHIE CHAN/SHUTTERSTOCK

ACMI

come-one-come-all joint, pumping out everything from blues and punk to retro.

JazzLab

Brunswick offspring of Melbourne's late, great jazz club Bennetts Lane, serving up top local and international sax seven nights a week.

Howler

In a Brunswick warehouse, Howler has courted the likes of British singer-songwriter SG Lewis and Aussie alt-rockers Middle Kids. Expect fresh, eclectic acts.

Words & Ideas

Wheeler Centre

Located at the State Library Victoria, the Wheeler Centre runs a busy program of public talks on topics ranging from art and literature to current affairs.

Readings

Voted the World's Best Bookstore in 2016, the Carlton branch of Melbourne's favourite independent bookstore chain hosts regular book launches and talks with lauded writers.

La Mama Courthouse

Playwriting greats including David Williamson cut their teeth at this intimate Carlton theatre, still a top spot to catch emerging local talent.

Melbourne by Design

Clementine's

Affordable, locally designed and made gifts in the CBD, from Melbourne-themed totes to ceramics, contemporary jewellery and even native skincare.

Alpha60

Statement-making threads designed by two Melbourne siblings. The label's Chapter House boutique occupies a beautiful vaulted hall by St Paul's Cathedral.

SMA1050/SHUTTERSTOCK

Clementine's

Gertrude Street

Fitzroy's hippest strip claims some of Melbourne's edgiest fashion labels, including Leonard St, Edgeley and Handsom.

Booze & Conversation

Marion $$

Sharp yet friendly staff, sophisticated small plates and out-of-the-box wines by the glass on Fitzroy's Gertrude St.

Carlton Wine Room $$

An understatedly refined Carlton favourite, complete with seasonally adjusted wine list and contemporary bites and mains.

Embla $$

In the CBD, congenial, intimate Embla has a New York vibe, an award-winning wine list and knockout dishes kissed by wood oven or grill.

Beermash $$

Laid-back and affable, Collingwood's Beermash pours a thrilling selection of craft brews, both draught and bottled. Niche ciders and wines add to the sense of adventure.

Vinesmith $$

Cellar door, wine bar, French-inspired bistro and wine shop rolled into a neat Flinders La package.

Commis $$

Cosy candlelit bar in Collingwood with free popcorn, interesting house cocktails and a short, smart menu.

City Cafe Culture

Seven Seeds $

House-roasted speciality coffee and a short, feel-good, all-day menu underscore this Carlton classic, hidden up a side street.

Wide Open Road $

Indie vibes, comforting toasties and house-roasted beans keep north-side hipsters purring at this super-local Brunswick stalwart.

Industry Beans $$

A Fitzroy-based coffee roaster revered as much for its next-level food options as for its signature blends, rotating single origins and speciality-coffee bubble cup.

Hardware Société $$

Gorgeous, Gallic-accented dishes, brunch cocktails and art by Melbourne illustrator Mads Francis, all hidden down a lesser-known CBD laneway.

Brother Baba Budan $

Serves just coffee and counter food, but both are excellent. On Little Bourke St; there are only a handful of seats inside.

Florian $

Be prepared to wait for a table at this popular Carlton North cafe. The filled baguettes, sandwiches and pastries are worth it.

Melbourne Foodie Hit List

Sunda $$

Young-gun chef Khanh Nguyen merges Southeast Asian flavours, native ingredients and new-school ingenuity to create headline-worthy dishes at his hip CBD eatery.

Anchovy $$

Critically acclaimed reinterpretations of Vietnamese cooking in Richmond. For a cheaper bite, grab a posh banh mi (Vietnamese baguette sandwich) from next-door sibling Ca Com.

HuTong Dumpling Bar $$

On a CBD laneway, dexterous chefs pleat Melbourne's best *xiao long bao* (steamed dumplings filled with broth and pork). There's a second branch in Prahran.

48h Pizza e Gnocchi Bar $$

A simple menu of award-winning wood-fired pizzas, plus pillowy gnocchi and graze-friendly antipasti and olives. Two restaurant locations: South Yarra and Elsternwick.

Attica $$$

Reserve months ahead to secure a table at Ben Shewry's world-famous Ripponlea restaurant, a bastion of contemporary Australian cooking at its most enlightened.

Farmer's Daughters $$$

A svelte ode to Gippsland produce in the CBD. Fine-dine in the restaurant, graze in the deli or sip cocktails on the rooftop.

AVANT VISUAL/SHUTTERSTOCK

Dandenong Ranges

Osteria Ilaria $$$

Thoughtful, modern Italo-Australian cooking in the CBD, with clever twists, house-cured meats and surprising wines.

Maha $$$

Chef Shane Delia puts an innovative spin on Middle Eastern cooking at his plush CBD restaurant. For something more casual, hit wine bar Maha East in Windsor.

Gimlet $$$

Contemporary European cuisine in a CBD heritage space reminiscent of a Viennese cafe.

Road-Trip-Worthy Meals

Brae $$$

In the Otways hinterland, acclaimed chef Dan Hunter mostly uses whatever's growing in the 12 hectares of organic gardens to create delightful gastronomic concoctions, all masterfully presented.

Royal Mail Hotel $$$

At the gateway to the Grampians, Dunkeld's main attraction is Wickens at the Royal Mail, with a daily-changing menu of local, seasonal produce. Also here is the Parker St Project bistro, a more affordable option that doesn't skimp on quality.

Lake House $$$

You can't talk about Daylesford without waxing lyrical about Alla Wolf Tasker's Lake House restaurant, long regarded as the region's top seasonal dining experience.

Great Outdoors

Main Yarra Trail

Snaking through fragrant bushland and skirting both Collingwood Children's Farm and Heide

KEITMA/ALAMY

Kayaks, Melbourne

Museum of Modern Art, this scenic, 35km cycling and walking trail connects Southbank to kangaroo-speckled Westerfolds Park.

Kayak Melbourne

Take in the city skyline on a guided kayaking tour along the Yarra River. Options include a sunset tour with dinner; no prior kayaking experience necessary.

Fitzroy Swimming Pool

Featured in Helen Garner's classic novel *Monkey Grip*, this historic 50m outdoor pool is more than a much-loved hangout; it's a character in Melbourne's collective imagination.

Dandenong Ranges

These lush, cool ranges 35km east of Melbourne harbour rainforest walks, elegant gardens and the thigh-busting 1000 Steps (Kokoda Track Memorial Walk).

Urbnsurf

Minutes from Melbourne Airport, Australia's first surf park rolls out wave after perfect wave, from gentle white water for rookies to 2m barrels for the next Molly Picklum.

BRISBANE & COASTAL QUEENSLAND

REEF ADVENTURES | BEACHES | WILDLIFE

RESEARCHED BY JESSICA LOCKHART AND SARAH REID

Visit the heart of the Daintree Rainforest at **Cape Tribulation** (p174)

1½hr from Cairns

Take a day trip to the glorious Great Barrier Reef from **Cairns** (p176)

2¼hr from Brisbane

BRISBANE & COASTAL QUEENSLAND

Trip Builder

Just call it 300 days of summer. That's how many days of annual sunshine you can expect in southeast Queensland (SEQ), which stretches from Brisbane to the NSW border. It gets steamier and wilder as you head north for teeming reefs and rainforests.

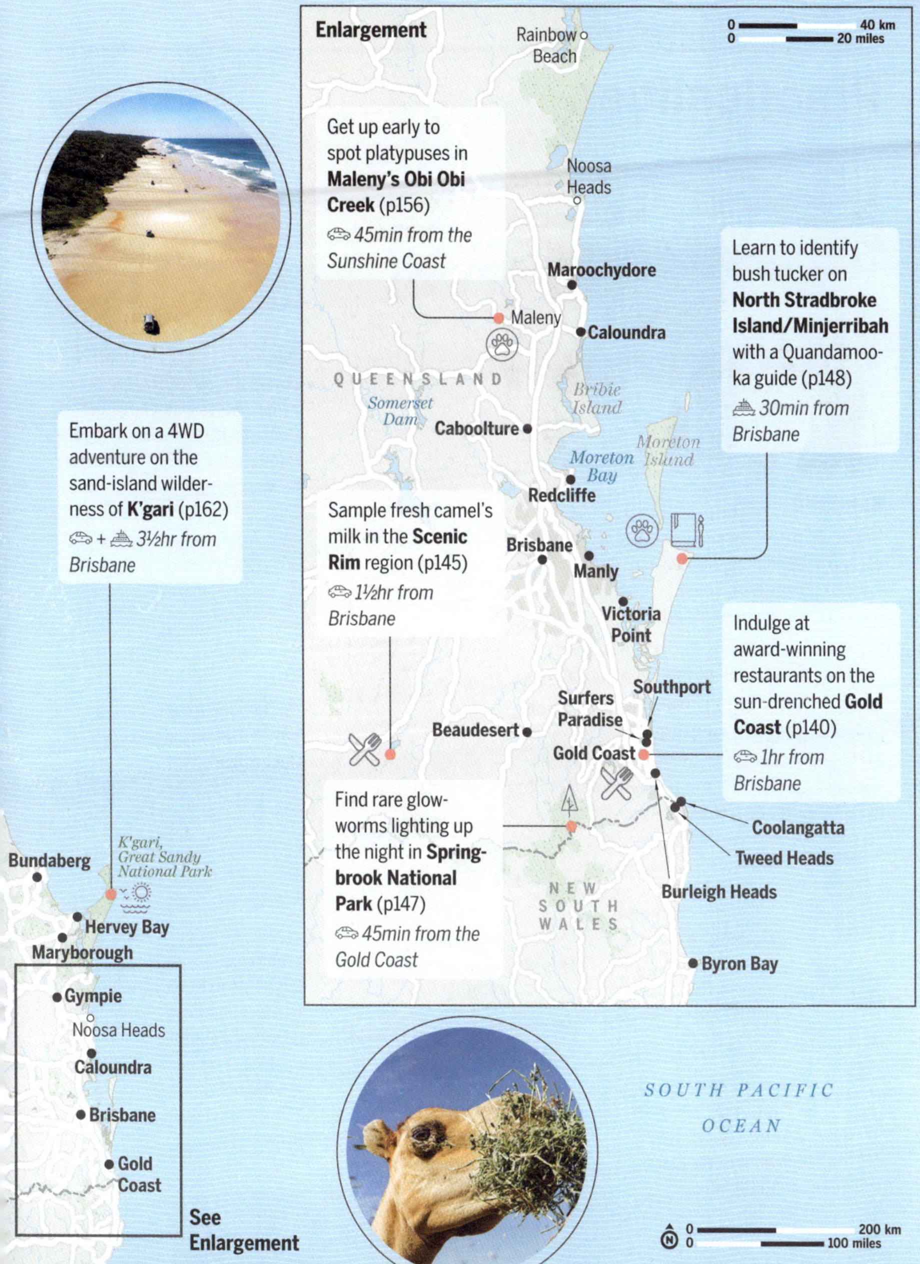
Enlargement
0 40 km
0 20 miles
Rainbow Beach
Noosa Heads
Get up early to spot platypuses in Maleny's Obi Obi Creek (p156)
45min from the Sunshine Coast
Maroochydore
Maleny
Caloundra
Learn to identify bush tucker on North Stradbroke Island/Minjerribah with a Quandamooka guide (p148)
30min from Brisbane
QUEENSLAND
Bribie Island
Somerset Dam
Caboolture
Moreton Island
Moreton Bay
Redcliffe
Sample fresh camel's milk in the Scenic Rim region (p145)
1½hr from Brisbane
Brisbane
Manly
Victoria Point
Indulge at award-winning restaurants on the sun-drenched Gold Coast (p140)
1hr from Brisbane
Southport
Surfers Paradise
Beaudesert
Gold Coast
Find rare glow-worms lighting up the night in Springbrook National Park (p147)
45min from the Gold Coast
Coolangatta
Tweed Heads
Burleigh Heads
NEW SOUTH WALES
Byron Bay
Embark on a 4WD adventure on the sand-island wilderness of K'gari (p162)
+ 3½hr from Brisbane
K'gari, Great Sandy National Park
Bundaberg
Hervey Bay
Maryborough
Gympie
Noosa Heads
Caloundra
Brisbane
Gold Coast
See Enlargement
SOUTH PACIFIC OCEAN
0 200 km
0 100 miles

Practicalities

CASEYJADEW/SHUTTERSTOCK

ARRIVING

Brisbane International Airport Queensland's largest and most centrally located airport (pictured). It's a 20-minute drive from the airport to the city; halfway between the Gold and Sunshine coasts.

Gold Coast and Cairns Airports Busy airports receiving domestic and some international flights.

Other regional airports Significant coastal domestic airports include Sunshine Coast Airport in Marcoola, Bundaberg Regional Airport, Whitsunday Coast Airport near Airlie Beach, Hamilton Island Airport and Townsville Airport.

HOW MUCH FOR A

Craft-beer tasting flight $15

SUP rental per hour $25

Outer Great Barrier Reef day trip $250

WHEN TO GO

JAN–MAR
Hot, humid and rainy, with temperatures that climb above 25°C.

APR–JUN
Clear skies and pleasant, mild weather.

JUL–SEP
Mild near the coast; chilly mornings and nights in the hinterlands.

OCT–DEC
Warm, sunny days; blooming jacarandas herald spring.

GETTING AROUND

Bus, ferry and train Translink covers the entire SEQ region, with services extending from Coolangatta in the south to Noosa Heads in the north. A commuter train runs from Varsity Lakes to Gympie North. Purchase a 'go card' from stations or retailers for discounted fares.

Car Renting a car is the best way to explore beyond coastal Queensland cities.

Island ferry SeaLink and Stradbroke Flyer car and passenger ferries go to North Stradbroke Island/Minjerribah. For Moreton Island/Mulgumpin, Micat operates on a demand-based timetable.

EATING & DRINKING

Like the rest of Australia's east coast, coastal Queensland is known for its seafood, including Moreton Bay bugs (pictured top right), a type of slipper lobster, and tropical reef fish and barramundi. Brisbane and the Gold Coast have fantastic food scenes with an emphasis on fresh flavours suited to warm climate, while Cairns leans into its proximity to Asia with a spicy kick. Surf clubs are great for a pub-style feed with sea views.

When it's time for a drink, choose from dozens of craft brewers and distillers along the coast.

Best cocktails Rosella's (p141), Gold Coast

Must-try bush honey Yura Tours on North Stradbroke Island (p149)

CONNECT & FIND YOUR WAY

Wi-fi Few cafes offer free wi-fi; try a library or one of the networks on the Gold Coast, in Brisbane, on the Sunshine Coast or in Cairns.

Navigation The newly widened M1 runs along the coast from the Queensland border to the Sunshine Coast, where it becomes the Bruce Hwy. The inland routes are less direct, but less hectic and more scenic.

WHERE TO STAY

Brisbane has accommodation for all budgets and tastes. Elsewhere, the further you are from the coastline, the more limited your choices become.

Place	Options
Gold Coast	Motels, apartments, midrange hotels and luxury accommodation are all within walking distance of the beach. In the hinterland there's camping, glamping and luxury health retreats.
Brisbane CBD, South Bank, West End and Fortitude Valley	Four- and five-star hotels in the centre of the action.
Sunshine Coast	Primarily tourist apartments and private rentals by the coast, and B&Bs, cottages and boutique family-owned inns high in the hinterland.
Fraser Coast and Bundaberg	Camping on K'gari is half the fun. Bundaberg also has camping, plus holiday apartments by the beach in Bargara.
Townsville and Cairns	Family resorts and hotels of all types dominate.

DISCOUNTS

The official regional tourism organisations – visitbrisbane.com.au, visitsunshinecoast.com, experiencegoldcoast.com and tropicalnorthqueensland.org.au – feature exclusive deals on accommodation and activities.

MONEY

Passion fruit, pineapples, avocados: you name it and you can probably find it being sold roadside. Most farm-gate stalls are unstaffed and cash only, operating on the honour system; have gold ($1 and $2) coins and $5 notes handy.

23 Glitz, Glamour & GLUTTONY

CAFES | COCKTAILS | DINING

Not long ago, food on the Gold Coast was synonymous with greasy takeaways. But over the past decade the place has been transformed into a five-star foodie destination, with top chefs from Sydney and Melbourne decamping to the stretch between Broadbeach and Burleigh. Family-friendly beachside venues, award-winning cafes and smart cocktail bars are all on offer.

THE MILKMAN'S DAUGHTER @THEMILKMANSDAUGHTER_GC

How to

When to go Cafe kitchens close as early as 2pm; dinner service starts around 6pm.

What's in a hat? 'Hats', indicating culinary excellence, are awarded annually by the Australian Good Food Guide. Confusingly, the *Good Food Guide*, a different entity, also awards hats to restaurants in NSW and Victoria.

Pace yourself Free-flowing drinks aren't restricted to weekends: bottomless brunches can be found up and down the coast on any day of the week.

MAYA SCHOLZ/PADDOCK BAKERY

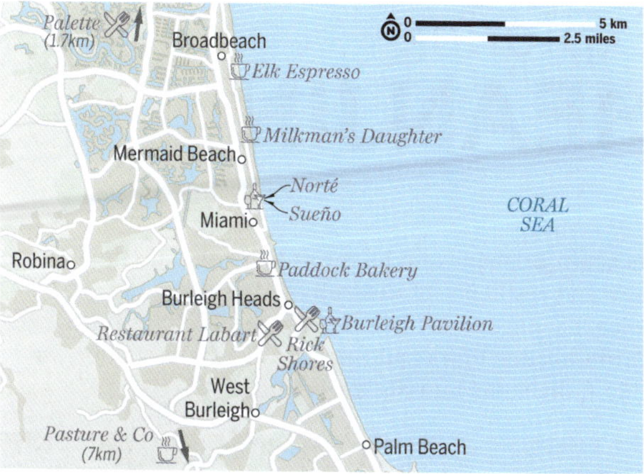

Early-morning indulgence Arrive early to score a seat in the garden at **Paddock Bakery** in Burleigh Heads, set in a 1950s cottage. Inside, watch pastry chefs at work whipping up Nutella cruffins or Paddock's trademark *crème brûlée* doughnuts. Or head to **Pasture & Co.** in Currumbin Village: surrounded by 100-year-old fig trees, the cafe caters to every dietary need imaginable, including paleo, vegan, nut-free and gluten-free. For a boozier brunch, there's **Elk Espresso** in Broadbeach, where bottomless mimosas are served daily from 10am to 1.30pm.

Afternoon tipple The mandate is endless summer at casual, beachside **Burleigh Pavilion**. Jugs of Pimm's, freshly shucked oysters and resident DJs are ensuring it meets its goal. To guarantee a seat with ocean views, make a reservation at the **Tropic**, the Pavilion's full-service establishment. Just up the road in Mermaid Beach, rooftop **Sueño** serves Latin-inspired cocktails and small plates. For a more substantial feed, head downstairs to **Norté**.

Get glammed up The Gold Coast has nearly two dozen hatted restaurants, including **Rick Shores** in Burleigh Heads, where the Moreton Bay bug roll is a perennial must-order, and **Palette** at HOTA in Surfers Paradise, where the menu names the farmer, producer, hunter or fisher behind every dish, from the Gold Coast prawns with scampi caviar to Waroo kangaroo with Davidson's plum.

Top left Dishes, Milkman's Daughter
Bottom left *Crème brûlée* doughnut, Paddock Bakery

From Dusk to Dessert

For brunch: Milkman's Daughter, Mermaid Beach This vegetarian cafe serves coffee with a conscience, which you can sip among an urban oasis of greenery.

For afternoon drinks: Rosella's, Burleigh Heads Enjoy innovative cocktails and a fun environment.

For dinner: The Collective, Palm Beach A great spot for group meals, and the rooftop bar is perfect for a sunset dinner.

For dessert: Scoop Gelati, Burleigh Heads It always has interesting flavour combinations, such as mango macadamia.

Alex Munoz Labart, *chef and owner of Restaurant Labart*
@restaurantlabart

24 Exploring MEANJIN

ART | CULTURE | HISTORY

Seek out Indigenous art in Brisbane and be rewarded with a fascinating window into the rich culture and resilience of Australia's Aboriginal and Torres Strait Islander peoples. Leaning on art to share stories as old as time, Indigenous-owned BlackCard Cultural Tours and Birrunga Art Gallery offer two of the city's most memorable Indigenous tourism experiences.

HAIREENA/SHUTTERSTOCK

How to

When to go Any time's a good time to visit, but summer can be hot. BlackCard Cultural Tours run year-round.

Getting around Translink buses, trains and ferries offer convenient transport around the city.

Preparation Wear comfortable shoes on tours and bring a reusable water bottle.

Original name The area occupied by Brisbane is known to the local Jagera and Turrbal peoples as Meanjin, meaning 'place shaped as a spike', in reference to a bend in the Brisbane River.

GARY YIM/SHUTTERSTOCK

Art Walk

Start your Indigenous art expedition in South Bank's Kurilpa Point and Cultural Precinct, where **BlackCard Cultural Tours**' dedicated Indigenous guides will lead you on a 90-minute excursion. Outside the **Gallery of Modern Art**, you'll see a bronze sculpture by Indigenous artist Judy Watson. Called *tow row*, the sculpture is a recreation of a traditional fishing net used by the Aboriginal people of the area. In the **State Library**, Dr Lila Watson's Kurilpa Country is a large-scale illuminated mural that tells the story of the habitat of the native water rat. Along the way, your guide will also tell you about the Indigenous Australians behind the city's public murals and share some of the area's lesser-known Aboriginal backstory.

Gallery Stop

Central Brisbane's **Birrunga Gallery**, an Indigenous-owned and -operated art space, houses contemporary art pieces by Aboriginal and Torres Strait Islander artists at all stages of their careers. Be sure to check out the 32m-long Rainbow Serpent, depicting the great life-giver of the Dreaming, which runs through several rooms. Some artwork is by students in Birrunga's Cultural Creative Development Program, which helps nurture Indigenous artists. Tiesha Martin's acrylic canvas *True* represents her totem, the kookaburra, a symbol of joy and fertility. There's also an on-site cafe showcasing native ingredients.

Top left Gallery of Modern Art and *tow row* by Judy Watson
Bottom left State Library

Look Deeper

Indigenous history is all too easily unseen by visitors as they move around contemporary Brisbane. Cultural art tours encourage you to analyse and reflect on the significance of First Nations experiences through art: history, politics and culture are intertwined in the narrative of each of the installations you'll see. For instance, the State Library of Queensland hosts a work by Aboriginal artist Fiona Foley called Black Opium, which refers to the Aboriginals Protection Act 1897, under which Indigenous people received opium as wages. Engaging with artworks such as these will give you fresh eyes for when you visit other places in the river city.

Mundanara Bayles, *managing director and co-founder of BlackCard @blackmagicwomanpodcast*

The Camel Connection

SEQ'S CAMEL DAIRIES REVEAL AN UNTOLD HISTORY

There will never been an animal more synonymous with Australia than the kangaroo, more beloved than the koala or more feared than the crocodile. Yet camels - despite not being an indigenous species - have managed to cement their place in the country's iconography.

CHERYL BRONSON/GETTY IMAGES

Camels in Australian Culture

At the turn of the century, camels were used by police officers to patrol rural areas, in Australia's very own version of the mounted police. In 1977 camels were the pack-animal companions to adventurer Robyn Davidson when she spent nine months trekking from Alice Springs to the Western Australian coast (a journey she wrote about in her 1980 book *Tracks*, the basis of the 2013 movie of the same name). Every year thousands of people descend upon Yulara in the Northern Territory to watch jockeys racing astride the ungulates, and as a tourist you can ride around Uluru on one.

Camel Milk

In southeast Queensland, entrepreneurial farmers are milking the invasive species for what they're worth – literally.

Some of the biggest camel dairies in the world are located just outside Brisbane, selling a product that's gaining superfood status. Camel milk is a low-lactose option that's touted as a cure for everything from eczema to diabetes. It's also arguably a more ethical animal milk. Unlike a dairy cow – which must be separated from her calf when it's born in order to give milk for just six to nine months – a camel can share her milk with the farmer and her calf for up to 18 months. Domesticating and milking the feral animals also saves them from being culled. With an estimated two million camels roaming freely through the outback, Australia is said to have the largest camel herd in the world.

JOHN WHITE PHOTOS/SHUTTERSTOCK

NJPHOTO/ALAMY

But a visit to one of SEQ's camel dairies isn't just a chance to learn about the burgeoning industry – it's also an opportunity to understand a piece of Australian history that could otherwise easily be missed.

Cameleers

The one-humped dromedaries were introduced to Australia in the 1840s. Identified for their suitability for the outback landscape, they were imported en masse, and became the primary means for transporting goods through the centre of the country. They didn't come alone, though – they were accompanied by camel drivers from what are now Afghanistan, Pakistan and India.

These cameleers and their steeds played a critical role in opening up the interior of Australia. In addition to hauling supplies, they helped build railways and the Australian Overland Telegraph Line between Adelaide and Darwin. But by the 1930s the introduction of the motor vehicle had rendered their services obsolete. Faced with hostility – including discriminatory government policies that prevented them from obtaining citizenship – many cameleers were forced to pack up and return home.

Yet you can still see traces of their impact on Australia. In Brisbane's Holland Park, for example, you'll find the site of Queensland's first formal mosque. Dating back to the 1880s, it's also home to Queensland's Muslim Museum, where you can learn about the cameleers' early contributions to the country. But one of the biggest marks they left on the landscape is the intelligent and resilient animals they had to leave behind.

Camel Cheese

In the Scenic Rim Region, 65km southwest of Brisbane, **Summer Land Camels** is the largest commercial camel dairy outside the Middle East, and the third largest of its kind in the world. At its cafe you can look out onto the paddocks as you sample camel cheese, camel gelato or a latte made with camel milk, and slather your hands with camel-milk beauty products. Family-friendly farm tours and camel rides are also available.

The award-winning **QCamel Milk Dairy** in the Glass House Mountains offers a similar experience, with meet-the-herd tours every Saturday and on school holidays. Bookings are essential.

25 Rainforest RETREAT

BUSHWALKING | GLOW-WORMS | SPAS

With its casinos, nightclubs and theme parks, the Gold Coast is renowned for being a bit extra. But go inland and you'll find excess of an entirely different sort. With a geological history dating back more than 225 million years, the Gold Coast hinterland is home to around 500 waterfalls, 390 wildlife species and hundreds of kilometres of bushwalking tracks.

JESSICA WYNNE LOCKHART

How to

Getting there Budget ample time. The road to Lamington National Park is single lane at times, with hairpin turns and monster potholes. Southern Cross Tours offers day trips.

When to go At an elevation of 1000m, the hinterland is 5°C to 8°C cooler than the coast. For gushing waterfalls, visit between November and March.

What to pack Wear long pants to ward off leeches, and a torch (flashlight) with a red light for nocturnal wildlife spotting.

JESSICA WYNNE LOCKHART

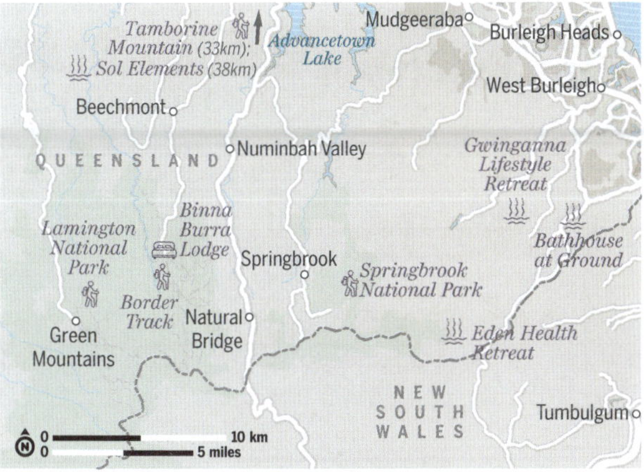

Top left O'Reilly's Rainforest Retreat
Bottom left Gwinganna Lifestyle Retreat

Bushwalking Although **Tamborine Mountain** has long been the go-to, many prefer the tranquillity of **Springbrook National Park** and **Lamington National Park**.

There are really only two spots to stay in Lamington: **Binna Burra Lodge** in the east and **O'Reilly's Rainforest Retreat** in the western Green Mountains section. Both offer glamping tents and lodge rooms, plus guided tours and direct trail access. The 21.4km **Border Track** – part of the longer Gold Coast Hinterland Great Walk – connects the two, with shuttles making it possible to walk one way. There are other trails for all skill levels, such as the 90-minute walk to 80m Morans Falls – listen for the mewling call of green catbirds and look for golden regent bowerbirds.

With limited accommodation, Springbrook is best as a day trip, though staying the night affords you the opportunity to see pademelons, which emerge at dusk, and rare glow-worms. Both parks have few amenities, so fuel up before you leave.

Adrenaline Opened in Beechmont in 2025, the Happitat 'cliff park' has two cliffside zip-line tours, a via ferrata course, cliffside viewing platforms and bushwalking trails.

Spas You're in Australia's spa capital, with some of the most luxurious hidden in the hinterland. **Gwinganna Lifestyle Retreat** in Tallebudgera Valley is a celebrity favourite; its award-winning spa is open only to guests. The same goes for treatments at the five-star **Eden Health Retreat** in Currumbin Valley. For day treatments, try the **Bathhouse at Ground** in Currumbin, with massages and cedar hot tubs. Or find your Zen at **Sol Elements**, a Japanese-inspired day bathhouse surrounded by a serene pond at Tamborine Mountain.

Glow Bright

Glow-worms – the larvae of *Arachnocampa* fungus gnats, and typically found in damp cave environments – are renowned for producing a blue-green bioluminescence, and this is one of the only places in the world to see it.

Australia's largest colony is under Springbrook National Park's **Natural Bridge**. In Lamington National Park, O'Reilly's Rainforest Retreat offers a glow-worm tour. If you're not a night owl, visit Tamborine Mountain's purpose-built caves during the day.

Fun/gross fact: it's the glow-worms' excrement that glows – but that doesn't make this experience any less ethereal. For the best viewing, avoid the use of flashlights and keep noise low.

26 Escape to a SAND ISLAND

BUSH TUCKER | WHALES | CULTURE

Fondly known as 'Straddie', North Stradbroke Island/ Minjerribah is the world's second-largest sand island. Swim in freshwater lakes, stroll along empty beaches, watch humpback whales from the shore and immerse yourself in Indigenous culture – it's all here, just 45km from Brisbane's CBD.

DARKBLUESHUTTER/SHUTTERSTOCK

How to

Getting here Ferries leave from Toondah Harbour in Cleveland (one hour by train from Brisbane's Roma St Station) and arrive in Dunwich.

When to go Whale season runs from May to November.

Getting around A car is handy but not necessary. A cash-only bus runs from Dunwich to Myora, Amity Point and Point Lookout, and tour operators pick guests up from the ferry terminal. Scooter and bicycle rentals are available.

Take It Slow

Straddie is SEQ's answer to K'gari (Fraser Island), but it's more accessible (you don't need a 4WD), making it possible to see on a day trip. But if your schedule allows, don't rush – this is the kind of place where time slows and folds in on itself in the best possible way.

Quandamooka Country

The Quandamooka (people of the bay) – including the Nughi, Nunukul and Gorenpul – have continuously occupied Minjerribah and neighbouring Moreton Island/Mulgumpin for tens of millennia. A visit is a chance to learn about their history, including at the **Myora Mission Site**. Now a place for quiet contemplation, you'll also find an award-winning bush-tucker garden trail.

Yura Tours takes visitors to key cultural and historical sites on the island. On the three-hour

TOBY ROBINSON/SHUTTERSTOCK

Top left Beach, North Stradbroke Island
Left Humoback whale

cultural excursion, Quandamooka woman Elisha Kissick shares her family's stories and helps guests identify and taste bush tucker, including honey produced by native stingless bees.

For another perspective, make an appointment to visit **Delvene Cockatoo-Collins' art studio** in Dunwich. Using techniques passed down by her grandmother, the Quandamooka artist makes ceramics, clothing and homeware with prints of *bunbiya* (turtles), *jalaman* (native bees) and *yalingbilla* (humpback whales). She also offers an art walk and workshop.

Thar She Blows

Straddie is the easternmost point in Queensland, so thousands of humpback whales pass by during the winter months as they migrate north from their Antarctic feeding grounds to mate and give birth. The best vantage point to watch for them is the 1.2km **Gorge Walk** boardwalk at Point Lookout, which sits about 30m above sea level. You might also see dolphins, sea turtles and manta rays in the waters below, and koalas,

Waterway Warnings

If you see ripples or waves on the surface of **Brown Lake/Bummiera**, proceed with caution. According to Quandamooka stories, it's a sign that the rainbow serpent has travelled from her home in **Blue Lake/Karboora** to play in its waters.

Like Bummiera, Karboora (meaning 'deep, silent pool') is a site of spiritual significance. To respect that, visitors are asked not to swim in Blue Lake regardless of the conditions. Instead, stick to the 5.2km walking track around its edges, and keep your eyes peeled for rare golden swamp wallabies, endemic to the island.

Ask an Elder

The **North Stradbroke Island Aboriginal and Islander Housing Co-Operative** is a 10-minute walk from the ferry terminal in Dunwich. Drop in to meet some of the Elders, and see the display of historical community photos, newspaper clippings and artefacts.

Elisha Kissick, *owner of Yura Tours @yura_tours*

YURA TOURS

eastern grey kangaroos and swamp wallabies in the surrounding bush.

Pure Shores

For many, the appeal of Straddie is having a wide stretch of sea and sand all to yourself. **Main Beach** is the spot for surf, patrolled **Cylinder Beach** is safe for swimming, and **Frenchman's Beach** is ideal for picnics.

But the freshwater lakes, perfect for a dip, are what truly set Minjerribah apart. **Brown Lake/Bummiera** may sound unappealing, but its waters are actually an inviting warm amber owing to tannins from the surrounding paperback eucalypts. It's not uncommon to see a koala on its shores. Or visit the freshwater **Myora Springs** at high tide, when seawater flows through the mangroves. Traditionally a favoured camping place of the Quandamooka peoples, the banks host large shell middens. You'll need a 4WD to access local favourite **the Keyholes**, just off Main Beach, or book a tour with 'barefoot' Dave from **Straddie Kingfisher Tours**. If you want to drive onto the beach in your own 4WD, you must purchase a permit online from Minjerribah Camping (minjerribahcamping.com.au).

RIGHT: JONO SEARLE/GETTY IMAGES; LEFT: THP CREATIVE/SHUTTERSTOCK

Left Blue Lake/Karboora
Above top Yura Tours (p149)
Above Gorge Walk boardwalk

BUSH TUCKER
of Southeast Queensland

01 Davidson's plum
Only distantly related to European plums, *Davidsonia johnsonii* is too sour to be eaten raw. Instead, it's used in jams, wines and ice cream.

02 Native ginger
The rhizomes, young shoots and blue berries of this plant have a mild, earthy ginger flavour.

03 Native raspberry
Found in sunlit rainforest areas, these prickly bushes produce sweet red berries, which can be eaten raw or made into jam or tea.

04 Lemon myrtle
The leaves of this fragrant and flavourful herb also have mosquito-repelling properties.

05 Pigface
The salty leaves, fruit and flowers of this succulent – which grows on sand dunes – can be eaten raw or boiled.

06 Australian finger lime
This prized fruit is known as 'citrus caviar' for good reason. Squeeze out the segments for a burst of flavour.

06

07

08

09

11

10

12

07 Macadamia nut
Most of the world's macadamias are grown in Hawaii, but they're indigenous to Australia. Scientists believe they may originate from a single Queensland tree.

08 Bunya nut
Growing up to 50m, this tree produces a seed that can be eaten raw, roasted or ground into flour for cakes.

09 Saltbush
An ingredient on menus at Australia's top restaurants, the salty leaves of this shrub are best fried.

10 Blue tongue
Not to be confused with the lizard of the same name, this evergreen has sweet blue fruit that will stain your mouth.

11 Native honey
This rare and intense sweet treat is produced by tiny stingless native bees, which are also called sugarbags.

12 Black apple
Ready to eat when they fall from the tree, these plum-like rainforest fruits can be eaten raw.

27 Seek Waterfalls & WILDLIFE

ROAD TRIP | PLATYPUSES | SHOPPING

The Sunshine Coast hinterland is only 30km from the ocean, but the region is a world apart from the hum of coastal activity. Ascend high the Blackall Ranges to be rewarded with lush rainforests, green pastures, eclectic mountain towns and made-for-postcards views.

FILEDIMAGE/SHUTTERSTOCK

How to

Getting around It's a 23km drive from Mapleton to Maleny, but plan for plenty of stops. To extend your exploration, make it a circuit by taking Hwy 22 from Maleny to Kenilworth, taking Obi Obi Rd to Mapleton, and then returning to Maleny via Hwy 23.

When to go During the summer months the hinterland is cooler than the coast – and the waterfalls should be full and flowing.

While you're out here Conondale National Park has great bushwalks and creekside campgrounds.

ALEX CIMBAL/SHUTTERSTOCK

Fill Your Belly & Your Bags

At the heart of the Sunshine Coast hinterland region are the townships of Maleny and Montville.

Appealing little **Montville** is known as the Blue Mountains of Queensland. Its buildings have a European Alps aesthetic, with storefronts mainly catering to visitors – which isn't necessarily a bad thing. There are numerous cafes, a chocolatier, a clockmaker, a tea shop and a handful of art galleries to explore.

Maleny is where locals from the surrounding area do their shopping – which is part of the reason you'll have a hard time finding parking. (Try behind the IGA.) Grab a coffee or a gelato at Maleny Food Co. to enjoy while wandering up the main street. Leave enough time to do the 900m walk to the Platypus

FILEDIMAGE/SHUTTERSTOCK

Mountain Views

Maleny's Mountain View Rd has unparalleled views of the Glasshouse Mountains, particularly from **Mountain View Cafe**, located near the entrance to the Mary Cairncross Scenic Reserve. Breakfast, lunch, coffees and local craft beers are available seven days a week. There's another good lookout spot 1.2km west.

Top left Montville
Left Viewpoint, Kondalilla Falls circuit (p156)
Above View of botanic gardens and Glasshouse Mountains from Maleny

Viewing Area, which can be found along the accessible boardwalk starting behind the Riverside Shopping Centre.

Further down the road is the village of **Mapleton**. Its pub, built in 1910, isn't known for its food but rather for its position – sitting at nearly 400m in elevation, it has a wrap-around veranda with clear views down to the coast and beyond.

Dive In

The ocean might be a half-hour drive away, but hinterland residents are spoilt for choice when it comes to wild swimming. One of the most accessible spots is at **Gardners Falls**, about 5km east of Maleny. From the car park, head downstream to find shady spots and rope swings. Another option is **Kondalilla Falls**, just southwest of Flaxton. For the best vantage point of the 90m drop, follow the

Platypus Whispers

You can find platypuses in the Mary River, in Peachester's creek and in Nambour, behind the train station. The national average is two platypuses for every kilometre of creek – but in **Maleny's Obi Obi Creek**, there are up to 10 per kilometre.

It's a misconception that platypuses are only active at dawn and dusk: they need to forage for up to 16 hours a day.

To spot them, look for a ring of low ripples on the water's surface that take a long time to dissipate. (By contrast, eastern water dragons produce very sharp ripples that dissipate quickly.)

Neil Andison, *photographer, tour guide and platypus whisperer. facebook .com/platypuswhisperer1*

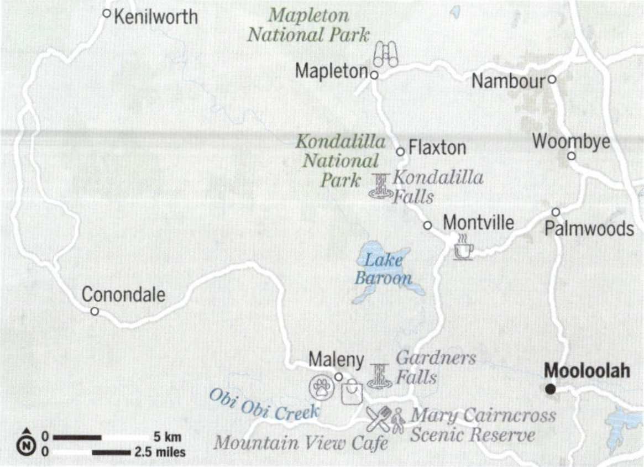

Left Platypus
Below Mary Cairncross Scenic Reserve

4.7km-circuit bushwalk to the bottom of the falls – but note that the best swimming is in the rock pools at the top.

If you have ample time, the 58.8km **Sunshine Coast Hinterland Great Walk** takes about four days to complete. Starting from the dammed Lake Baroon, it passes by Kondalilla Falls, Baxter Falls, Mapleton Falls and Gheerulla Falls. Along the way, keep an eye out for yellow-tailed black cockatoos, snakes, goannas and, if you're lucky, koalas.

Ancient Remnants

When colonists arrived in the Sunshine Coast in the 1870s, they quickly set to work logging the area's red cedar and beech trees. The bush you see today is largely regrowth, with one notable exception: the 55-hectare **Mary Cairncross Scenic Reserve** outside Maleny. A remnant subtropical lowland rainforest, its trees have stood for hundreds of years, sheltering endemic species that you're unlikely to see elsewhere. Its three walking circuits and wheelchair-accessible Butterfly Walk provide an opportunity to spot red-legged pademelons, squirrel gliders, paradise riflebirds and rare plant species. Entry is by gold-coin donation, with guides on-site to help you identify birdlife in the canopy.

28 Through Indigenous EYES

TOURS | BUSH TUCKER | CULTURE

More than 70 Aboriginal and Torres Strait Islander groups have lived alongside the Great Barrier Reef for millennia. There have never been more opportunities to explore the region with Indigenous guides, particularly in the following tourism hubs.

CHAMELEONSEYE/SHUTTERSTOCK

How to

Etiquette Always ask before taking photos on an Indigenous-led tour, as it may not be allowed for cultural reasons. And remember that no question is too silly if it's asked respectfully.

Tours Discover and book more Indigenous experiences via Discover Aboriginal Experiences (discoveraboriginalexperiences.com).

Eat Enjoy a sumptuous tropical feast featuring native ingredients at the Indigenous Culture Experience, run by Aboriginal-owned Flames of the Forest, near Port Douglas.

Cooktown

The first recorded act of reconciliation between Indigenous and non-indigenous people in Australia occurred in Cooktown. This is just one fascinating fact you'll learn on a self-guided tour of the **Cooktown Museum**, which recounts Captain James Cook's landing here in June 1770 from an Aboriginal perspective. Just south of Cooktown, interpretive panels offer insights into the cultural significance of the unusual **Kalkajaka** (Black Mountain) boulder field. Nearby, at **Rossville Retreat**, Kuku Nyungkul Elder Harold Tayley or 'Mooks' leads popular bush food and medicine walks on his traditional homeland. It's a two-hour drive west from Cooktown to Laura, the jumping-off point for Kuku Yalanji man Johnny Murison's highly regarded two-day **Jarramali Rock Art Tour**.

BMPHOTOGRAPHER/SHUTTERSTOCK

Top left Cooktown Museum
Left Tour boat, Great Barrier Reef

Cairns & Daintree

Cairns' first Indigenous-led Great Barrier Reef tour, **Dreamtime Dive & Snorkel**, weaves Indigenous storytelling, music and dance throughout its outer-reef day trip. On a half-day experience with **Mandingalbay Authentic Indigenous Tours** you'll cruise from Cairns Marina to the East Trinity Wetlands to connect with culture on the homelands of the Mandingalbay Yidinji people.

Nearby, in the Daintree region – the traditional home of Eastern Kuku Yalanji people – there are a number of Indigenous experiences. On a Ngadiku Dreamtime Walk, organised by the Indigenous-run **Mossman Gorge Centre**, your guide will tell you about the special relationship their people share with the unique tropical environment during a meandering rainforest stroll. You can also explore the Daintree region with Kuku Yalanji guides from **Walkabout Cultural Adventures**. Or take a cultural walk

Indigenous Must-Reads

Dark Emu, by Bruce Pascoe (2014) Reexamining colonial accounts of Indigenous people in Australia, this ground-breaking non-fiction tome challenges long-held perceptions of Australia's first peoples.

Welcome to Country: A Travel Guide to Indigenous Australia, by Marcia Langton (2018) Cultural etiquette tips, plus insights into Aboriginal languages, customs, art and more.

The Yield, by Tara June Winch (2019) Evocative, Miles Franklin Literary Award–winning novel about a man's determination to preserve his people's language and culture.

Australia Day, by Stan Grant (2019) Excellent backgrounder on Aboriginal Australia, with uncomfortable truths about colonial history.

Indigenous Art

The mid-year **Cairns Indigenous Art Fair** (ciaf.com.au) offers an unrivalled opportunity to purchase Indigenous art and handicrafts directly from artists. Throughout the year, northern Queensland's Indigenous art centres such as the Yarrabah Art Centre, near Cairns, as well as the Cairns Art Gallery, host excellent exhibitions.

SUZANNE LONG/ALAMY

along Cooya Beach near Mossman with brothers Linc and Brandon Walker of **Kuku Yalanji Cultural Habitat Tours**. Feeling creative? Sign up for an art class with renowned Aboriginal artist Brian 'Binna' Swindley at **Janbal Gallery**.

Townsville

A central theme in Indigenous culture, caring for Country (traditional lands) is woven into each instalment of the Townsville region's **Museum of Underwater Art** (MOUA). On dry land, **Gudjuda Tours** runs a bush-tucker and rock-art tour in the Townsville region. Its owners, the Gudjuda Reference Group Aboriginal Corporation, have been conducting marine-turtle tagging and monitoring for more than 20 years. Contact them for more information about upcoming turtle rescue tours.

Fraser Coast

Walk in the footsteps of Butchulla people on the **Djinang Cultural Walking Tour** in Hervey Bay. Learn more about significant sites to the Butchulla in Hervey Bay and nearby K'gari (Fraser Island), sample local bush tucker, and get creative using natural materials. The tour is run in partnership with Hervey Bay Eco Marine Tours, which also runs a cultural sunset cruise with a Butchulla guide on board.

LEFT: MARCO TROVALUSCI PHOTOGRAPHY/ALAMY STOCK; FAR LEFT: MOSSMAN GORGE CENTRE

Left Mossman Gorge Centre
Above top Cairns Indigenous Art Fair
Above Torres Strait Islander dancer, Cairns

29 Get Off-Grid on K'GARI

FRESHWATER FUN | 4WD ADVENTURE | WILD CAMPING

Once known as Fraser Island, K'gari is the world's largest sand island – and one of Australia's greatest adventures. Join an organised tour or tackle the island's 4WD-only trails in your own vehicle in search of waterholes, historical traces, dingoes and more. There are guesthouses and two resorts, but bush and beach camping is a highlight of the K'gari experience.

PETER UNGER/GETTY IMAGES

How to

Getting here Take a ferry or barge from River Heads (south of Hervey Bay) to the western side of K'gari, or the barge from Inskip Point to Hook Point at the island's southern tip.

When to go K'gari is a year-round destination, but the summer months are ideal for swimming.

Hot showers Bring $2 coins to operate the showers at Central Station, Dundubara and Waddy Point Top camping areas.

MATT MUNRO/LONELY PLANET

CAM LAIRD/SHUTTERSTOCK

Far top left Lake Wabby
Bottom left Dingo, Great Sandy National Park
Near left SS *Maheno* wreck

Swimming spots K'gari's beaches are among the world's most dangerous due to strong currents and sharks, but its idyllic freshwater lakes and seaside rock pools make up for it. Chief among them are **Lake McKenzie** and similarly azure **Lake Birrabeen**. Strolling the 200m Eli Creek Boardwalk, then floating back downstream, is another K'gari must-do. Just north of Indian Head, the **Champagne Pools** 'fizz' as seawater spills into the rock pools. And after the 4.1km bushwalk to **Lake Wabby**, you'll be ready for a dip there, too.

Drives and walks Days on K'gari are best spent exploring by car or on foot. Four scenic inland driving routes offer hours of bumpy fun; allow extra time for bogged-vehicle traffic jams.

Part of the **Great Sandy National Park**, the island's 40-odd marked walking trails immerse you in surreal landscapes, from tall rainforest to striking sand blows. Look out for cute Krefft's river turtles on the **Lake Allom Circuit** (1.4km).

Cultural and historical sites The history of the Butchulla people goes back at least 5000 years. Sharp-eyed visitors may spot middens, artefact scatters and scarred trees that bear witness to the first inhabitants' deep and continuing connection to K'gari.

The rusting wreck of the **SS *Maheno***, which ran aground in 1935 just north of Eli Creek, is one of K'gari's best-known sights. Learn more about the island's maritime incidents and WWII history on the Sandy Cape Lighthouse Walk (4.8km return) at the island's northern tip.

Dingo Safety

Around 200 dingoes are thought to roam K'gari in about 30 packs. To ensure a safe encounter (for you and for the sandy-hued wild native dogs), the Queensland National Parks & Wildlife Service advises:

Never feed dingoes.

Always stay within arm's reach of children.

Walk (never run) in groups and carry a stick.

Camp in fenced areas when possible.

Keep food stores locked and never store food or food containers in tents.

Secure all rubbish. With limited garbage bins on the island, it's best to pack it out with you, too.

30 Townsville Island HOPS

ISLAND HIKING | BEACHES | INDIGENOUS CULTURE

The only Great Barrier Reef island with wild koalas, Magnetic Island offers a unique escape. It's a great base for exploring the Museum of Underwater Art (MOUA) at John Brewer Reef. But it's not the only island you can visit near Townsville, which is preparing to open its showpiece Great Barrier Reef Aquarium in 2029.

LISA HOLMEN PHOTOGRAPHY/SHUTTERSTOCK

How to

Getting here and around Magnetic Island Ferries (which takes cars) and SeaLink run daily services from Townsville to Magnetic Island (25 to 40 minutes). SeaLink runs to Palm Island Wednesday to Monday (one hour 45 minutes). Miniature 'Barbie Cars' can be rented on Magnetic Island.

When to go May to September, when the humidity's lower and stinger suits aren't required.

Snorkel Great options at Magnetic Island beyond MOUA include the snorkel trails at Nelly Bay and Geoffrey Bay.

BMPHOTOGRAPHER/SHUTTERSTOCK

Magnetic Island

Laid-back 'Maggie' boasts palm-fringed beaches, good snorkelling, scenic hiking trails and a robust koala population. Taking you to WWII fortifications with epic views (with koala spotting on the way), the 4km-return **Forts Walk** is the island's top trail. Pack a picnic and continue from Forts Junction around to Horseshoe Bay via Radical Bay, a 7.5km trail linking the island's most beautiful beaches. Come for the day or stay longer, with plenty of holiday accommodation options.

Orpheus Island

Well-heeled guests are helicoptered to the island national park's luxurious **Orpheus Island Lodge**, the only place to stay. But mere mortals can also visit on a day trip from Townsville with SeaLink, with three hours to swim, snorkel impressive reefs and tackle the island's only trail, the 450m-return **Yanks Jetty Walking Track**.

Palm Island

Known for its troubled history, the former Aboriginal mission of Palm Island (Bwgcolman) is now looking to tourism to future-proof its economy. A major project to develop 70km of walking trails is underway. Until its completion, local Indigenous guides can take you on walks to cultural sites and remote snorkelling spots.

Top left Orpheus Island jetty
Bottom left Koala, Magnetic Island

Plan Your Palm Island Visit

Etiquette For independent visits, it's best to contact the local council to let them know you're coming. They can connect you with guides and provide information about visiting respectfully.

Whale watching In July and August you can often spot migrating humpback whales on the boat trip to Palm Island from Townsville. If the whales are close, the boat stops for a while to let you watch.

Culture Start your visit at the Bwgcolman Indigenous Knowledge Centre, near the jetty, for a primer on local culture. We have lots of celebrations during NAIDOC Week in July, so that's a good time to come to experience culture.

Vicki Saylor, *Manbarra Traditional Owner and cultural adviser*
@vickeranne

31 Retreat to the WHITSUNDAYS

ISLAND HOPPING | TROPICAL HIKES | ABORIGINAL CULTURE

From living it up at luxury island resorts to slamming down drinks in the backpacker bars of Airlie Beach, there are plenty of ways to 'do' the Whitsundays. A day trip to the mesmerising swirl of powder-white sand and turquoise water known as Whitehaven Beach is obligatory. But there's plenty more to do. Here's a taste.

JOAO INACIO/GETTY IMAGES

How to

Getting here Flights land at Hamilton Island Airport and Whitsunday Coast Airport, 30 minutes from Airlie Beach.

When to go Join in the Airlie Beach and Hamilton Island Race Week yachting festivities in August, or beat the crowds during the April–May and November–December shoulder seasons.

Sunset There's only one place to be on Hamilton Island (affectionately known as 'Hamo') as the sun goes down, and that's hilltop bar One Tree Hill.

BEN CALLAHAN/SHUTTERSTOCK

DAVID PRUTER/SHUTTERSTOCK

Far top left Whitehaven Beach
Bottom left Hamilton Island
Near left Sailing, Whitsundays

Airlie Beach The mainland hub of 'Airlie' is the most affordable base for exploring the 74-island Whitsundays archipelago, part of the Great Barrier Reef Marine Park, with outer-reef and island-hopping excursions available daily. While there's no shortage of backpacker bars and hostels, you'll find family-friendly resorts here, too. For one of the best views in the Whitsundays, make the 8.2km return hike to Honeyeater Lookout; allow three hours.

Hamilton Island hikes The largest inhabited island of the Whitsundays is laced with more than 20km of scenic trails to explore. Leading you to a blissfully secluded cove with a giant timber hammock to laze on, the 5.1km-return Escape Beach Trail is the perfect excuse to stretch your legs. Allow two hours to complete the return hike from the Scenic Trail entrance, or loop back via South East Head, which adds an additional hour of walking.

Island hopping Bounce between Airlie, Daydream Island and Hamilton Island with **Cruise Whitsundays** (cruisewhitsundays.com) or sign up for one of the many Whitsundays day cruises on offer. More adventurous travellers can join a multi-day sailing adventure, or skipper your own barefoot charter. This is one of the world's only sailing destinations that don't require you to have a boating licence – a half-day training session is all you need to set sail.

Ancient Trail, New Hike

The Whitsundays is the traditional home of the Ngaro people, whose connection to the archipelago dates back some 9000 years. Learn more about Ngaro history and culture via interpretative signage and artworks on the **Ngaro Track** (ngarotrack.com.au), a 32km, three-day hiking trail weaving across uninhabited Whitsunday Island. Opened in 2026, the trail was developed in partnership with Ngaro knowledge holders to showcase the natural beauty and rich stories of Ngaro Country. Hikers can tackle the trail independently or book a guided adventure with **World Expeditions** (worldexpeditions.com) – stay on the trail to avoid disturbing sacred places.

WILDLIFE

of the Wet Tropics World Heritage Area

01

02

03

05

06

04

01 Ulysses Butterfly
Seen throughout the region, particularly in Cape Tribulation, the star of the Wet Tropics' insect world has huge, electric-blue wings.

02 Amethystine python
Named for its iridescent scales, Australia's largest snake (also called the scrub python) is as beautiful as it is docile.

03 Spotted-tailed quoll
The famously elusive ground-dwelling predator is mainland Australia's second-largest native carnivore, after the dingo.

04 Lace monitor
Known to skulk around campgrounds looking for an easy snack, these beautifully patterned lizards can grow up to 1.5m long.

05 Boyd's forest dragon
Look for these colourful 'dragons' clinging to tree trunks along the pathways of Mossman Gorge.

06 Herbert River ringtail possum
Affectionately known as 'Herbie', the nocturnal emblem of the Queensland Parks & Wildlife Service is found at highland altitudes.

07

08

09

10

12

11

07 Mahogany glider
Increasingly threatened by land clearing, this endangered sweet-toothed glider is one of six glider species found in the Wet Tropics.

08 Tree kangaroo
Two arboreal kangaroo species live in the Wet Tropics. Try your luck spotting the Lumholtz's tree kangaroo in the Atherton Tablelands.

09 Southern cassowary
The dinosaur-like icon of the Wet Tropics faces an uncertain future, with fewer than 4400 of the formidable birds estimated to remain in the wild.

10 Musky rat-kangaroo
This adorable pint-sized roo is diurnal, meaning it can often be seen foraging on the forest floor during the day.

11 Platypus
Sit quietly alongside Peterson Creek in Yungaburra, in the Atherton Tablelands, ideally at dawn or dusk, for a good chance of observing these quirky monotremes.

12 Saltwater crocodile
The world's largest living reptile patrols the rivers and beaches of the Wet Tropics and beyond.

01 ALICE-PHOTO/SHUTTERSTOCK, **02** KEN GRIFFITHS/ALAMY, **03** ENCYCLOPAEDIA BRITANNICA/GETTY IMAGES, **04** PAUL LOOYEN/SHUTTERSTOCK, **05** BIRDIMAGES/GETTY IMAGES, **06** MARKKU MURTO/ART/ALAMY STOCK PHOTO, **07** BLUEDOG STUDIO/SHUTTERSTOCK, **08** FRANK FICHTMUELLER/SHUTTERSTOCK, **09** SANIT FUANGNAKHON/SHUTTERSTOCK, **10** WILDSCOTPHOTOS/ALAMY STOCK PHOTO, **11** MATIS75/SHUTTERSTOCK, **12** BINTURONG-TONOSCARPE/SHUTTERSTOCK

32 Sundowners in CAIRNS

CRAFT COCKTAILS | SEA VIEWS | GOOD TIMES

With year-round balmy weather, the buzzy Tropical North Queensland holiday hub of Cairns was made for sunset drinks by the sea. The city's bar scene has exploded in recent years, with craft breweries joined by slick rooftop bars and moody laneway speakeasies.

OCHRE RESTAURANT AND CATERING

Trip Notes

Getting around The bars of central Cairns are all within easy walking distance.

Don't miss Near Cairns Airport, the Stratford neighbourhood is an emerging drinking hub; here Barrier Reef Brewing Co. is joined by The Fox Small Bar and Narrow Tracks Distilling, which opens its tasting room from 1pm Wednesday to Sunday.

Happy hour Cairns' bars offer great happy-hour deals, but Queensland law prohibits advertising them externally. Contact venues for current deals.

Dinner Time

Ochre Restaurant (pictured) Cairns' best waterfront fine dining uses native ingredients creatively.

Tokyo Dumpling Serves the best Japanese curry outside Japan.

NuNu This Palm Cove fine diner also serves the best beachfront breakfast around.

CC's Bar & Grill Ideal for date night, with a high-end fit-out and top-quality steaks.

Darren Barber, *co-owner of the Hospo Group @darrenjbarber*

01 Start on a high – literally, at Cairns' most elevated bar. Perched on the 12th-floor rooftop of the Crystalbrook Riley hotel, Mediterranean-inspired **Rocco** calls for an Aperol spritz (or two).

02 Soak up more epic Coral Sea sunset views at **Whiskey & Wine**, on level two of the Riley's sister hotel, Flynn, where you can choose from more than 80 local and imported whiskies.

03 With a prime location on Cairns' marina, swanky **Salt House** (pictured left) is a superb spot to watch the sun go down with a cocktail in hand.

05 You won't be able to see the sunset from **Three Wolves**, but you'll be happy you found this Prohibition-inspired laneway bar when you sample its theatrical cocktails.

04 When only a craft beer will do, **Hemingway's Brewery** is the place to pair a frothy one with views across Chinaman Creek towards the forested peaks of the Great Dividing Range.

FROM TOP: PAUL KINGSLEY/ALAMY STOCK PHOTO, CLAUDINE VAN MASSENHOVE/SHUTTERSTOCK

Daintree Dreaming

FEEL THE ANCIENT ENERGY

An ecosystem so spectacular that Sir David Attenborough called it 'the most extraordinary place on Earth', Queensland's Daintree Rainforest is a real-life Jurassic Park, home to descendants of plants and animals from the era of the dinosaurs. This biodiversity powerhouse is not only ecologically significant but also culturally important to its Traditional Custodians, the Eastern Kuku Yalanji rainforest people.

Left Daintree Rainforest
Centre Magnificent tree frog
Right Southern cassowary

AUSTRALIANCAMERA/SHUTTERSTOCK

Covering more than 1200 sq km between Mossman Gorge and the Bloomfield River, the otherworldly Daintree is estimated to be around 180 million years old. So it's no wonder that visiting this verdant corner of Queensland feels like stepping (a long way) back in time.

Part of the Wet Tropics World Heritage Area (WTWHA), the ancient rainforest is also protected by Daintree National Park, which has two sections: Mossman Gorge and Cape Tribulation. Just 20 minutes from Port Douglas, the **Mossman Gorge Centre** (mossmangorge.com.au) at the national park's southern end is the most accessible section. Here you can take self-guided or Indigenous-led walks and swim in the idyllic Mossman River, which tumbles between huge granite boulders. On the northern side of the Daintree River, accessed by a car ferry, the Cape Tribulation section (110km north of Cairns) feels even more wild, but like Mossman Gorge it also has a handful of easily accessible walking trails, as well as accommodation and ecotours.

Historic Handback

In 2021, more than 160,000 hectares of land in Tropical North Queensland, including the Daintree Rainforest, were officially handed back to the Eastern Kuku Yalanji people.

Central to the culture and spirituality of the Eastern Kuku Yalanji people, who have an intimate knowledge of the rainforest, passed down through generations, the handback means that Daintree National Park is now jointly managed by Traditional Custodians and the Queensland Government. At the time of research, construction was un-

ANDREJ BLAGOJEVIC/SHUTTERSTOCK

TORSTEN PURSCHE/SHUTTERSTOCK

derway on the Eastern Kuku Yalanji Bamanga Muruku Tourism Hub at Kulki on Cape Tribulation (p174), which will offer visitors new ways to engage with this ancient landscape.

Heritage Under Threat

Having survived for so long, the Daintree might seem pretty resilient. But research has found that the WTWHA, home to 36% of Australia's mammal species alone, is highly susceptible to climate change. Current modelling predicts that global warming of just 1°C – which science suggests has already been reached – could decrease the distributional range of the region's endemic vertebrate species by 60%. At 3.5°C, approximately 65% of endemic vertebrates are projected to disappear from the WTWHA, leading to a likelihood of mass extinctions, beginning with frogs and possums.

> In 2021, more than 160,000 hectares of land in Tropical North Queensland, including the Daintree Rainforest, was officially handed back to Eastern Kuku Yalanji people.

Additional threats to the rainforest identified by the Wet Tropics Management Authority include invasive species such as feral pigs and yellow crazy ants, increased demand for infrastructure, and a significant decline in research and investment due to a lack of government funding. And while tourism, too, has the potential to create negative impacts, it's impossible to visit this special place without being inspired to help protect it.

Daintree Experiences

Croc cruise Operating on the Daintree River, Solar Whisper (solarwhisper.com) boats are both ecofriendly and super-quiet, so you can glide up to salties and other wildlife without scaring the animals.

Daintree Discovery Centre In the Cape Tribulation section, this attraction has a treetop walkway that immerses you in the canopy – look for cassowaries down below.

Rainforest lodges Stay at a rainforest lodge at Cape Tribulation or near Mossman Gorge. Treat yourself to a stay at Silky Oaks Lodge.

Indigenous experiences See p158 for more info.

33 Cape Tribulation ESCAPE

RAINFOREST TRAILS | ROAD TRIP | SWIMMING HOLES

When you drive off the ferry that shuttles vehicles across the Daintree River, it feels like you've entered another realm. The Daintree Rainforest and the Great Barrier Reef meet at 'Cape Trib', a magical place dotted with rainforest trails and freshwater swimming holes. Most visitors only come for a day, but it's worth carving out three to connect more deeply with this off-grid wonder.

AUSTRALIANCAMERA/SHUTTERSTOCK

How to

Getting here and around The Daintree Ferry is a 1½-hour drive north of Cairns. Once across, it's about an hour to Kulki Lookout at the northern end of Cape Trib (if you don't stop).

When to go Avoid (most of) the rain during the May–November dry season.

Where to stay More than a dozen guesthouses (some with their own natural swimming holes) dot Cape Trib. Several camping spots include a basic national-park campground at Noah Beach.

MICHAEL SMITH ITWP/SHUTTERSTOCK

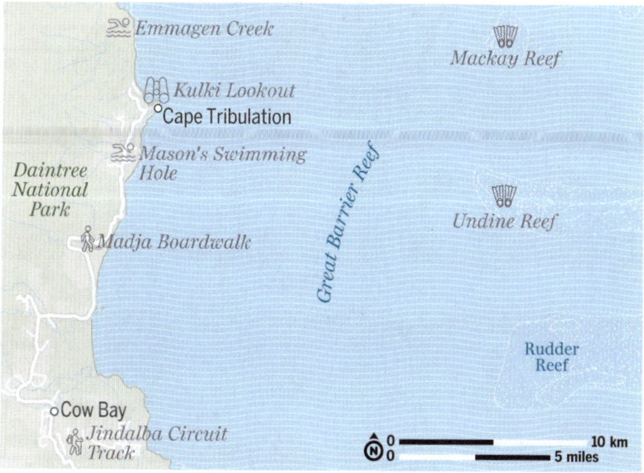

Rainforest trails Overnight stays allow for tackling Cape Trib's longer walks, including the lush Jindalba Circuit Track (3km) and the 7km-return slog up Mt Sorrow for spectacular views (allow six hours). Weaving through coastal mangroves, the elevated Madja Boardwalk (1.2km) is one of the world's most scenic wheelchair-accessible trails. Learn more about this ancient ecosystem on a walk with long-time local Neil Hewett (coopercreek.com.au). Cassowaries are spotted on most of his tours.

Next-level snorkelling If you only do one Great Barrier Reef snorkelling tour, make it this one. It only takes 25 minutes on Ocean Safari's inflatable boat to reach Mackay and Undine Reefs. Part of the Great Barrier Reef, these neighbouring reefs teem with marine turtles, tropical fish and some of the most beautiful, untouched corals accessible to snorkellers in the entire World Heritage Site. Gin-clear waters and shallow reef systems create ideal conditions for underwater photography.

Magical waterholes Cape Trib's beautiful beaches are off-limits for swimming due to 'salties' (saltwater crocodiles), but some of Australia's best (and croc-safe) freshwater swimming holes are found here. Don't miss Emmagen Creek (3.5km along the Bloomfield Track) and Mason's Swimming Hole (behind Mason's Cafe; gold-coin – $1 or $2 – donation). There's another beautiful waterhole you may hear about but won't find signposted, and for good reason: it's a sacred site for Kuku Yalanji Traditional Custodians.

Top left Daintree Rainforest
Bottom left Marine turtle

4WD Adventure

One of Australia's most legendary 4WD trails, the Bloomfield Track links the northern end of Cape Trib to the Aboriginal community of Wujal Wujal, from where a sealed road runs to Cooktown. The Bloomfield is only 30km long, but it's a famously challenging drive, with creek crossings, ultra-steep hills, and potholes the size of people. An extra 40km past Wujal Wujal (don't miss its Indigenous arts centre), the historic Lion's Den Hotel is an obligatory post-Bloomfield stop.

If one celebratory beer turns into a few – which can easily happen here – you can camp on the property. The pizzas are excellent.

34 Great Barrier Reef ADVENTURES

DIVING | ISLANDS | CONSERVATION

With 2300km of the Great Barrier Reef (GBR) to explore, where does a traveller begin? Hint: the outer reef is generally the best place to snorkel and dive, from top to bottom. Pinpoint your perfect base with this quick guide.

RANI ZERAFA/GETTY IMAGES

How to

Getting here It takes around 90 minutes to reach the outer reef on a motorised catamaran from Port Douglas and Cairns, and around two hours from Townsville and Bundaberg.

When to go The comfortably warm May–October dry season proffers the best conditions for diving and snorkelling, though many operators run trips year-round.

Reef-safe sunscreen Protect the reef by using sunscreens that contain only mineral UV-blocking ingredients such as oxide and titanium dioxide.

Northern Great Barrier Reef

Stretching from the Torres Strait to Hinchinbrook Island, north of Townsville, the Northern GBR is typically accessed from the holiday resort hubs of Cairns and Port Douglas, with smaller operators running trips from Cape Tribulation and Mission Beach. Or base yourself on luxe Lizard Island, reached by plane.

Visitors are spoilt for choice when it comes to reef operators. While bigger boats offer a smoother ride, they also hold more people. Day and overnight trips to Green and Fitzroy Islands are also available from Cairns.

Northern reefs are more susceptible to extreme weather events, including cyclones and ocean warming (which causes coral bleaching), yet these reefs tend to have more vibrant corals than the southern, more temperate

TANYA PUNTTI/SHUTTERSTOCK

Top left Lady Musgrave Island (p179)
Left Copperband butterflyfish

end of the reef. Tourist boats visit some of the healthiest corners of the marine park.

Central Great Barrier Reef

The Central GBR runs from the Townsville region down to Mackay, with outer-reef day trips available from Townsville, Orpheus Island, Magnetic Island, Airlie Beach, the Whitsundays and Mackay.

The Townsville region is home to the Museum of Underwater Art (MOUA) as well as the **SS *Yongala***, Australia's best wreck dive. There's decent snorkelling around the islands of the Central GBR, but this region doesn't compare to the quality of outer-reef locations like John Brewer Reef (accessed from Townsville) and Hardy Reef in the Whitsundays area. Visited by Cruise Whitsundays day trips from Airlie and the Whitsundays, Hardy Reef's **Reefworld Pontoon** also has two underwater hotel rooms (Reefsuites) and an upper-deck camping experience (Reefsleep).

Give Back to the Reef

Get involved with citizen science. Every visitor can help to safeguard the reef by uploading data via the Eye on the Reef app.

Visit with a **High Standard Operator** (see gbrmpa.gov.au); many have a Master Reef Guide on board.

Support reef-friendly businesses; most are Advanced Ecotourism certified by Ecotourism Australia.

Join the Citizens of the Great Barrier Reef by making an online pledge to take reef-friendly actions at home, including taking steps to reduce your emissions.

Follow the Reef Authority's motto: See the Reef, Love the Reef, Protect the Reef.

David Wachenfeld, *Research Program Director, Australian Institute of Marine Science @australianmarinescience*

Meet Turtles on Dry Land

Mon Repos Turtle Centre From November, nightly ranger-led tours observe marine turtles coming ashore near Bundaberg to lay their eggs. Hatchlings appear January to late March.

Cairns Turtle Rehabilitation Centre This Fitzroy Island centre cares for sick and injured turtles. Book a turtle tour to meet the patients.

NICO FARAMAZ/SHUTTERSTOCK

Southern Great Barrier Reef

Ending at **Lady Elliot Island**, home to the reef's foremost eco-resort, the lesser-visited southern fringe of the GBR has much to offer. Anchored near uninhabited Lady Musgrave Island on the outer reef, Lady Musgrave HQ is a pontoon that's used as a base for day and overnight trips from Bundaberg. The calm, shallow surrounding lagoon is fantastic for families.

Lady Musgrave Island day trips are also available from Seventeen Seventy, while overnight stays on **Heron Island** and nearby **Wilson Island** depart from Gladstone. Closer to the mainland yet still within the Great Barrier Reef Marine Park, the **Keppel Islands** can be visited from Yeppoon.

While the coral tends to be slightly less colourful than in the north, the Southern GBR, which has the highest percentage of hard coral cover, is widely regarded to be in better health overall, making for some epic diving and snorkelling. Enjoy manta ray sightings galore at Lady Elliot Island, and plenty of turtle action around Heron and Lady Musgrave Islands.

RIGHT: HOTFLASH/SHUTTERSTOCK; LEFT: PHMARCOSBORSATTO/SHUTTERSTOCK

Left Green turtle
Above top Manta Rays, Lady Elliot Island
Top left Coral polyp

Listings

BEST OF THE REST

Wondrous Waterfalls

Barron Falls

Take the elevated, wheelchair-accessible Barron Falls Lookout Track (1.2km return) for a front-on view of this dramatic waterfall near Kuranda. Alternatively, view it from the Skyrail Rainforest Cableway or Kuranda Scenic Railway.

Millaa Millaa Waterfall

Arguably the most photogenic waterfall in the Atherton Tablelands, near Cairns, surrounded by lush rainforest.

Josephine Falls

The crystal-clear pool at the bottom of this cascade in Wooroonooran National Park, an hour's drive south of Cairns, is one of Queensland's most idyllic freshwater swimming spots. It's a 1.2km return walk from the car park.

Wallaman Falls

Southwest of Ingham in Girringun National Park, the highest permanent single-drop waterfall in Australia plunges 268m into the gorge below. There's a viewing platform on the edge of the gorge, from where you can hike down to the base of the falls.

Little Crystal Creek

Cascading under a heritage-listed stone arch bridge, this series of small waterfalls is a picturesque spot to cool off in Paluma Range National Park, near Townsville.

Finch Hatton Gorge

Hike alongside a turquoise cascade tumbling through Finch Hatton Gorge in Eungella National Park, an hour's drive west of Mackay. There are natural swimming pools at the ends of the Wheel of Fire Track (4.2km return) and the Araluen Cascades Track (2.8km return).

Kondalilla Falls

After tackling the 300 stairs on the 4.7km-return Kondalilla Falls Circuit, a dip in the pool at the top of this 90m-high waterfall in the Sunshine Coast hinterland is obligatory.

Curtis Falls

In Tamborine Mountain National Park, a 1.1km-return trail leads to this lovely small waterfall spilling into a pool surrounded by lush rainforest. Keep an eye out for basking turtles on fallen logs, or come at night to look for glow-worms in the surrounding cliffs.

Seaside Pubs

Court House Hotel $$

Housed in a gorgeous old Queenslander on Wharf St, the 'Courty' in Port Douglas oozes old-school Aussie pub charm. The premium location has prices to match.

Mission Beach Tavern $$

A block from Mission Beach, this relaxed neighbourhood pub serves good-value classic

ARTHERNG/GETTY IMAGES

Millaa Millaa Waterfall

pub grub, from mackerel and chips to chicken parmigiana. It's a 200m stroll from Mission Beach Camping & Caravan Park.

Dingo Beach Hotel $$

Right on Dingo Beach, a 40-minute drive north of Airlie Beach in the Whitsundays, this relaxed, unassuming pub is a choice spot to while away an afternoon with a coldie in hand.

Eimeo Pacific Hotel $$

Perched at the edge of a cliff in Mackay's northern suburbs with cracking views towards the Cumberland Islands, this historic pub is a fantastic lunch spot.

1770 Beach Hotel $$

Ease into the relaxed vibe of Seventeen Seventy at this rustic pub, just paces from the peaceful 1770 Inlet Beach.

Bargara Beach Hotel $$

Tucked behind the esplanade on the Bundaberg coast, the recently renovated Bargara Beach Hotel has a sweeping deck, craft brews and an extensive pub-grub menu.

Quirky Attractions

Historic Village Herberton

With more than 50 restored period buildings, this outdoor museum is an unmissable Atherton Tablelands attraction.

Paronella Park

This tropical pleasure garden, south of Cairns, has a Spanish castle built by emigrant José Paronella in the 1930s.

Big Mango

You can't miss the 10m-high mango statue on the Bruce Hwy in Bowen. The next-door Bowen Visitor Information Centre sells tasty mango ice cream.

ALIZADA STUDIOS/SHUTTERSTOCK

Big Pineapple

Capricorn Caves

Half an hour north of Gladstone, the series of beautiful limestone caves can be visited on three types of guided tour.

Big Pineapple

Because one 'big thing' selfie is never enough, this Sunshine Coast icon is just off the M1 at Woombye.

Streets Beach

Brisbane may not be located on the ocean, but that doesn't mean it lacks a beach. This artificial inner-city beach is fringed by white sand and subtropical plants.

Hidden Beaches

Etty Bay Beach

Cassowaries are often spotted foraging on this small beach surrounded by rainforest near Innisfail. Has a popular beachfront campground.

Horseshoe Bay Beach

Linked to similarly pretty Rose Bay and Murray Bay beaches by the stunning 2.5km Cape Edgecumbe Walking Trail, this tiny curve of golden sand fringed by turquoise water is a gorgeous place for a swim in Bowen.

Coral Beach

Take the 1.1km rainforest track in Conway National Park, east of Airlie Beach, to this secluded coral rubble beach.

Cape Hillsborough Beach

Famous for its kangaroos that gather on the beach at dawn, attracted by food provided by the local council, this remote beach is beautiful for a stroll at any time of day. For great views, hike up the Andrews Point Track at the southern end of the beach (5.2km return).

Springs Beach

Enjoy a dip at picturesque Springs Beach, just south of Agnes Water, or head south along the trail linking it to Red Rock Beach to find a series of small coves and rock pools.

Tea Tree Bay Beach

Follow the Noosa Coastal Walk for 20 minutes to this lovely aquamarine bay in Noosa National Park.

Tallebudgera Creek

It's not exactly hidden, but when the Gold Coast's beaches are blown out, the sandy banks of this azure estuary separating Burleigh Heads and Palm Beach offer protected bliss.

Epic Food Markets

Rusty's Market

Cairns' iconic tropical fresh produce market (Friday to Sunday) is surrounded by street-food stalls.

Yungaburra Markets

On the fourth Saturday of each month, local growers, producers and artisans gather in the historic Atherton Tablelands village, with up to 260 stalls.

Eat Street Northshore

This Brisbane street-food market is known for its global, 'grammable dishes, from doughnut fries to handmade Hong Kong dumplings. With over 70 traders, including five themed bars, there's a dinner option for the whole family. Friday to Sunday.

HOTA Farmers & Artisan Markets

One of the Gold Coast's biggest and most popular weekly farmers markets takes over the Home of the Arts precinct in Surfers Paradise on Sunday mornings.

Family Fun

Fitzroy Island

Ideal for a half-day out with small kids, this lush coral-reef-fringed isle offers a Great Barrier Reef island experience just a 45-minute boat trip from Cairns.

Cairns Esplanade Lagoon

This fantastic public saltwater swimming pool is fringed by a sandy beach and lush lawns with barbecue facilities.

Buderim Ginger Factory

Set in 9 hectares of subtropical garden, this place offers factory tours and tastings. Kids will love jumping aboard the 100-year-old sugar-cane train.

GARY YIM/SHUTTERSTOCK

Eat Street Northshore

Mary Valley Rattler

Departing from Gympie Station, this refurbished steam train travels through the Mary Valley to the cute country communities of Dagun and Amamoor.

QAGOMA

The Queensland Art Gallery and Gallery of Modern Art are housed in two buildings in Brisbane. At the Kids' Art Centre, young artists can get their hands busy creating. Entry is free.

Moreton Island

Delight bigger kids with a day trip from Brisbane to Moreton Island (Mulgumpin) to snorkel the Tangalooma Wrecks. Hosted by Tangalooma Island Resort.

Bim'bimba Park

This award-winning nature-based park in Pimpama has a 14m-high play tower, outdoor table tennis, and 3km of walking and cycling trails.

Distilleries & Drinks

Wild Flower

Distilling what it calls 'Burleigh in a bottle', the Gold Coast's Wild Flower produces gins and spirits, including speciality blends such as lamington-flavoured vodka. Sourdough pizzas are available on Friday and Saturday.

Howard Smith Wharves

Nestled under Brisbane's Story Bridge, along the historic wharves on the banks of the Brisbane River, are cocktail bars, restaurants and a brewery with wood-fired pizzas.

Piggyback

Run by Tony Kelly, known for Sunshine Coast institutions such as Rice Boi, Piggyback in Palmwoods serves up Asian street food and creative cocktails.

MITCHELL DANN/SHUTTERSTOCK

Tangalooma Wrecks, Moreton Island

Beachtree Distilling Co.

Infusing native botanicals with organic and traditional ingredients, this Caloundra distillery makes animal-themed spirits, such as its Quokka native berry gin. Its cellar door is open Tuesday to Saturday.

Handmade Sunshine Coast Souvenirs

Artisan

Since 1970, Artisan has been the home of art and design in Queensland. Head to the store in Brisbane's Bowen Hills for Aboriginal textiles, opal jewellery and ceramics painted with native wildflowers.

Pottery Classes

Learn to shape clay by hand, throw pottery on a wheel, glaze your work and fire up the kiln. Classes in its Maroochydore studio include the 90-minute Make a Platter workshop.

David Linton Furniture & Timber Works

Showcasing the work of local artists, this expansive shop in Maleny sells beautifully carved objets d'art made from Australian woods, such as Huon pine and Bunya pine.

TASMANIA

HISTORY | OUTDOORS | FOOD

RESEARCHED BY ANDREW BAIN,
CHARLES RAWLINGS-WAY AND SARAH REID

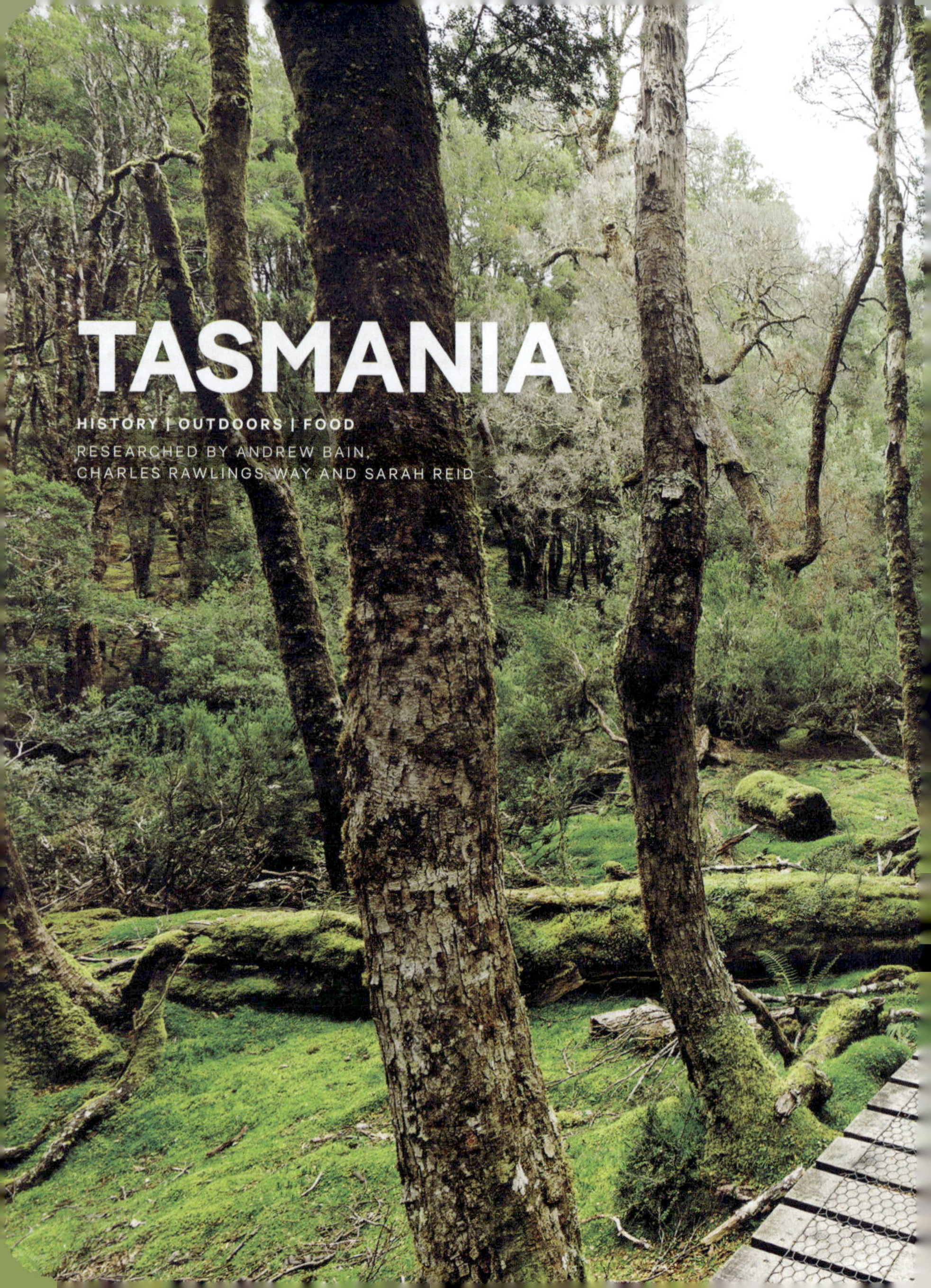

Experience Tasmania's alpine heart at Cradle Mountain's **Dove Lake** (p200)

2½hr from Launceston

TASMANIA

Trip Builder

Explore Hobart's art scene and heritage before embarking on outdoor adventures, from wonderful wilderness hikes to wildlife spotting. The compact state, also known by its Aboriginal name Lutruwita, is ideal for road tripping, with gourmet delights around every corner.

Go chasing waterfalls across the island, such as terraced **Liffey Falls** (p201)
+ 1¾hr from Launceston
Sip and swill your way between cool-climate wineries in the **Tamar Valley** (p206)
20min from Launceston
See fabulous **Freycinet** on foot, from the water and even by air (p202)
3hr from Hobart
Hang out with wombats (pictured above) on the former penal settlement of **Maria Island** (p204)
+ 2hr from Hobart
Immerse yourself in Hobart's famously quirky art scene at **MONA** (p190)
20min from Hobart
Explore Tasmania's convict past at **Port Arthur** (p194)
1½hr from Hobart
Embark on an easy gourmet adventure on **Bruny Island** (p196)
+ 1hr from Hobart
Flinders Island
Cape Barren Island
Clarke Island
Noland Bay
George Town
Bridport
Eddystone Point
Ulverstone
Devonport
Tamar River
Scottsdale
larapuna/ Bay of Fires
Sheffield
Exeter
Pyengana
St Helens
Launceston
TASMAN SEA
Deloraine
Westbury
St Marys
Fingal
Walls of Jerusalem National Park
Yingina/ Great Lake
Bicheno
Cranbrook
Derwent Bridge
Great Oyster Bay
Tarraleah
Oatlands
Schouten Island
Little Swanport
Bothwell
Hamilton
Kempton
Orford
Mt Field National Park
Buckland
Maria Island
Lake Gordon
Bridgewater
New Norfolk
Sorell
Maydena
Hobart
Bellerive
Forestier Peninsula
Lauderdale
Lake Pedder
Kingston
Tasman Peninsula
Eaglehawk Neck
Huonville
Southwest National Park
Geeveston
Woodbridge
Storm Bay
Bruny Island
Dover
Bathurst Harbour
New River Lagoon
Southport
Prion Bay
Cockle Creek
Maatsuyker Group

Practicalities

REDZAAL/GETTY IMAGES

ARRIVING

Hobart Airport Tasmania's main international (with seasonal flights from New Zealand) and domestic airport is located 19km east of the city in Cambridge. A taxi to central Hobart is around $45. SkyBus shuttles meet every flight and stop at six locations around the city.

Launceston Airport (pictured) Domestic flights only. Door-to-door shuttle buses and taxis (around $40) travel 14km north to the city centre.

Devonport Arrival city for the *Spirit of Tasmania* vehicle ferry from Geelong near Melbourne.

HOW MUCH FOR A

Curried scallop pie $10

Local craft beer $12

Two-month parks pass per vehicle $95.50

WHEN TO GO

DEC–FEB
Warmer and drier weather. Lots of summer festival action.

MAR–MAY
Mild days and cooler evenings. Good walking weather.

JUN–AUG
Crisp mornings and shorter days. Perfect for a whisky beside the fire.

SEP–NOV
Warming up in spring. Great Eastern Wine Week and Launceston's Junction Arts Festival.

GETTING AROUND

Car Tasmania is perfect for a road trip, with recommended routes including the east coast, the Tarkine Drive and the Tamar Valley Wine Route. Roads can be wet and icy during the winter months, and wildlife is often plentiful on rural roads. Avoid driving at dawn, dusk and nighttime, when native animals are more active.

Bus Services link Hobart and Launceston through central Tasmania, travel along the east coast via Freycinet National Park, and run from Burnie southwest to Strahan. Frequency of departures can be limited.

Plane There are flights from Launceston to Flinders Island and from Burnie-Wynyard to King Island and Flinders Island. Some King Island flights originate in Melbourne (Essendon).

EATING & DRINKING

Culinary highlights include export-quality oysters, scallops and lobster, as well as grass-fed Cape Grim beef. Popular wine regions are the east coast and the Tamar Valley, while craft breweries and distilleries are increasingly widespread. Road-trip dining opportunities include village bakeries turning out delicious savoury pies, popular weekend farmers markets, and innovative eateries in Hobart and Launceston harnessing an island bounty of seasonal ingredients. In the northwest, Tasting Trail Tasmania (tastingtrail.com.au) guides you to artisanal producers.

Best Tassie tasting menu
Dier Makr (p210) in Hobart

Must-try seafood with a view
Lobster Shack (p209) in Bicheno

CONNECT & FIND YOUR WAY

Mobile phones There is limited or no mobile-phone reception in more remote locations, notably on the west coast and in the northwest. Telstra is the only telco with service on King and Flinders islands.

Wi-fi A map of free wi-fi locations and access details can be found at freewifi.tas.gov.au. It is usually free at public libraries.

WHERE TO STAY

Motels and B&Bs are widespread throughout regional Tasmania, while Hobart has a wider range of accommodation, with hostels, hotels and waterfront apartments.

City	Pro/Con
Hobart	Good range of accommodation and Tasmania's best eating and drinking scene.
Launceston	Excellent B&B accommodation and a lively food, arts and culture scene. Near the Tamar Valley.
Coles Bay	Convenient access to Freycinet National Park but expensive. Consider Bicheno as an alternative.
Devonport	Emerging restaurant and bar scene and well placed for exploring Cradle Country and along the north-west coast.
Stanley	Heritage accommodation and good access to the Tarkine Drive. Limited eating and drinking opportunities.
Cradle Mountain	Right by the national park, but expensive accommodation.

FILL 'ER UP

Around the west coast, always take the opportunity to refuel your car, as petrol stations are few in more remote areas.

MONEY

ATMs are widely available, even in smaller towns. Most businesses accept contactless payment.

In Launceston, save money by using the free Tiger Bus service that loops around key attractions in the city.

35 Putting the Art in HOBART

ART | CULTURE | GALLERIES

Few cities have been so immediately and irrevocably changed by a single cultural moment as was Hobart when MONA opened in 2011. But even beyond David Walsh's subversive underground art gallery, this city has an unexpected art pedigree.

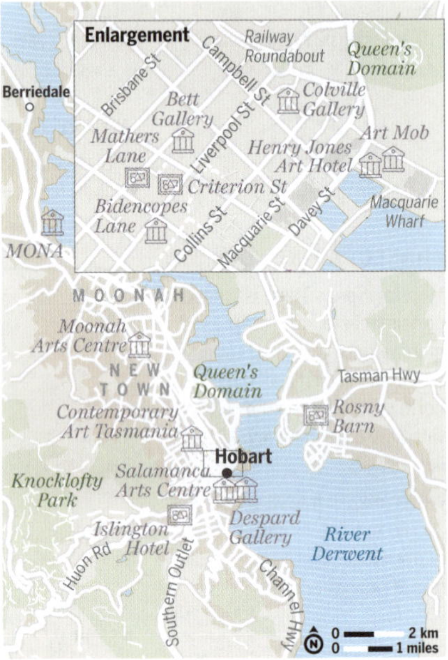

How to

Getting there The best way to MONA is on the MONA ROMA ferry, which sails from the Brooke St Pier. Posh Pit tickets add wine and canapés to the journey.

When to go MONA is open Thursday to Monday.

Pedalling art MONA sits just 800m from Hobart's Intercity Cycleway, making it a simple pedal to the gallery – it's 12km from the city. Pick up a bike from Hobart Bike Hire.

Artfully MONA

Behind all of **MONA**'s self-styled 'wank', there is the art, which ranges from the sublime to the shocking. Australia's largest private art gallery fills three subterranean levels in a maze-like bewilderment of art and antiquities. Among it all are some signature works, such as Sidney Nolan's 1620-panel **Snake**, a painting so large it had never been publicly displayed until MONA built a room especially for it. Irreverently nearby is Wim Delvoye's **Cloaca Professional**, aka the 'poo machine', an installation that replicates the human digestive tract, complete with faeces and associated smells. There's a wall of 152 anatomically correct **porcelain vulvas** moulded from real subjects, while the very cathartic **MONA Confessional** offers the chance to broadcast your sins anonymously to random listeners far above.

R WAREHAM/ALAMY

Hobart Street Art

Venturing into Hobart's many lanes, you'll find a somewhat hidden but vibrant street-art scene. **Bidencopes Lane**, a favourite hangout for taggers, reveals myriad artists' work, including the distinctive work of local hero Tom O'Hern. Just around the corner in **Mathers Lane**, O'Hern strikes again with *Terraform*, a 4.5m-by-11m mural he describes as 'a foresty thing'. Stormie Mills' *Lost Giant* towers grimly over latte sippers in **Criterion St**, while the back alleys of Elizabeth Mall reveal an endangered spotted handfish lurking opposite Jae Mills' 3.5m-high figures in antique chairs, a nod to the long-gone Purdy's Mart emporium.

Emma Bett, *co-director of Bett Gallery @bettgallery*

Gallery Days

Hobart's love affair with art long preceded MONA. The city is rich in vibrant local spaces, such as the **Rosny Farm**, the **Salamanca Arts Centre**, **Moonah Arts Centre** and **Contemporary Art Tasmania** (CAT), presenting arts-based exhibitions and experimental performances. Well-established commercial galleries are plentiful. **Bett Gallery** is one of Australia's foremost contemporary galleries. Waterfront **Despard Gallery** and **Colville Gallery** feature regular exhibitions and art auctions, while **Art Mob** specialises in Aboriginal art from across Australia. Take in an opening night or find exhibition programmes through gallery websites.

Above MONA

ARCHITECTURAL
Hobart

01

02

03

04

01 MONA
So much here takes place underground, away from the eye, but even the Corten and concrete exterior, with its newer pyramidal Pharos extension, is commanding.

02 Silos Apartments
Standing tall at the end of Salamanca Pl, this 11-storey building has been transformed from what it still resembles – grain silos – into apartments.

03 Menzies Institute Building
The facade divides opinion, but the fluid lattice lines represent the contours of the land and are a louvre system to passively shade the windows.

04 Shot Tower
Built to make gun shot, the chimney-like structure – one of only three shot towers in Australia – was, for four years in the 1870s, Australia's tallest building.

05 Hobart Synagogue
Australia's oldest synagogue, built in rare Egyptian Revival style, has early links to the convict said to have inspired the character Fagin in *Oliver Twist*.

06

07

08

09

10

05

06 Wrest Point

When built in 1973, this cylindrical Sandy Bay building was Australia's first legal casino. It remains Hobart's tallest building (64m).

07 Cascade Brewery

The striking, stepped sandstone facade, standing in repose before Kunanyi/Mt Wellington, was said to have been designed in a jail cell by brewery founder Peter Degraves.

08 General Post Office

One of Hobart's landmark buildings, modelled on London's Big Ben, though it took a public subscription to raise the money to build the tower in 1906.

09 St David's Cathedral

Leading British architect George Frederick Bodley's finest Australian work, and the seat of the Bishop of Tasmania.

10 Henry Jones IXL Jam Factory

The warehouses along waterfront Hunter St are Hobart's oldest. The IXL jam factory filled much of the space, and is today a hotel filled with 19th-century industrial design and features.

01 MONA/JESSE HUNNFORD, ARCHITECT: NONDA KATSALIDIS **02** DESIGNIUM/SHUTTERSTOCK, ARCHITECT: HBV **03** SLOVEGROVE/GETTY IMAGES, ARCHITECT: LYONS **04** KYLE TOWNS/SHUTTERSTOCK **05** CHAMELEONSEYE/SHUTTERSTOCK **06** SLOW WALKER/SHUTTERSTOCK **07** DARYL ARIAWAN/SHUTTERSTOCK **08** BENNY MARTY/SHUTTERSTOCK **09** TRABANTOS/SHUTTERSTOCK **10** VIPERSNIPER/GETTY IMAGES

Australia's Alcatraz

ONE NARROW DETAIL PREVENTED CONVICTS FROM ESCAPING PORT ARTHUR

Freedom teased at Port Arthur. The surrounding bush promised cover, and it might have appeared a simple task to break out, but this remote convict settlement had one ingenious bit of escape-proofing, and it was provided by nature: the Teralina/ Eaglehawk Neck isthmus.

Left and right Port Arthur historic buildings
Centre Eaglehawk Neck isthmus

SARAWUT KONGANANTDECH/SHUTTERSTOCK

As if being sent to one of the furthest-flung corners of an island in one of the furthest-flung places on the planet from Britain wasn't demoralising enough, nature and human nature conspired to make Port Arthur almost escape-proof. Turrakana/Tasman Peninsula clings to the Tasmanian mainland by a literal thread – the Teralina/ Eaglehawk Neck isthmus, which, at its narrowest, is little more than 100m wide. To prevent convicts from escaping, all authorities had to do was guard this filament of land and stop the convicts from taking to the water.

Barking Mad

Preventing escape via the water was largely achieved through the age-old tactic of fear, with convicts told that the local waters were infested with sharks (only a white lie, really). Which just left the isthmus. In 1831, following a number of escape attempts in the first year of the penal settlement's existence at Port Arthur, sentries were posted at Teralina/Eaglehawk Neck, though they were ineffective because the noise of the surrounding ocean masked the sound of any convicts trying to slip through. That's when an officer came up with the idea of stringing a line of savage dogs across the isthmus.

The so-called Dog Line involved up to 18 dogs tethered across the sandy isthmus, with wooden barrels as kennels and spaced so that their snouts almost touched when they reached the end of their chains. Other dogs were placed on platforms in the sea, to detect any escapees trying to swim past the isthmus. Shells were also spread across the narrow neck of land. Any approaching convict

GREG BRAVE/SHUTTERSTOCK

ONPATROLPHOTO/GETTY IMAGES

would have to crunch over the shells – no dog was going to miss the sound or the stench of an unwashed convict.

Today, a bronze statue of a tethered dog on Teralina/ Eaglehawk Neck marks the site of the Dog Line.

Escape Attempts

Desperate times call for desperate measures, and bolts for freedom were still occasionally made. Most famously, bushranger Martin Cash managed to twice slip through the Teralina/ Eaglehawk Neck dog fortress. The first time he succeeded in swimming across Eaglehawk Bay, the narrow bay on the isthmus' western side, though he was soon recaptured and returned to Port Arthur. In 1842, with two other convicts, he again swam past the Neck to freedom – note the attempt by water again, which is testament to the deterrent effect of the dogs.

George 'Billy' Hunt, who was transported to Australia for stealing a handkerchief, wrapped himself in the skin of a kangaroo and endeavoured to hop across the isthmus.

The most entertaining escape attempt belonged to George 'Billy' Hunt. The Scotsman, who was transported to Australia for stealing a handkerchief, wrapped himself in the skin of a kangaroo and endeavoured to hop across the isthmus. It all came undone because the rationed and hungry guards saw a potential meal hopping past, rather than a convict in disguise. When they raised their guns to shoot the roo, Hunt threw off the hide and surrendered.

Cashing In

When Martin Cash escaped from Port Arthur on Boxing Day in 1842, he set out on a crime spree that lasted for eight months, immortalising himself as one of Australia's most notorious bushrangers. His rampage only ended when he headed to Hobart in August 1843, vowing to kill his cheating girlfriend and her new beau. Confronted by a constable, he shot and killed the policeman and was sentenced to death. A last-minute reprieve saw him sent to Norfolk Island instead. He later became a constable at Hobart's Cascades Female Factory and overseer at the Royal Hobart Botanical Gardens.

36 BRUNY Escapes

NATURE | FOOD | WALKS

Bruny is the island every city wishes it had within a 30-minute drive of the city centre. Wrapped in beaches, cliffs and surf, and magically held together by the narrowest of sand isthmuses, it's a place devoted to nature and nurture in equal measures, with its coastal walks matched in quality only by the freshness of the island produce.

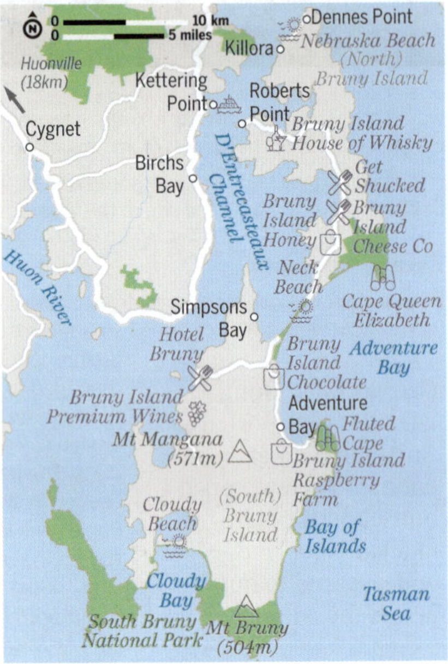

How to

Getting here The island ferry (sealinkbruny island.com.au) departs multiple times a day from Kettering.

When to go Long queues for the ferry aren't uncommon during school holidays. To avoid them, November, early December, February and March are good times to visit.

Happy housemates Stick around at night to watch little penguins coming ashore at the Neck, where the birds have the rare habit of sharing their burrows with migratory muttonbirds (September to April).

Bruny Bites

By day, Bruny Island is a veritable providore (by night it's a dining desert, with **Hotel Bruny** likely to be the only dinner option – try the house-made cider), demanding at least a few hours of idle grazing time. Pair cheese and craft beer under the gum trees at **Bruny Island Cheese Co**, slurp oysters at **Get Shucked** (complete with a drive-through oyster window), sip a smooth spirit at **Bruny Island House of Whisky** and a fine drop at **Bruny Island Premium Wines**, Australia's southernmost winery. **Bruny Island Honey**, **Bruny Island Raspberry Farm** and **Bruny Island Chocolate** sweeten the deal.

Walk This Way

Bruny's coast is as exceptional as it is varied. Walk to

NIGEL KILLEEN/GETTY IMAGES

Cape Queen Elizabeth at low tide and it's possible to squeeze through gaps in the cliffs to find an arch of rock curling out of the Moorina Bay sand. The **Fluted Cape** walk passes through the remains of a whaling station before climbing atop some of Australia's highest cliffs – this is also the walk on which you might sight one of Bruny's rare white wallabies. Inland, an ascent through rainforest leads to the island's highest point, 571m **Mt Mangana**. The messy summit might appear to have no views, but all is revealed if you find the trail to the right, heading to an open boulder field.

Bruny Beaches

Some of my favourite Bruny beaches are known by many people, but are large enough to make you think you're alone.

For a lazy swim, I love the crystal-white sands and blue water of **Nebraska Beach** – out to the mooring buoys and back. **Neck Beach** is long and usually deserted, with a nice surf break when the banks are working. **Adventure Bay** leaves you spoilt for choice – it's great for families. Further south, **Cloudy Bay** ticks all the boxes: the best surf and a long stretch of beach to explore.

The great secrets, though, are to be found by boat or kayak. Tiny little sandy coves reminiscent of the Greek islands emerge everywhere at low tide.

Lee Macefield, *owner of Get Shucked oyster farm*

@get_shucked_oysters

Above Neck Beach

37 Walker's PARADISE

WILDERNESS | FALLS | WILDLIFE

Walks here clamour over each other as the most iconic, most beautiful, most photographed, most popular... From seasoned and experienced walkers to those who want a gentle meander in nature, this truly is a walker's paradise.

FILEDIMAGE/SHUTTERSTOCK

How to

Getting here You can get buses (or even a ferry) to the start and end of these walks, but for day walks it's best to drive yourself.

When to go Even summer can feel like winter in these parts. All but the hardiest walkers should avoid the depths of winter.

Be prepared This region is remote. Check weather warnings, pack for four seasons, carry enough water and do your research.

FILEDIMAGE/SHUTTERSTOCK

Overnight Walks

The **Overland Track**, six days and 65km of one-way dazzling wilderness in a UNESCO World Heritage area, is deservedly known as Australia's premier alpine walk. Beginning at Cradle Mountain and ending at Leeawuleena/Lake St Clair, there are no shops, no roads, no supplies on this trek; you'll reach the end of the trail enlightened (or just lightened, which may feel like the same thing).

Walls of Jerusalem National Park also borders on a spiritual experience: the three-day 23km circuit (with multiple variations) starts with a 3km walk up the Walls – climbing 600m until it feels like you have reached the heavens. Amenities are limited, so you will be carrying your life on your back as you ascend; pack sparingly but wisely – and definitely read all the advice you can find. Here, up top, you

PIP STRICKLAND/SHUTTERSTOCK

Guided Walks

From the luxury guided Overland Track tour with sumptuous food, wine and accommodation every night to following professional walking guides, you can explore the region with the benefit of local expertise. If you haven't done much walking or aren't familiar with Tasmanian conditions, this is for you!

Top left and above Overland Track
Left Walls of Jerusalem National Park

will find dolerite peaks, ancient pencil pine groves, rich cultural heritage and plenty of wildlife.

Taking It a Day at a Time

There are numerous day and half-day walks here – too many to mention and way too many to choose from – of varying grades and lengths, but here are a few favourites to consider. There are many and varied walks around iconic Cradle Mountain, from **Dove Lake** (two- to three-hour loop, with some lovely diversions along the way) to the more challenging **Cradle Summit** (eight hours return). You'll easily find a walk that suits your time, mood and motivation – and the weather! Snow is not uncommon here: a white fluffy flurry is a delight to walk in; sideways streaming sleet not so much...

The **Western Tiers** is the lesser-known cousin to destinations like Cradle and the Walls, but its appeal is rich variety and it should not be underestimated. Some walks

Wall in the Wilderness

Derwent Bridge is a small Tasmanian town in the midst of walking country, with little more than a takeaway store and 'The Wall'. Since 2005, sculptor Greg Duncan has been slowly carving a timber wall 3m high and over 100m in length. For a break between walks, why not stop in and admire this feat of patience and quiet respect for the history, hardship and perseverance of the people of the Central Highlands? This is a unique and dramatic piece of sculptural art in the middle of nowhere.

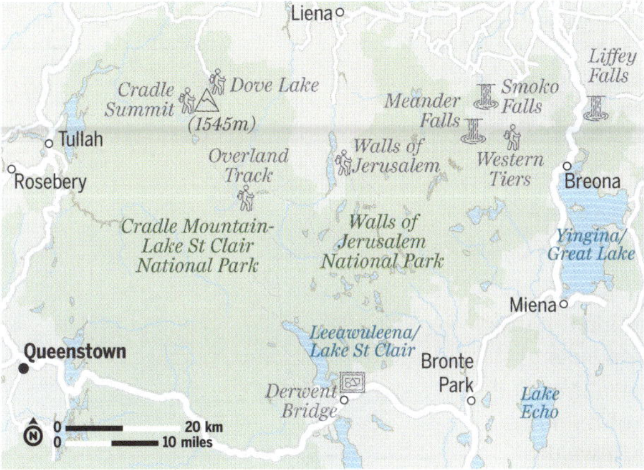

in the area include **Mother Cummings** (five to six hours), **Quamby Bluff** (four to five hours), and the easy and wheelchair-friendly 20-minute **Pine Lake** walk.

Walks with Waterfalls

Ah, the magic of falling water in the wilderness! **Meander Falls** is a five- to six-hour challenging out-and-back walk that follows the Meander River to the 130m falls that dramatically cascade over the Great Western Tiers. You will see iconic Tasmanian trees like King Billy pine, Celery Top pine and myrtle as you pass through this part of the Tasmanian Wilderness World Heritage Area.

Alternatively, for a shorter walk in the same area, **Liffey Falls** is a truly stunning waterfall that is just a 45-minute walk from the picnic ground. You can also choose your own waterfall adventure if you head along the Mother Cummings walk – you will come across the picturesque **Smoko Falls** after an hour and that may be as far as you want to go. Sit down, pop your feet in the water and have a bite to eat.

Left Dove Lake
Below Liffey Falls

38 Freycinet FUN

WINEGLASS BAY | BEACH WALKS | KAYAKING

Tasmania's oldest national park (with Mt Field) is also its top coastal park, sheltering one of Australia's most famous beaches, one of its most colourful mountain ranges, a wealth of wildlife and a host of other natural features. Best of all, there are myriad ways to explore Freycinet National Park.

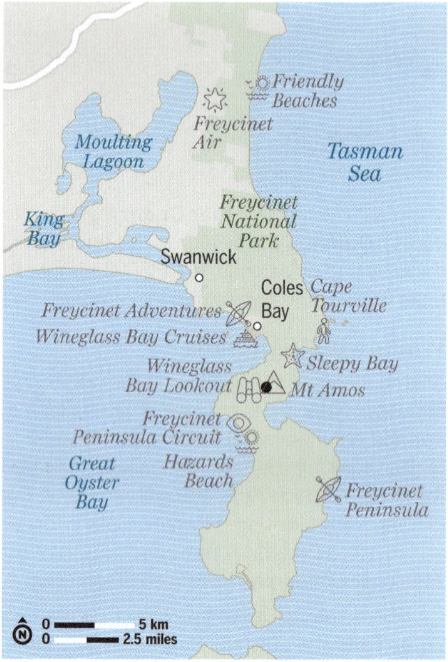

How to

Getting here Tassielink buses connect Hobart to Bicheno, with one daily (except Sunday) bus continuing to Coles Bay, at Freycinet National Park's edge.

When to go Beach life is best in summer, but Freycinet remains (relatively) mild year-round.

Give it a pass A valid park pass is required for entry to Freycinet National Park. Purchase online (parks.tas.gov.au), at the park visitor centre, or at ticket machines at the Wineglass Bay car park.

Freycinet on Foot

Almost every visitor to Freycinet comes for a peep at Wineglass Bay. You can catch a distant glimpse from the accessible **Cape Tourville** boardwalk (a 20-minute walk) while the traditional look is from the **Wineglass Bay Lookout** clipped onto the slopes of the Hazards mountains – continue down the slopes and you get the pleasure of stepping out onto the bay's sands, perhaps returning via **Hazards Beach** as part of an 11km loop. The loftiest and best view is found atop **Mt Amos**, though the climb, at times a scramble, requires sure-footedness and confidence.

Elsewhere, consider the short walk down into **Sleepy Bay**, a lingering beachcomb along the **Friendly Beaches**, or even the two- to three-day **Freycinet Peninsula Circuit**.

TOM JASTRAM/SHUTTERSTOCK

One Perfect Day

A great way to begin the day at Freycinet is on our 25-minute flight over Wineglass Bay – that'll get you started and get your bearings from the air. Then do the Wineglass Bay Lookout walk and see the bay yourself, and enjoy the Cape Tourville walk. Finally, you've got the nice granite rocks and the red lichen at Honeymoon Bay.

The region is also home to many excellent vineyards and eateries, where you can savour local produce, fresh seafood and spectacular views of the Hazards and surrounding coastline.

Greg and Gabby Ross, *the owner-operators of Freycinet Air.*

Water & Air

To see Wineglass Bay from the water, hop aboard a five-hour tour with **Wineglass Bay Cruises**, rounding the southern point of the peninsula and heading into the bay. You won't see Wineglass from a kayak, but a morning or twilight paddle with **Freycinet Adventures** will have you skimming along the base of the granite Hazards and gliding into the romance of Honeymoon Bay.

Hire an SUP from **Freycinet Paddle Boards** and gently punt your way around the calm waters of Coles Bay with an eyeful of the Hazards, or take to the skies with **Freycinet Air** for a godly view of the peninsula and its famous beach.

Above View of Wineglass Bay from Mt Amos

39 WILDLIFE Wonders

WILDLIFE | NATIONAL PARKS | SANCTUARY

Tasmania's east coast is sparsely populated, except when it comes to wildlife. Wallabies, Forester kangaroos, wombats, Cape Barren geese and even Tasmanian devils flourish here, roaming a string of national parks that line the coast and an island once known as Australia's Noah's Ark.

How to

Getting here Car is the best way to get between the national parks and Bicheno. Maria Island is car-free and reached by the Encounter Maria Island passenger ferry from Triabunna.

When to go It's less about seasons and more about time of day. Tasmania's native critters are at their most active around dawn and dusk.

Viewing behaviour Don't ever feed or touch wild animals, and give them a few metres of space.

Park Residents

On the lawns around the World Heritage–listed Darlington Probation Station on **Maria Island**, the one thing you're unlikely to see is emptiness. The island was used in the 1960s as a 'Noah's Ark' experiment to preserve native species, and it now bustles with animals – most notably wombats (we counted 132 one day), Forester kangaroos, Cape Barren geese and, if you're lucky, Tasmanian devils, which were released on the island in 2012 in an attempt to save the iconic species from extinction after the population was devastated by devil facial tumour disease.

Take a morning or evening drive around the 12km Forester Kangaroo Drive in **Mt William National Park**, at the foot of low Wukalina/ Mt William, and you'll find a similar suite of native animals roaming the marsupial lawns.

Callous Maria

Wildlife is just one of Maria Island's callings in life. The island is entirely national park and Darlington Probation Station, which predated Port Arthur, is part of the Australian Convict Sites World Heritage Site. You can stay in basic bunkhouse-style accommodation inside the old convict cells (guaranteeing you a front lawn with wombats), from where you can venture out on walking trails to the likes of the whimsically patterned Painted Cliffs, the spire-topped Bishop and Clerk, and the island's highest point, 711m Mt Maria, peering directly down onto the island's paper-thin isthmus.

Marching on Bicheno

Bicheno's wildlife credentials are twofold. Each evening after dusk, little penguins puff up their courage, marching ashore and making for their burrows along the town's coast. Join a guided tour with **Bicheno Penguin Tours** to watch their tentative arrival and view life among the burrows. At **East Coast Natureworld**, 7km north of town, you can meet Tasmanian devils on a Devils in the Dark tour and, by day, meet and greet echidnas, wombats, sugar gliders and the cutest critters of all – baby devils (mid-September to March/April) – on personalised Encounter experiences.

MICHAL PESATA/SHUTTERSTOCK

JANE RIX/SHUTTERSTOCK

Above Forester kangaroos
Left Tasmanian devil

40 Valley of VINES

DRIVING ROUTE | CELLAR DOORS | RIVER VIEWS

The Tamar Valley is Tasmania's premier wine region, encompassing more than 30 vineyards spread over both banks of Kanamaluka/Tamar River. It's a region celebrated for its sparkling wines, pinot noirs and aromatic whites. Plot a road trip with water views and wine intentions.

GIONNIXXX/GETTY IMAGES

Trip Notes

Getting around The West Tamar and East Tamar Hwys connect across the Batman Bridge, making for an easy driving loop. Or leave the car keys in your hotel room and book a day among the wineries with Tamar Valley Wine Tours.

Need to know On the eastern side of the river, the Pipers Brook and Legana areas produce some of the world's best sparkling wines, with the awards to back it up.

Non-Alcoholic Attractions

There are plenty of alcohol-free attractions through the Tamar Valley to keep the designated driver happy. **Notley Fern Gorge** is a fern-filled wonderland and **Brady's Lookout** offers a commanding view over Kanamaluka/Tamar River. **Tamar Island Wetlands** has a bird-filled, over-water boardwalk out to Tamar Island in the middle of the river.

PHILIP GAME/ALAMY

01 The beautiful rammed-earth and rusted-steel cellar door at **Clover Hill Wines** looks out over a natural amphitheatre of vines, with most varietals on the tasting list exclusive to the cellar door.

02 Book ahead at **House of Arras** for a tasting or a Wine and Wildlife walking tour. In 2024 this vineyard became the first in Australia to win the coveted Chairman's Trophy at the Champagne and Sparkling Wine World Championships.

03 The chardonnay, pinot noir and pinot gris at family-owned Rowella winery **Holm Oak** are worth a stop, but it's also fun just feeding apples to Pinot d'Pig, the pig with the grand job of Holm Oak's general manager.

04 Stake a spot on the deck overlooking the vines at **Moores Hill Estate**, Tasmania's first off-grid winery, and run through a tasting of the wine range over a grazing board or seafood platter.

05 **Swinging Gate Vineyard** is a rustic cellar door that turns out everything from pinots to pét-nat, with Domescapes glamping domes on-site if you fancy staying the night.

Listings

BEST OF THE REST

Scenic Spots

Russell Falls

The 1.4km-return trail to the pinnacle of Mt Field National Park is wheelchair accessible. Walk the 6km Three Falls Circuit for a waterfall feast.

Lake Mackintosh

A beautiful lake near Tullah managed by Hydro Tasmania, stocked with trout and surrounded by myrtle, sassafras and eucalypt forest. There are walking tracks around the lake and plenty of picnic spots.

Donaghys Hill

Easy 2.2km return walk to a lookout point with wide views of the Franklin River and Frenchmans Cap. The gradual uphill track passes through cool temperate rainforest, past mosses and lichen.

Mt Murchison

One of Tassie's best day walks for experienced hikers. Expect rock scrambling and steep sections on your way to the summit of the highest peak in the West Coast Range. Well worth it for the wilderness panoramas.

Spion Kop Lookout

Short but steep 300m walkway on the eastern edge of Queenstown. Named after a Boer War battle, the walk is paved and includes several mining exhibits and interpretive boards along the way.

Mole Creek Karst National Park

Among the 500-plus caves that puncture this karst landscape, two are open for ranger-led guided tours. The larger of the pair, Marakoopa, has glow-worms for bright company.

Cosy Corner

If you have to pick just one Larapuna/Bay of Fires beach, it might as well be the comfortingly named Cosy Corner with its artistically jumbled granite boulders and coating of orange lichen.

Boat Harbour Beach

Stop, relax; you've found one of Tasmania's most beautiful beaches on its northwest coast.

Cataract Gorge Reserve

A stunning gorge and basin, just a 15-minute walk from central Launceston and cut by the longest river in Tasmania, the South Esk.

Straight from the Source

Coal River Farm

Stock up on chocolate and cheese, or come for a 'high cheese', which comprises a sample of four cheeses paired with a Tassie tipple.

Willie Smith's Apple Shed

Check out the display of almost 400 apple varieties at this former apple barn turned bar, restaurant, apple distillery and cider cellar door in Grove.

LKONYA/SHUTTERSTOCK

Cataract Gorge Reserve

Pyengana Dairy

Enjoy a true paddock-to-plate experience with a tasting board of award-winning, handcrafted cheeses. From your table, watch the cows let themselves in and out of the robotic milking shed.

Lease 65

Grab freshly shucked oysters from the shed door at this oyster farm on the shores of Georges Bay between St Helens and Binalong Bay. It's takeaway only, but it's only right that you take them to a beach to enjoy. Cash only.

Waubs Harbour Distillery

Everything but the growing of the grain is done on-site at this pure whisky distillery, housed in a former oyster hatchery at the Gulch in Bicheno. Book ahead for a distillery tour or a one-hour guided tasting.

Kate's Berry Farm

Popular berry farm at Swansea's southern edge looking over Great Oyster Bay to the peaks of Freycinet Peninsula. The picking season is November to May; the cafe's ice creams and scones are delicious.

Devil of a Time

Devils@Cradle

At the entrance to Cradle Mountain National Park, this conservation facility is dedicated to ensuring the survival of Tasmania's most unique species, the Tasmanian devil.

Bonorong Wildlife Sanctuary

Visiting the animals in Bonorong's care supports its wildlife hospital, which treats more than 2500 animals per year.

Tasmanian Devil Unzoo

A new take on zoos – unfenced (except for the enclosed Tasmanian devils), with animals free to come and go as they choose. Join a Devil Tracker tour to help with local devil research.

YIFEN WU/SHUTTERSTOCK

Oysters, Bruny Island

Super Seafood

Flippers $$

Grab waterside fish and chips from this fish-shaped floating caravan at Hobart's Constitution Dock. Dessert is 10 steps away at the neighbouring Van Diemens Land Creamery mooring.

Mures $$

Upstairs is high-end; downstairs has oysters, ice-cream cones to go (promenade past the local yachts and fishing boats) and the best seafood chowder in Hobart. Opens early.

Blue Eye $$$

Seafood linguine, char-grilled octopus, sashimi, garlic-butter abalone, all sluiced down with Tasmanian wines and beers. A Salamanca stalwart.

Doo-Lishus $

It's just a caravan in a car park (at the Blowhole in Doo Town) and yet it's held by many to serve up Tasmania's best fish and chips.

Lobster Shack $$

Tasmania's best lobster roll? You be the judge at this Bicheno waterfront cafe.

Cannery $$

Don't muck around – order a seafood platter and head for the deck at this former fish cannery in Dunalley, down by the canal.

Foreshore $$

Local favourite on the Burnie beachfront serving up quality Tasmanian seafood alongside burgers, breakfasts, a decent wine list and Bass Strait views.

Hursey Seafoods $$

Look beyond the warehouse-like exterior – with its own fishing fleet moored metres away, you know things are fresh at this Stanley restaurant with takeaways downstairs.

City Criminals

Hobart Penitentiary

The gallows still work in this hellish city-centre penitentiary, with courtrooms and tunnels. Its solitary cells are built immediately beneath the chapel – so the convicts could still benefit from the sermons, of course.

Cascades Female Factory

This haunting former prison in Hobart tells the story of the displacement, mistreatment and forced migration of convict women and girls, and their contribution to colonisation.

Premium Dining Stars

Templo $$$

With only 20 seats, most of them around a communal table, and only three or four Italian-inspired mains to choose from, it's an exercise in selectivity and sharing at this tucked-away Hobart treasure.

Fico $$$

This Hobart award-winner puts magical spins on local produce, from risotto with mountain pepperberries to sea-urchin tortellini. It's the nine-course set menu or nothing.

Dier Makr $$$

Nothing this good should come from a kitchen this bare-bones. It's all innovation in Hobart's tasting-menu-only Dier Makr. Finish the evening in the front-of-house Lucinda wine bar.

Stillwater $$$

Launceston's best restaurant is housed in an 1830s flour mill, with boutique accommodation above. Excellent service and a big focus on local produce. A real treat.

Clover Hill $$$

The beautiful Lebrina cellar door is just the wrapping for a weekend multi-course, Japanese-style *omakase* (chef's choice) dining experience.

Josef Chromy $$$

Upmarket winery and restaurant 10 minutes' drive south of Launceston. Beautiful local produce cooked with care and delivered with fine vineyard views.

Outdoor Adventures

Three Capes Track

The final leg of the Turrakana/Tasman Peninsula's famed multiday hike also makes a great day walk to the spectacular dolerite cliffs of Cape Huay, topped off with a dip in idyllic Fortescue Bay.

Floating Sauna Lake Derby

A wood-fired sauna atop a pontoon on Lake Derby. Bake yourself then plunge into the lake's frigid waters as mountain bikers swirl around you. Great post-ride therapy, or just a treat for anytime.

Bay of Fires Trail

St Helens' hero mountain-biking trail propels riders 42km from the top of the Blue Tier mountains to the sands of Larapuna/Bay of Fires. The blue (intermediate) trail takes at least 4½ hours to complete.

Franklin River Rafting

One of the world's great rafting adventures, running the mythologised Franklin in an off-grid, eight- to 10-day adventure through the heart of Tasmania's Wilderness World Heritage area. Guided trips are run by several professional companies.

Franklin Nature Trail

Scenic short walk (1km return), partly on boardwalk, through mossy rainforest to the bank of Tasmania's most celebrated river. A great place to stop and stretch your legs on the drive between Queenstown and Derwent Bridge.

Meander Wilderness Experiences

Plunge into the rapids of the Meander River with a Lilo-like 'sled' and pilot yourself downstream on this gentle guided tour at the edge of the World Heritage area.

Launceston Walking Tours

Explore the streets of Launceston and Cataract Gorge with Tasmanian Aboriginal historian Geoff McLean.

Penny Royal Adventures

This kids' favourite has rock climbing, zip lining, cliffside boardwalks and the chance to jump off the cliffs by the mouth of Cataract Gorge in Launceston.

Gordon River Cruises

Cruise upstream from Strahan on the Gordon River, where the reflections of riverside rainforest on the tannin-darkened waters are typically mirror-perfect.

West Coast Wilderness Railway

Step back in time on sections of a 35km track between Queenstown and Strahan – a reconstruction of the route used from the late 1890s by the Mt Lyell Mining and Railway Company.

Arthur River Canoe & Boat Hire

Paddle up the Arthur River for a takayna/Tarkine picnic, or set out on a two- or four-day self-guided wilderness paddle down the river.

ANDREW BAIN/ALAMY

Rafting, Franklin River

Perfect Pubs

Winston $$

It's all craft beer, mac 'n' cheese and wings (go near the Atomic sauce at your peril) at this brilliant US-style pub at the far end of the North Hobart dining strip.

Preachers $$

If the patio heaters aren't enough to take off the chill, take your craft beer or wine into the bus or onto the retro sofa inside. In Hobart.

New Sydney $$

Every city has its classic boozer, and in Hobart it's the New Sydney. The twist is in the taps – 15 of them, pouring craft beer. Winter gets the fire cranking.

Salty Dog Hotel $$

Beachside hotel in Kingston Beach serving better-than-most pub food, with a raucous beer garden that's the drinking place to be in summer. Live music Sunday afternoons.

Empire Hotel $$

This 1901 Queenstown institution has a lovely traditional dining room, open fire, heritage-listed staircase and a menu of traditional Tassie pub grub.

ADELAIDE & SOUTH AUSTRALIA

FESTIVALS | WINE | WILDERNESS

RESEARCHED BY JOSH WEST AND SARAH REID

ADELAIDE & SOUTH AUSTRALIA

Trip Builder

Located in the heart of Australia's sun-drenched expanse, South Australia emerges with ancient landscapes, rugged coastlines, a thriving food and wine scene, and an action-packed event calendar. Embracing an array of experiences, the state attracts festival-goers, foodies and nature-lovers alike.

Get a taste of life underground in outback **Coober Pedy** (p230)
9hr from Adelaide

Uncover the dawn of animal life at **Nilpena Ediacara National Park** (p221)
6hr from Adelaide

Ride through the vines on a Segway tour of **Seppeltsfield Wines** (p223)
1hr from Adelaide

Slurp freshly shucked oysters on the **Eyre Peninsula** (p224)
7½hr from Adelaide

Dance into the wee hours at **WOMADelaide** (p217)
15min from Adelaide

Admire wildlife and rock formations in Kangaroo Island's **Flinders Chase National Park** (p228)
+ 4hr from Adelaide

PREVIOUS SPREAD: MAJONIT/SHUTTERSTOCK
FROM LEFT: ALEXANDRE ROSA/SHUTTERSTOCK, DADEROT/WIKI COMMONS

Practicalities

ARRIVING

Adelaide Airport Most visitors will arrive at Adelaide's international airport, 6km west of the city. Car rental and public buses are available on the ground level.

FIND YOUR WAY

Adelaide's grid layout and short-lived peak hour ensure quick and easy navigation by car.

MONEY

SA is blessed with free conservation parks, campsites and beaches. Fees apply for national-park entry and amenities.

WHERE TO STAY

Place	Pro/Con
Adelaide city centre	Festival hub with parklands and thriving cafe culture. Sleepy on weekends.
Clare Valley	Laid-back wine country with quirky B&Bs.
The Riverland	Casual agricultural towns with calm river currents. Gateway to regional Victoria and NSW.
Kangaroo Island	Beachfront holiday homes, isolated wilderness and native animals. Pricey ferry, very remote.

GETTING AROUND

Public transport Adelaide Metro trains service the north and south of the outer sprawl, with the iconic tram linking the city to Glenelg on the coast. Metro and LinkSA coach buses connect to suburbs and regions.

Driving A rental car is necessary for exploring the regions, and especially to reach remote beaches, trails and wineries.

EATING & DRINKING

South Australia tantalises with diverse flavours. From Coffin Bay's ocean-fresh oysters (pictured top left) to Adelaide Hills' all-seasons fruit basket and the Barossa Valley's prized shiraz, the state delivers destination dining. At its heart lies Adelaide Central Market, a bountiful buzz of farm-to-market producers, cheesemongers, chocolatiers and artisanal bakers. Nearby, Adelaide's Chinatown features affordable eateries serving authentic Asian cuisine.

Must-try oysters Oyster HQ (p225)

Best wine trail Clare Valley's Riesling Trail (p233)

DEC–FEB
Hot, dry weather; keep cool at the beach or hills.

MAR–MAY
Warm days but nights becoming cool; peak festival season.

JUN–AUG
Chilly urban temps; mild Flinders Ranges days ideal for hiking.

SEP–NOV
Warm days and frosty nights; spring wildflowers bloom.

41 Four Seasons of FESTIVALS

ARTS | MUSIC | YEAR-ROUND CELEBRATIONS

South Australia's licence plates flaunt 'Festival State' and 'Creative State' for good reason. Artistic celebrations are an all-year affair in SA, and locals have etched festival living into their identity. Across Adelaide, creative events embrace an array of disciplines, generations, cultures and tastes, attracting attendees and artists from around the world, brought together by their shared love of the arts.

PETERTEA/FLICKR/WIKI COMMONS/ CC BY-ND 2.0 DEED

How to

Getting around Adelaide's festival sites are typically located in or around the city centre and are easily accessible by taxi, bus, free tram and e-scooter.

When to go Autumn boasts ample sunshine and pleasant temperatures hovering in the low to mid-20s.

Mad March South Australia's peak festival season features three show-stopping events: the Adelaide Fringe Festival, the Adelaide Festival and WOMADelaide. Book your tickets and accommodation well in advance.

MARIANGELA CRUZ/SHUTTERSTOCK

BING CHEN CHUAH/GETTY IMAGES

Summer As Adelaide's summer sun blazes into late February, beachgoers re-emerge from the western shores, turning the city into a hub of impromptu acts and pop-up galleries. The month-long **Adelaide Fringe** electrifies the whole state, hosting international artists, musicians and comedians, and blending spontaneity and entertainment in an infectious celebration of the arts.

Autumn This season of irresistible performances embraces a blend of innovative domains. March heralds a convergence of global rhythms and cultural performances with the four-day **WOMADelaide** arts festival and the 17-day **Adelaide Festival**. As the city's deciduous leaves fall, the biennial **DreamBIG Children's Festival** arrives in May, inviting young minds to explore their imaginations.

Winter Through the depths of winter, Adelaide's creative spirit brightens the city centre. June welcomes the **Adelaide Cabaret Festival** with an ensemble of music, theatre and comedy. As the nights grow longer, the city's urban environs radiate with sparkling installations of **Illuminate Adelaide**.

Spring In October, three creative events take flight. The **Adelaide Film Festival** serves as a stage for cinematic ingenuity, while the **OzAsia Festival** celebrates cultures and ideas. **Tarnanthi** embarks on a creative journey until summer, spotlighting First Nations art and culture at the Art Gallery of South Australia and beyond. November arrives with the three-week **Feast Festival**, celebrating Adelaide's LGBTIQ+ community and bringing the year's arts extravaganza to a fabulous close.

Far top left WOMADelaide
Bottom left Adelaide Fringe
Near left OzAsia Festival

Live Music

In the rare event an official festival isn't on in Adelaide, live-music venues can be found scattered around the city.

Perpetual city-centre pub-jam favourites include the **Crown & Anchor** (aka the 'Cranker', operating out of the Ed Castle until mid-2027), **Grace Emily Hotel** and **Exeter Hotel**. Ten minutes away on the free tram to Hindmarsh, the legendary **Governor Hindmarsh Hotel**, aka 'The Gov', is Adelaide's home of live music, featuring rock, folk, jazz, blues, salsa, reggae and dance.

A winery and wine bar housed in a heritage-listed church in Bowden, **Oddio** serves up wine, aperitivos, food-truck chow and good times. It opens on a sometimes basis; keep an eye on Instagram for details @oddiobowden.

OLDEST, LARGEST
& Most Distinctive

01

02

04

03

05

01 Farmer's Union iced coffee
South Australia is the only market in the world where a milk-based drink outsells its cola rivals. As the motto goes, 'It's a Farmer's Union Iced Coffee, or it's nothing'.

02 Ediacaran golden spike
This fossilised spur in Ikara-Flinders National Park marks the Ediacaran period 635 million years ago.

03 Heysen Trail
Australia's longest marked walking trail stretches from the untamed southern coast through lush forests and vineyards to the arid outback in the north.

04 World's oldest shiraz vines
Preserving the Barossa Valley's viticultural heritage, Langmeil Winery safeguards the world's oldest surviving shiraz vineyard, planted in 1843.

05 Pie floater
Taste South Australia's street-food heritage: an upturned meat pie submerged in hearty pea soup. Traditionally sold from carts, pie floaters

06

10

08

07

09

are available at Bakery on O'Connell, North Adelaide (and elsewhere).

06 Opals
In the heart of South Australia's outback, the remarkable subterranean enclave of Coober Pedy supplies 70% of the world's opals.

07 Adelaide Fringe Festival
Each February, Adelaide hosts the largest arts festival in the southern hemisphere.

08 Aboriginal artefacts
The South Australian Museum houses the world's most comprehensive Aboriginal collection, collaborating with First Nations communities to share their stories.

09 Great white sharks
On the Eyre Peninsula, Port Lincoln is home to one of the world's few shark cage-diving experiences.

10 Australian giant cuttlefish
Chameleon-like cephalopods make a pilgrimage to rocky outcrops off Point Lowry from May to August, delivering a psychedelic spectacle.

01 CTR PHOTOS/SHUTTERSTOCK, **02** JAMES ST. JOHN/FLICKR/WIKI COMMONSCC BY 2.0 DEED, **03** BJORN SVENSSON/ALAMY STOCK PHOTO, **04** JOHN DZIEKAN/CHICAGO TRIBUNE/GETTY IMAGES, **05** DARIAKM/SHUTTERSTOCK **06** BJOERN WYLEZICH/GETTY IMAGES, **07** RYAN SMITH/FLICKR/WIKI COMMONS/CC BY-NC-SA 2.0 DEED, **08** SIA DUFF/SOUTH AUSTRALIAN MUSEUM **09** WILDESTANIMAL/SHUTTERSTOCK, **10** WILDESTANIMAL/GETTY IMAGES

Fossilised Flinders

THE DAWN OF ANIMAL LIFE

Within the scorched expanse of Adnyamathanha Country, the central and northern Flinders Ranges reveal ancient tales of colliding mountains and inland seas. Decipher the stone-scripted narrative chronicling life's origins within a landscape so unique that Sir David Attenborough named it one of his favourite places on Earth.

Left Flinders Ranges
Centre Arkaroo Rock
Right View from Tanderra Saddle

SOUTHERN LIGHTSCAPES-AUSTRALIA/ GETTY IMAGES

Spanning an impressive 430km from the shores of Gulf St Vincent to the dry, salty expanse of Lake Callabonna, the Flinders Ranges have unfolded across 800 million years. An ancient sea laid the mineral-rich groundwork during that era, depositing sediments within the Adelaide Geosyncline basin. Around 300 million years later, the once-docile deposits had undergone a dramatic transformation: colliding tectonic plates had contorted and reshaped them into dominant mountains. Time has since weathered the mighty peaks, leaving behind saw-toothed ranges formed from sandstone, mudstone, limestone and quartzite.

The Golden Spike

Around 430km north of Adelaide, **Ikara Wilpena Pound**, inside **Ikara-Flinders Ranges National Park**, is the Flinders' most iconic geological formation. Surrounded by semi-arid plains deep in Adnyamathanha Country, this ochre-tinted sandstone valley is fringed by amphitheatrical rock walls, creating a microclimate flush with vegetation and endemic forests. This surprisingly green oasis is revered for its deep-rooted Aboriginal Dreaming, flourishing biodiversity, scenic bushwalks and scientific discoveries.

The sedimentary sequences buried in Flinders Ranges rocks provide a glimpse of the Ediacaran period – dubbed the 'dawn of animal life'. This one-time seafloor unveils a geological archive spanning 350 million years, showcasing the dynamic shifts in climate and habitable ecosystems that laid the fertile foundations for Earth's earliest species.

Named for the Flinders' Ediacara Hills, this period is officially marked by the presence of a Global Stratotype Section and Point (GSSP) Boundary at Enorama Creek

PHOTON-PHOTOS/GETTY IMAGES

HANS WISMEIJER/SHUTTERSTOCK

within Ikara-Flinders Ranges National Park. This is the only such internationally recognised indicator in the southern hemisphere. Nicknamed the 'Golden Spike', the Ediacaran GSSP is a 10-minute stroll along the shaded creek bed from **Trezona Campground**, roughly 30km north of Wilpena Pound.

Palaeontologists' Paradise

Adjacent to the ephemeral Lake Torrens west of Ikara-Flinders, **Nilpena Ediacara National Park** presents the world's most comprehensive repository of Ediacaran fossils. The groundbreaking excavation has unearthed 40 sandstone beds, revealing tens of thousands of impeccably preserved fossils. These prolific strata sites tell of ancient squalls, with layers of stormy sands smothering creatures inhabiting the ocean floor. Across millennia, this sediment hardened into solid rock, immortalising their imprints from below.

Recognised as an area of international importance, Nilpena has reshaped our understanding of Ediacaran evolution, its habitats, and the complex interactions within ancient marine environments. Without natural predators, the soft-bodied inhabitants of this underwater world blazed an evolutionary trail, pioneering movement, sexual reproduction and scavenging behaviour, all while building intricate ecosystems among their seabed communities.

Guided tours take in audiovisual displays and walks across the deserted fossil-infused seafloor. This rare opportunity delivers up-close encounters with these delicate prints, providing insights into the creatures that lived 550 million years ago. For bookings and information, go to ediacarafoundation.org/visit. Note that the park is closed through the summer months due to extremely high temperatures.

Adnyamathanha Experiences

Aboriginal rock art Ascend the mild incline to **Arkaroo Rock**, discovering ancient ochre and charcoal paintings, or explore **Sacred Canyon** on an Adnyamathanha-guided tour booked at **Discovery Resorts – Wilpena Pound**, the only place to stay inside the national park.

Tanderra Saddle circuit hike Within the Ikara-Flinders Ranges National Park, the 21km round-trip to soaring St Mary Peak is steeped in Adnyamathanha creation stories. The peak is sacred to Indigenous peoples, so hikers are requested to not proceed beyond **Tanderra Saddle**, trimming 3km from the hike but offering equally stunning views.

Yura Udnyu walking tour Setting off from **Discovery Resorts – Wilpena Pound**, this two-hour Adnyamathanha-led tour unpacks the region's Aboriginal and European histories from an Aboriginal perspective.

42 More than Just WINE

WINERIES | ACTIVITIES | REGIONS

Going beyond the swirl-and-sip and boozy lunches, South Australia's wine country has rich experiences for everyone. From vineyard tours and epicurean dinners to heritage exhibits, art displays and nature walks, cellar doors cater to young adventurers, nondrinkers and palates at all stages of development.

MIKE BRAND/ALAMY STOCK PHOTO

Trip Notes

Getting around Unless you've arranged a tour, the most convenient way to explore is by car. The 223km Epicurean Way driving trail winds through the McLaren Vale, Adelaide Hills, Barossa and Clare Valley wine regions.

When to go Visit in early autumn (March to April), when temperatures are lower, vines shimmer gold and vintage celebrations kick off.

Top tip An 11am start allows enough time to explore, lunch and relax.

Australia's Wine State

It's irrefutable: SA is the home of Australian wine, crafting half the nation's bottled drops and 80% of its premier labels. Adelaide is listed as one of the world's Great Wine Capitals. With more than 340 cellar doors dotted across 18 distinct vine-covered regions, you won't need to travel far in SA to find a place to imbibe.

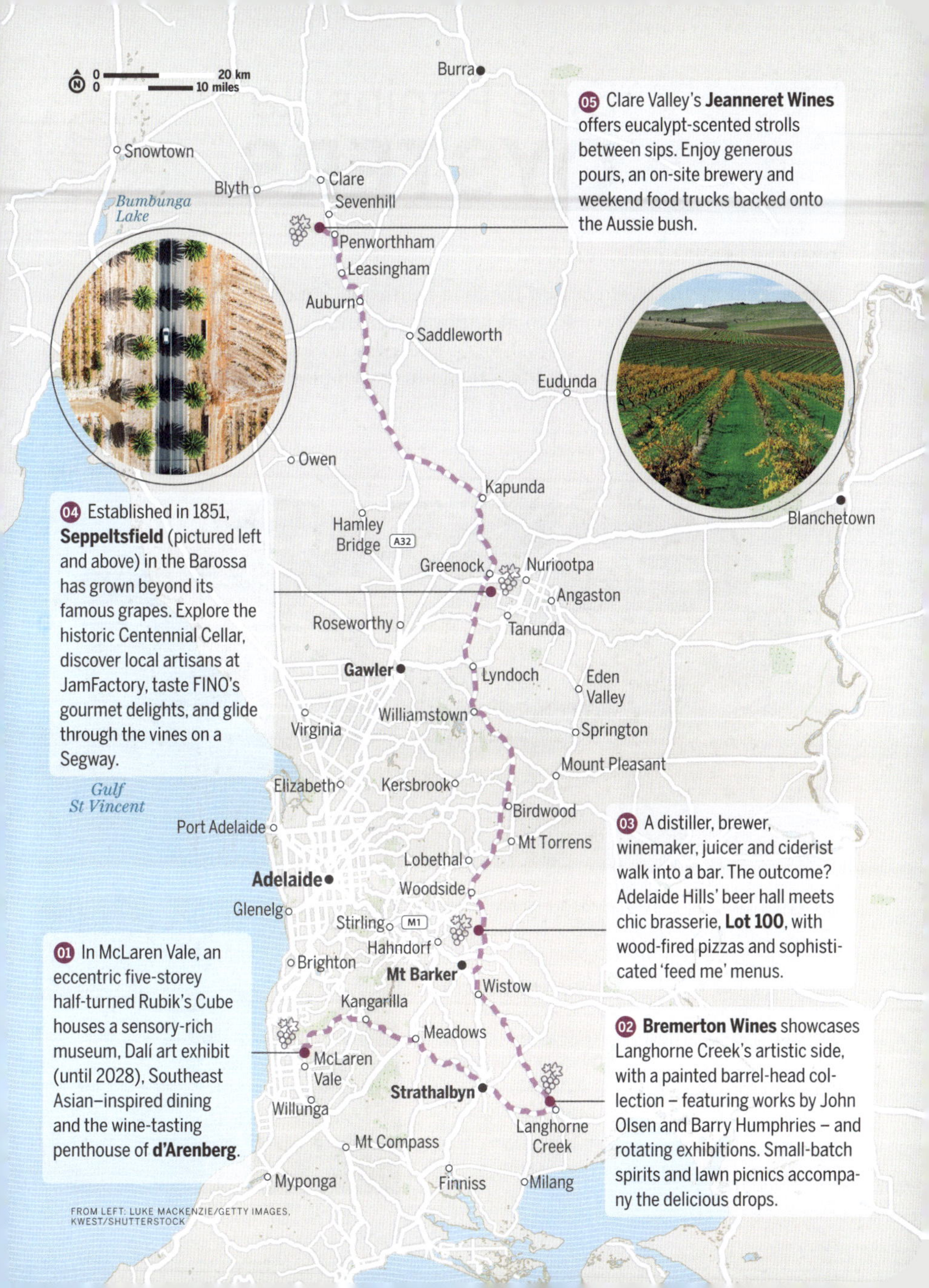

01 In McLaren Vale, an eccentric five-storey half-turned Rubik's Cube houses a sensory-rich museum, Dalí art exhibit (until 2028), Southeast Asian–inspired dining and the wine-tasting penthouse of **d'Arenberg**.

02 **Bremerton Wines** showcases Langhorne Creek's artistic side, with a painted barrel-head collection – featuring works by John Olsen and Barry Humphries – and rotating exhibitions. Small-batch spirits and lawn picnics accompany the delicious drops.

03 A distiller, brewer, winemaker, juicer and ciderist walk into a bar. The outcome? Adelaide Hills' beer hall meets chic brasserie, **Lot 100**, with wood-fired pizzas and sophisticated 'feed me' menus.

04 Established in 1851, **Seppeltsfield** (pictured left and above) in the Barossa has grown beyond its famous grapes. Explore the historic Centennial Cellar, discover local artisans at JamFactory, taste FINO's gourmet delights, and glide through the vines on a Segway.

05 Clare Valley's **Jeanneret Wines** offers eucalypt-scented strolls between sips. Enjoy generous pours, an on-site brewery and weekend food trucks backed onto the Aussie bush.

FROM LEFT: LUKE MACKENZIE/GETTY IMAGES, KWEST/SHUTTERSTOCK

43 Eyre Peninsula OYSTERS

OYSTERS | TOURS | FESTIVALS

Explore the west coast of the Eyre Peninsula, shucking oysters on farm tours, slurping them down at highway-side oyster bars and revelling in exuberant oyster festivals. Or just buy a takeaway dozen and head for the beach. Out here, oysters are a way of life – the industry employs around 100 locals in Coffin Bay alone – and visitors can't get enough.

BEYONDIMAGES/GETTY IMAGES

How to

Getting here You can drive seven hours from Adelaide, or take a 50-minute flight into Port Lincoln. Hire a car at the airport.

When to go Local oysters are at their most succulent in winter. Plus the roads are empty, and you can pick and choose your accommodation.

She sells seashells Pay top dollar for oysters in restaurants, or buy a fresh dozen at budget prices from oyster farms or roadside seafood shacks.

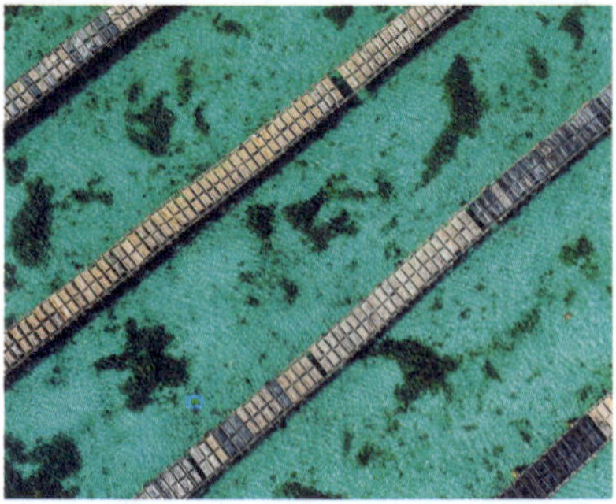
LYNDONOK/SHUTTERSTOCK

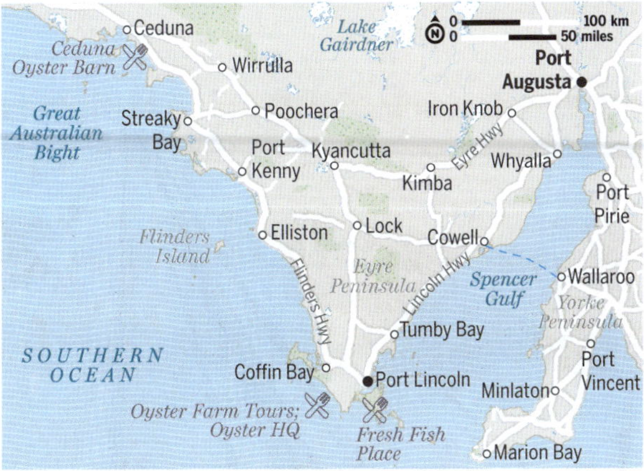

Oyster Extravaganza

It's rare that a meal on the vast, sea-salty Eyre Peninsula transpires without some seafood: tuna, whiting, squid...and especially oysters. From Port Lincoln to Ceduna, here's where to get yours.

Fish of the day Check the specials on the blackboard outside the **Fresh Fish Place** in Port Lincoln. Inside you can buy 'EP' seafood straight off the boats, and Coffin Bay oysters for around $2.50 each. Grab a box to go.

Oysters and Coffin Bay Oysters are this little town's financial and culinary lifeblood. Take a 90-minute tour with **Oyster Farm Tours** (oysterfarmtours.com.au) to see what all the fuss is about. Wade into the water, harvest your own oysters and learn to shuck 'em, sitting on a semi-submerged tour deck called the 'Salt Water Pavilion'. Afterwards, the **Oyster HQ** cafe is on hand (with great views).

Ceduna scenes Smoky Bay, Streaky Bay and Ceduna are big on oysters, too. If you're out this way in late September or early October, check out the **Ceduna Oysterfest** (cedunaoysterfest.com.au), the undisputed king of Australian oyster parties. Throughout the rest of the year, you can pick up a box of molluscs from the **Ceduna Oyster Barn** (facebook.com/cedunaoyster). Head for the grassy shoreline, or sit on the roof under an umbrella and watch the road trains rumble in from Western Australia.

Top left Coffin Bay oysters
Bottom left Oyster farm, Coffin Bay

The Coffin Bay Industry

Every year, hundreds of tonnes of briny bivalves from Coffin Bay are shipped around Australia and overseas. Oysters grow fast and fat in the town's bays, which have a narrow entrance to the open ocean, trapping plenty of plankton for the oysters to eat. Native angasi oysters have always been here, growing on shallow reefs, but by 1890 they were all but fished out. Then, in 1969, Pacific oysters from Tasmania and Japan were successfully introduced. Today you'll see up to 40 oyster boats working the leases offshore, employing more than 100 people – and conservation efforts are bringing back the angasi, too.

44 Nature's PLAYGROUND

ISLAND LIFE | OUTDOORS | WILDLIFE

Kangaroo Island offers secluded surf beaches, wildlife havens, and a string of eco-conscious adventures. Set aside a few days to explore it, but don't be surprised if your itinerary stretches well beyond a week. This scenic island is surprisingly big!

MPIX/SHUTTERSTOCK

How to

Getting around Your own wheels are a must, as public transport isn't available. Rent a car, join a tour or bring your vehicle aboard the SeaLink ferry.

When to go Summer steals the show for peak island time, offering long, sunlit days and inviting warm beaches.

Parks pass Access Flinders Chase National Park, Seal Bay and the Kelly Hill caves with a Kangaroo Island Tour Pass (parks.sa.gov.au).

Top left and below Vivonne Bay
Bottom left Admirals Arch (p229)

EMMA SHAW/LONELY PLANET

Sand & Surf

Spanning 540km of golden shores and craggy cliffs, Kangaroo Island's sun-kissed coastline has rightfully earned international acclaim.

The north coast offers safer swims in warmer waters with fewer rips. Enjoy **Emu Bay**'s broad sands or explore **Stokes Bay**'s secluded rock pools through cliff-carved tunnels. **Snelling Beach**'s 660m sandy arc boasts sheltered swims and enchanting vistas, but mind the rocky rips at either end. New to ocean dips? Dive into the **Kingscote Tidal Pool** for a salt-water experience minus the shifting currents.

The island's main surf spots are in the south, with the best swells through winter. **Vivonne Bay** has uncrowded breaks for all abilities, while the more powerful waves of **Pennington Bay** are suited to intermediates and above. Experts can tackle the right-hand point break at

PHUONG D NGUYEN/SHUTTERSTOCK

Island Bushfires

Like the mainland, Kangaroo Island faces seasonal bushfires. The 2019–20 Black Summer fires deeply scarred its native habitats and inhabitants, and their supporting environments. Despite these challenges, the island's resilience fuelled positive change by prioritising sustainable tourism and revamping infrastructure, focusing on conservation and accessibility while fostering wildlife recovery.

D'Estrees Bay and **Hanson Bay**, a hazardous reef break. Get boards on the mainland before arriving; rentals aren't available on the island.

Island Trails

On the island's west in **Flinders Chase National Park**, a slew of wildlife-rich bushwalks fan out from Rocky River, weaving among hidden lagoons and native woodlands. Fifteen minutes south, coastal walks navigate windswept heath between clifftop lookouts.

Venture an hour north to embark on the stunning 7km-return Ravine Hike in the **Ravine des Casoars Wilderness Protection Area**. Descend through mallee vegetation, watching as the earth transitions from auburn to bone white, unveiling a sandy bay punctured with coastal caverns – ideal for spelunking.

After a truly immersive experience? Embark on the intrepid **Kangaroo Island Wilderness Trail**, a 66km, five-day trek across Flinders Chase. Journey through wildflower-strewn scrubland, across ivory shores and along majestic cliffs, discovering the park's geological wonders along the way. Remote camp sites provide overnight comforts for hikers.

Seeing KI's Animals

In Penneshaw, walk the 4km up-and-back **Ironstone Hill Hike**, sharing the trail with **Tammar wallabies** as **bottlenose dolphins** splash about the bay.

At the **Admirals Arch** viewing platform, see **long-nosed fur seals** basking on the rocks.

Observe endangered **Australian sea lions** up close with a guided tour at **Seal Bay Conservation Park**.

Koalas and **platypuses** found sanctuary in **Flinders Chase National Park** during the 1920s, when it was feared they would become extinct on the mainland. Unhindered by predators, they've flourished.

At nightfall, witness **little penguins** waddling ashore, led by guides from the **Penneshaw Penguin Centre**.

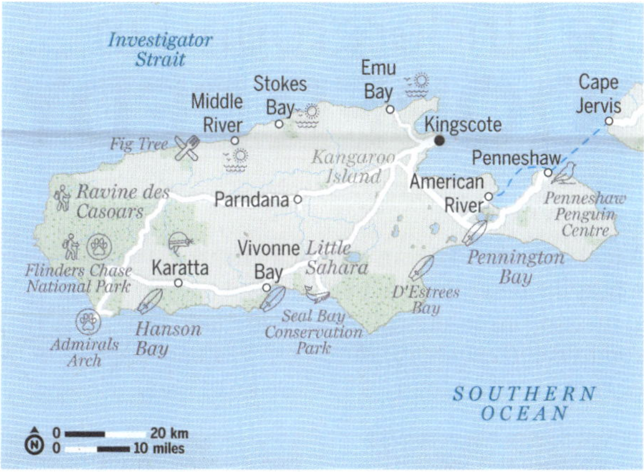

Left Seal, Seal Bay Conservation Park
Below Koala, Kangaroo Island

Natural Wonders

The scrub-bordered road south of Rocky River leads to Cape du Couedic. A series of boardwalk switchbacks passes a colony of playful long-nosed fur seals to **Admirals Arch**. This awe-inspiring archway, embellished with weather-shaped stalactites, offers a glimpse of nature's powerful forces. The iconic **Remarkable Rocks**, a Dalí-esque collection of giant granite boulders atop a windswept plateau, have been shaped by centuries of Southern Ocean storms.

Beneath the eucalypt-draped **Kelly Hill Caves Conservation Park** lies a labyrinth of ancient limestone sinkholes and caves, lined with intricate stalagmites and stalactites. Accompanied by an experienced ranger, take an underground tour with expert commentary and a light display.

Unexpected Adventures

Surfing isn't just saved for the waves here. Along the island's south coast, **Little Sahara** has a ripple of sandboard-safe and toboggan-ready sand dunes. Dune-buggy rides and fat-tyre-bike tours are also available.

Even Kangaroo Island's dining invites adventure. Immerse yourself in the **Fig Tree**, a Mediterranean-inspired feast served among the entangled branches of a majestic 120-year-old fig tree.

LEFT: IGNACIO PALACIOS/GETTY IMAGES;
RIGHT: TIER UND NATURFOTOGRAFIE J UND C SOHNS/GETTY IMAGES

45 Life Underground in COOBER PEDY

HISTORY | ARCHITECTURE | GEM-HUNTING

Opal deposits were found in Coober Pedy in 1915, and miners in this quirky outback town beat the desert heat in underground houses. Later, filmmakers flocked to these plains to shoot films such as *Mad Max Beyond Thunderdome* and *Priscilla, Queen of the Desert*. Visitors can sleep, go to church or explore historic homes – all below street level.

ALEXANDRE ROSA/SHUTTERSTOCK

How to

Getting here Coober Pedy is a nine-hour highway drive from Adelaide or a 90-minute flight. Hire a car at the airport, or get walking.

When to go Time your trip for winter so you can wander around without the dangerous heat.

On set Get a feel for Coober Pedy filmmaking with a visit to the huge spaceship on Hutchison St – an unexpected and rather unnerving leftover prop from the film *Pitch Black*.

FRITZ16/SHUTTERSTOCK

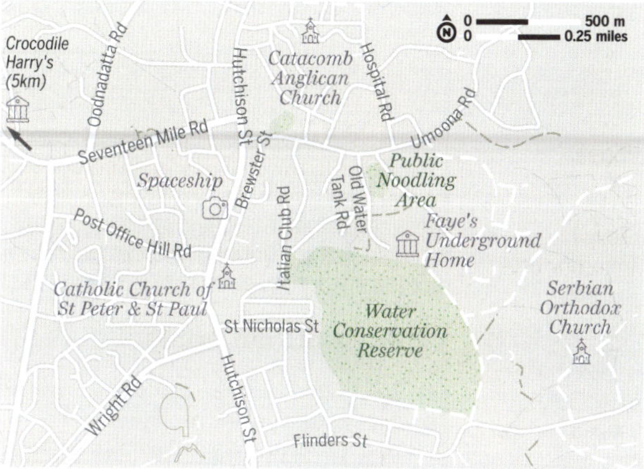

Coober Pedy gets face-meltingly hot in summer – up to 50°C. But the early miners soon figured out that underground, the temperature would never rise above 23°C.

Underground houses See how the locals do it on a tour of **Crocodile Harry's**, a wildly eccentric subterranean abode that was once home to Arvid Blumenthal, a Latvian-born runaway who covered the walls in graffiti, sculptures, posters, hats and relics of his love life. More modest is **Faye's Underground Home**, hand-dug by three women in the 1960s – it's a time-warp museum and a window into underground life last century.

Take me to church Get reverent at one of Coober Pedy's **underground churches** (cooberpedy.com/underground-churches). The diminutive **Catholic Church of St Peter & St Paul** on the main street has a sweet appeal, with statue-filled nooks and hushed classical music. Over the hill, **Catacomb Anglican Church** is a simple, cross-shaped bunker with plenty of pews. East of town, the **Serbian Orthodox Church** is Coober Pedy's most impressive subterranean church, with intricate carvings, stained glass and a gorgeous vaulted ceiling. Flip the lights off on your way out.

Sleep below the streets Some Coober Pedy hotels have both above-ground and underground rooms, but hey – you may never be here again. *Carpe diem* and descend. You won't need to turn on the air-con.

Top left Faye's Underground Home
Bottom left Crocodile Harry's

Mine Tours & Noodling

Coober Pedy's opal fields are extremely dangerous, with more than one million unmarked shafts, some up to 30m deep. Instead of wandering around, take a guided or self-guided tour through any of the town's original mines. Or try 'noodling' (aka fossicking), where you sift through surface rubble looking for opal that was missed by early miners. The public noodling area in town is safe, free, and open 24/7. People have found $4000 stones here. You can't detect opal underground, so opal mining is a game of luck. There could be billions of dollars' worth of opal just waiting to be unearthed.

Brilyanz Mance, *Office Assistant at Umoona Opal Mine & Museum.*
@umoonaopal

Listings

BEST OF THE REST

Adelaide's Global Flavours

Adelaide Pho $

This unassuming Waymouth St soup house plates up piping-hot bowls of comforting broth and classic Vietnamese dishes in a flash.

Parwana Afghan Kitchen $$

A vibrant, family-owned Afghan eatery in inner-west Thebarton serving delectable dumplings, flavourful dhals, chickpea curries and Adelaide's finest aubergine.

La Popular Taqueria $$

Housed in a heritage Port Adelaide building, this is SA's top choice for authentic Mexican tacos jammed with braised pork, beef cheek, marinated chicken, battered fish and vegetarian options, coupled with tequila and mezcal.

Daughter in Law $$

Embodying the motto 'unauthentic Australian Indian', this colourful Rundle St restaurant packs a culinary punch. Try the mint-infused 'Ball of Happiness (Gol Gappa)'.

Golden Boy $$

Grab a stool at a lively communal table or snuggle into a cosy booth at North Terrace's energetic Thai hot spot. Embrace the set menu packed with spicy, authentic flavours.

Africola $$

A whimsical South African restaurant where gourmet barbecue meets extravagant banquets, paired with warm, attentive service in a classical East Terrace bluestone.

Restaurant Botanic $$$

A haute seasonal tasting-menu experience set within the Adelaide Botanic Garden's heritage rotunda.

Osteria Oggi $$$

Exceptional Italian dining in an award-winning interior, with time-honoured pastas, innovative plates, sweet treats and an ever-evolving wine list. Settle in at the glamorous bar or dine outside for people-watching on Pirie St.

Regional Craft Drinks

Grünthal Brew $$

This quirky Adelaide Hills microbrewery concocts beers, ciders and gins, complemented by modern Australian shared plates and gourmet pizzas. Udder Delights hosts cheesemaking classes in its sunlit greenhouse.

Never Never Distilling Co. $

Part of McLaren Vale's Chalk Hill Collective, this top-tier distiller presents premium gin tastings, seasonal cocktails and engaging masterclasses with neighbouring Chalk Hill Wines and Cucina di Strada's Italian street food.

Kangaroo Island Spirits $$

Australia's first gin distillery is 10km from Kingscote. Join a masterclass that dives into the country's gin history and botanical science, or craft a blend as unique as the island itself.

BOAZ ROTTEM/ALAMY STOCK PHOTO

Africola

Seppeltsfield Road Distillers $

This feisty little distiller makes a curated blend of locally crafted, award-winning gins, bravely bucking the Barossa Valley's wine traditions.

23rd Street Distillery $$

Renmark's spacious highway moonshiner has an impressive spread of handcrafted spirits. Book online for tastings, tours and classes, or pop in for tapas and wood-oven pizzas.

Robe Town Brewery $

The family-owned Robe brewhouse crafts speciality small-batch ales with a focus on sustainability and organic practices. Its locally harvested ingredients deliver a distinctive Limestone Coast flavour.

Adventures on the Water

Kangaroo Island Marine Adventures

Take an Ecotourism Australia–certified guided marine tour for a chance to see and swim responsibly with wild dolphins. The dolphins are not fed and guests are not allowed to use fins.

Spirit of the Coorong

Stretching 145km along the Fleurieu Peninsula's southern coast, Coorong National Park is a sanctuary for native and migrating birdlife. Departing from Goolwa, half- and full-day boat tours glide among the waders, waterfowl and migrating species of this protected habitat.

Adventure Kayaking SA

Just north of Port Adelaide, you can paddle a kayak through the Adelaide Dolphin Sanctuary, where around 40 bottlenose dolphins live and play among the mangroves, seagrass and ghostly ship graveyard.

Calypso Star Charters

This shark-centric Port Lincoln operator offers full-day cage-diving experiences off the Eyre Peninsula, plus swims with Australian sea lions. Note that research suggests human interaction may impact marine mammal behaviour.

Australiana Bushwalks

Three Falls Grand Hike

This shady 7km circuit lies within the Morialta Conservation Park in Adelaide's northeast ranges, 20 minutes from the city centre. Take in waterfalls, cliff-edge views, and wildlife-rich bushland; arrive early to find a parking spot.

Alligator Gorge Ring Route

This 9km loop trail in Mt Remarkable National Park leads into an ochre-hued ravine, along a rippled quartzite staircase and through an expanse of scrub lined with spring wildflowers.

Deep Creek Circuit Hike

Encompassing the full array of the Fleurieu Peninsula's diverse coastal ecosystems, this challenging 11km loop takes in yakka-lined slopes, eucalypt woodlands, a steepling inlet and the gushing Deep Creek waterfall. Entry fees apply for Deep Creek National Park.

Wine by Bike

Riesling Trail

Around 90 minutes north of Adelaide, the 35km gum-lined path between Clare and Auburn is a fusion of history, vineyards and pull-in wineries. Avoid the post-tasting return leg by booking a one-way rental and convenient pickup.

Barossa Trail

Breathe in the Barossa Valley amid historic vineyards and charming German villages along this fuss-free bikeway. Stretching 40km between Gawler and Angaston, the Barossa Trail is ready-made for lycra-clad wine buffs or multiday leisure riders.

Coast to Vines Rail Trail

From Adelaide's southern suburbs to McLaren Vale, the trail spans seaside views, heritage towns and prodigious vineyards, following the retired Willunga Railway for 38km. Catch a train to the Seaford Terminus to trim 23km off Adelaide's urban sprawl.

PERTH & WESTERN AUSTRALIA

BEACHES | OUTDOORS | CITY LIFE

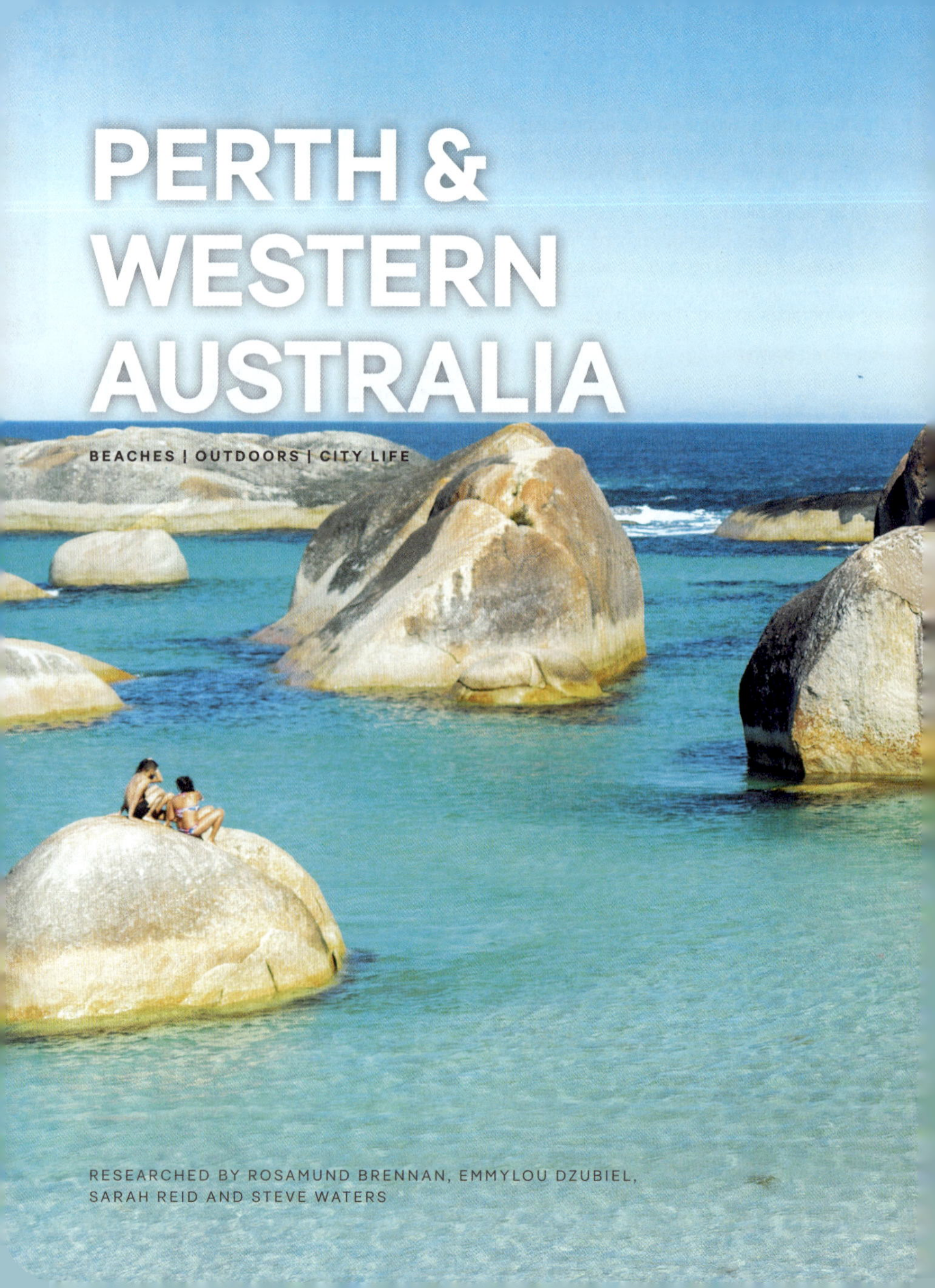

RESEARCHED BY ROSAMUND BRENNAN, EMMYLOU DZUBIEL, SARAH REID AND STEVE WATERS

PERTH & WESTERN AUSTRALIA
Trip Builder

The sun-kissed capital of Perth is the gateway to the state's wild and wondrous landscapes, from idyllic white-sand beaches to world-class wineries, blooming wildflowers to biodiverse reefs, and gourmet adventures galore. Welcome to the good life.

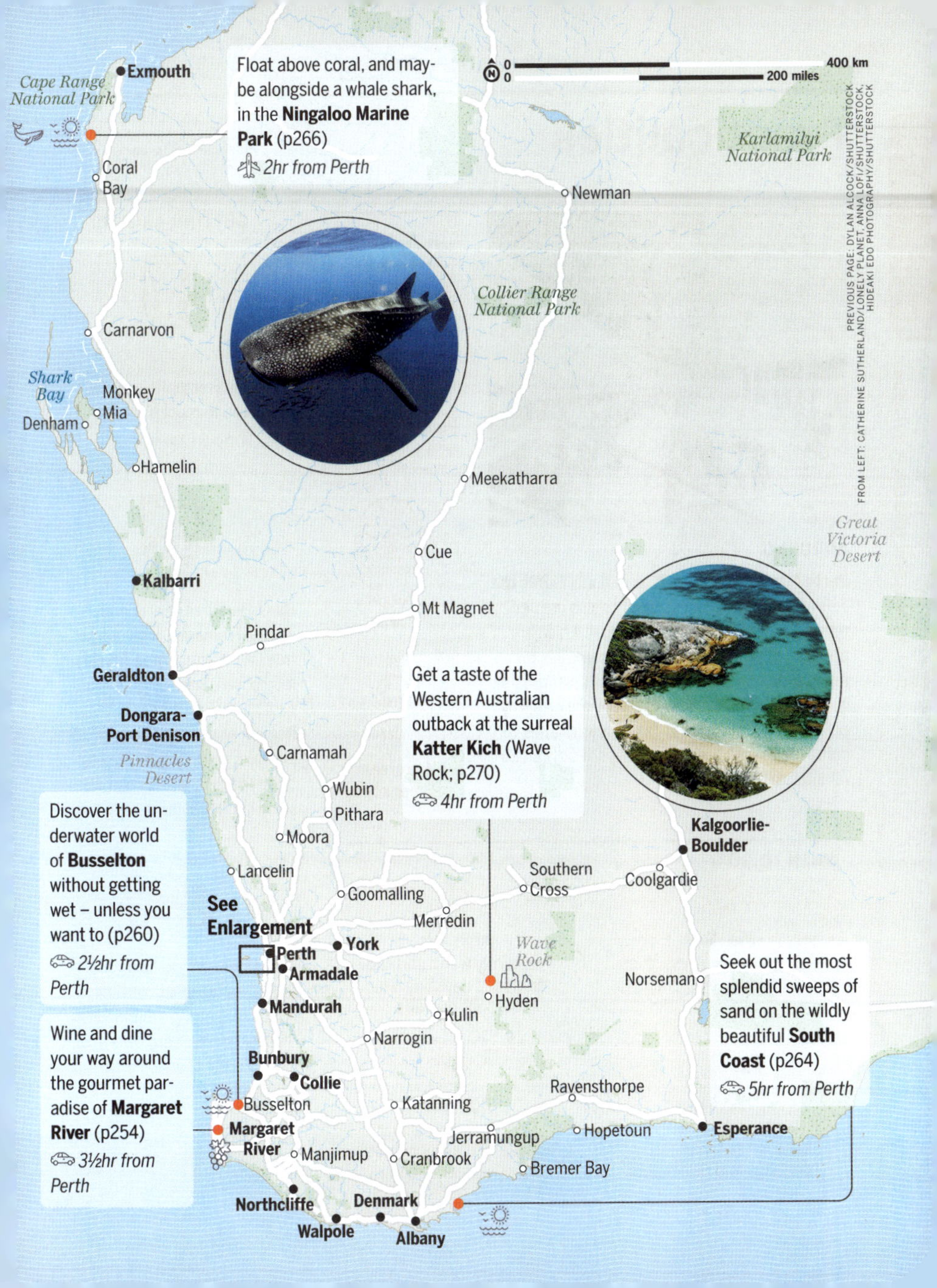
Float above coral, and maybe alongside a whale shark, in the **Ningaloo Marine Park** (p266)
2hr from Perth
Get a taste of the Western Australian outback at the surreal **Katter Kich** (Wave Rock; p270)
4hr from Perth
Discover the underwater world of **Busselton** without getting wet – unless you want to (p260)
2½hr from Perth
Wine and dine your way around the gourmet paradise of **Margaret River** (p254)
3½hr from Perth
Seek out the most splendid sweeps of sand on the wildly beautiful **South Coast** (p264)
5hr from Perth
0 400 km
0 200 miles
Cape Range National Park
Exmouth
Coral Bay
Karlamilyi National Park
Newman
Collier Range National Park
Carnarvon
Shark Bay
Monkey Mia
Denham
Hamelin
Meekatharra
Great Victoria Desert
Cue
Kalbarri
Mt Magnet
Pindar
Geraldton
Dongara-Port Denison
Pinnacles Desert
Carnamah
Wubin
Pithara
Moora
Kalgoorlie-Boulder
Lancelin
Southern Cross
Coolgardie
Goomalling
See Enlargement
Merredin
Perth
York
Armadale
Wave Rock
Hyden
Norseman
Mandurah
Kulin
Narrogin
Bunbury
Collie
Ravensthorpe
Busselton
Katanning
Margaret River
Jerramungup
Hopetoun
Esperance
Manjimup
Cranbrook
Bremer Bay
Northcliffe
Denmark
Walpole
Albany

Practicalities

BEEBOYS/SHUTTERSTOCK

ARRIVING

Perth Airport (pictured) International flights use Terminal 1. Some domestic flights also use Terminal 1, as well as Terminals 3 and 4, which are about 15 minutes' drive away. Terminal 2 is for regional airlines. There are taxi ranks just outside T1 and T3, or you can call an Uber from a nearby parking area; they usually take a few minutes to come to the rideshare pickup bays. It's about 25 minutes to the city centre.

HOW MUCH FOR A

Pint of craft beer
$14

Burger
$25

Ice cream
$6 per scoop

GETTING AROUND

Train The Fremantle line will whisk you to most places you're likely to want to see.

Bus In inner-city Perth and central Fremantle, look out for free CAT (Central Area Transit) loop buses. Several routes run past places of interest to visitors. Regular public buses can be complicated, unless you're staying close to the inner city and can avoid connections.

Taxi, Uber and car Taxis and Ubers are the most convenient option for getting around Perth. It's best to have your own wheels for exploring beyond Perth and Fremantle.

WHEN TO GO

JAN–MAR
Hot, sunny, cloudless skies perfect for the beach.

APR–JUN
Pleasantly warm and sun-drenched days; ideal for outdoor pursuits.

JUL–SEP
Winter brings rainfall between sunshine, crisp mornings and cold nights.

OCT–DEC
Spring's reawakening heralds wildflower carpets and warmer airflow.

TOP: MELBOURNEKOREA/SHUTTERSTOCK; BOTTOM: IGOR KOSTENKO/SHUTTERSTOCK

EATING & DRINKING

Perth's food is influenced by its location: it's isolated from Australia's east coast and looks more to neighbouring Asia for inspiration. You'll find an inventiveness to its modern-fusion fare. In recent years, indigenous ingredients have come to the fore as well. Marron (freshwater crayfish) is a regular on upmarket menus, perhaps garnished with the citrus twang of Geraldton wax, while kangaroo (pictured top right), served rare for its leanness, may be dusted with pepperberry or quandong (native peach) powder. Margaret River is another major wining and dining destination.

Best negroni
Darling Darling (p241)

Must-try marron
Wildflower (p277)

CONNECT & FIND YOUR WAY

Wi-fi Perth's inner city and busy urban villages such as Leederville, Fremantle and Subiaco have free hot spots, as do most cultural institutions. However, a prepaid or digital SIM gives you the most flexibility.

Drive or fly Western Australia is enormous, with flights to regional hubs such as Exmouth and Broome a handy option for visitors short on time.

CYCLING

Many Perth hotels now offer free bikes; the city's bike paths have been well developed in recent years, with good lighting and safety.

WHERE TO STAY

Staying central in Perth means more hotels and easier public transport; if hiring a car, go suburban.

Suburb	Pro/con
Central Perth	New, flashy, overlooking the river. Shopping, nightlife and dining pockets. Easy transiting. Midrange to high-end prices.
Northbridge	Nightlife, small bar buzz, Chinatown, some trashy streets. Fast access to cultural hubs and transit links, neighbours Perth CBD. More affordable.
Cottesloe	Beach frontage, posh-casual, cafes. Car required. Expensive.
Fremantle	Characterful port town, backpacker magnet, historic streets, away from centre. Caters to all price points.
Margaret River	Boutique B&Bs, cosy cottages, holiday apartments, caravan parks, motels and a couple of beach resorts dot the region.
Albany	South Coast hub with hotels, motels, holiday apartments, caravan parks and B&Bs.

MONEY

Almost anything can be paid for by card or smartphone in Perth. Carry cash for small items and for some purchases in remote areas. Many Perth parking zones offer the first hour for free, with ticket.

46 FREMANTLE Nooks & Crannies

SECRET SPOTS | LOCAL PICKS | ENTERTAINMENT

Freo, as it's affectionately referred to by locals, is Perth's characterful port town and a well-trodden traveller fave, but there are still a few secret spots. Let us lead you to a hidden-in-plain-sight rooftop bar, a tiny drinking den that evokes 1800s-era seafaring and the place for the tastiest 'cheap cut' of fish you may ever try.

RUBEN M RAMOS/SHUTTERSTOCK

How to

Getting here If you're not already staying in Fremantle, take the Fremantle train line in. The station is close to everything.

When to go To avoid extreme heat or rainy days, visit March to June or September to December. Weekends are twice as busy as weekdays; from day to night, families give way to evening revellers.

Good to know Freo is a hot spot for buskers, especially around the Fremantle Markets, so keep a few coins handy.

JASON KNOTT/ALAMY

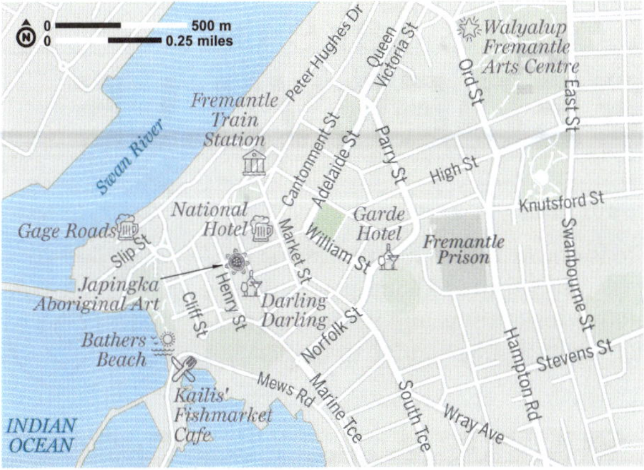

A rooftop secret You'll hear the **National Hotel** before you see it. The multilevel Federation-era pub usually has live music playing in the main bar, but don't stop there. Go in the narrow side entrance and up the stairs. Take them slowly, not only so you don't puff but also so you'll have time to take in the gallery of art the owners have curated on the colourful walls. Reaching the top, you'll walk out onto a sun-drenched deck with clusters of couches and tables. Locals converge here to take in Fremantle's rooftop, ocean and working port views.

A merchant vessel on land As the sun goes down, slip into the 25-seat **Darling Darling** and be transported to another time. The bijou bar (walk-ins only) seems to breathe low-lit, mahogany-hued history from every surface, but it's all a carefully created illusion. Marvel at the weathered ropes, the wooden ship wheels, the barrels topped with free, crack-'em-open peanuts and the chainlink light fittings. There's atmosphere in spades. Expect a queue at weekends.

A cheap feed For the best-value bites in Freo, head directly to **Kailis Fishmarket Cafe** on the pretty harbourfront and order the $16 fish wings. Forget any ideas you have about fillets – this is better. A wing is a cut from around the fish fin, and it's one of the tenderest, sweetest parts you can savour. Trust us, you'll never go back.

Top left National Hotel
Bottom left Kailis Fishmarket Cafe

Tips from a Freo Fan

Gage Roads This brewery faces Fremantle Harbour; you can watch tugboats and cargo ships pass by.

Japingka Aboriginal Art Support Aboriginal artists at this High St gallery.

Walyalup Fremantle Arts Centre Catch a free outdoor concert on Sunday in the warmer months.

Garde Hotel This central Fremantle precinct combines the heritage Warders Hotel, set in former prison-guard cottages, with the contemporary Garde development. Stay overnight, sip wine at micro-bar Gimlet or dine at Emily Taylor restaurant, all in one place.

Bathers Beach Take a dip where the first Europeans of the Swan River colony came ashore in August 1829.

Ryan Mossny, *Tour Guide with Two Feet & a Heartbeat walking tours @twofeetperth*

47 A Local's Take on LEEDERVILLE

URBAN | NEIGHBOURHOOD | CULTURE

Inner-city Leederville is one of Perth's most idiosyncratic neighbourhoods, loved for its eclectic mix of boutiques and bars, its approachable but distinctive restaurants and its light-strung laneways and street art. Here's our insider's guide to Leederville.

JACK LOVEL

How to

Getting here From Perth centre, take the Yanchep train line one stop to Leederville, or catch the number 15 bus; both drop you on Leederville's main cafe strip, Oxford St. From there, stick to walking.

When to go Leederville is fun year-round. During the day it's all about the shopping and people-watching, whereas at night the bars, pubs and restaurants bustle.

Top tip If you're driving, there's a large public car park hidden just behind Oxford St, with access via surrounding side streets near the Good Grocer.

BIG STATE IMAGES/ALAMY

FLEUR BAINGER/LONELY PLANET

Far top left Servo
Bottom left Perth train
Near left Urban Depot

At first glance, Leederville looks like an easy-to-read, eclectic inner-city suburb. Its streetscape is dotted with stripy umbrellas, alfresco dining nudges out onto car parking spaces and every shopfront is individual. But there's more to it.

Take **Babylon Cafe**, a narrow coffee house that's found down a side street and behind a rug shop. Its sign gives nothing away, but walk past the forest of potted plants and mismatched garden chairs, duck your head under the low, vintage brick doorway, and you find a buzzing caffeine den.

A short wander away is one of Oxford St's long-timers. **Urban Records** does what it says on the label. But edge further down the aisles and you'll find **Urban Depot**, a shop within a shop. It's a haven of the unlikely, with mind-tickling books by The School of Life sitting alongside risqué greeting cards and women's fashion.

Cross Oxford St to find the landmark **Leederville Hotel** on Newcastle St. Bypass the main bar and restaurant and order a craft brew from the beer bar, Sandgropers (it's the name of a local dune-loving insect and what Western Australians affectionately call themselves). Every month, a different small-batch brewery takes over the taps.

Head to the back of the Leederville Hotel and find **Servo**, an energetic restaurant that edges Electric Lane. Its food is wonderfully adventurous: think mussels with fennel pollen on squid-ink baguette.

Leedy Must-Dos

Luna Leederville An iconic cinema, showcasing international and Australian films in nostalgic surrounds. It also has an outdoor screen.

Bunn Mee A foodie escape to Vietnam, via authentic banh mis and Vietnamese ice coffees. You can smell the grilled pork belly from 50m away and you'll be well fed for $10 to $20.

Roberts on Oxford A quaint, small bar that is homey yet upmarket. Rob, the owner, built the bar himself.

Jenny Lam, *former MasterChef contestant and the whiz behind Bunn Mee and Phat Lon in Leederville @jennylamau*

WA'S WEIRD &
Wonderful Wildflowers

01

02

03

04

01 Wasp imitator
The carousel spider orchid *(Caladenia arenicola)* impersonates native wasps so convincingly – pheromones and all – that male insects try to mate with it.

02 Scented blossom
The *Eucalyptus kingsmillii* can be seen in Kings Park in Perth, as can all the flowers here. Australia has loads of perfumed flowering trees.

03 Grevillea variifolia
There are hundreds of types of *Grevillea variifolia*, known as the spider plant. This drought-hardy shrub grows happily in the sand and gravel along the Ningaloo Coast.

04 Sun worshipper
The scented sun orchid *(Thelymitra macrophylla)* pops up everywhere during wildflower season, which runs from June (in the mid-north) to late October (in the south).

05

06

07

08

05 Bug beater

The wily triggerplant *(Stylidium araeophyllum)* dusts visiting insects with pollen by smacking them with a hidden swat that's triggered by the touch of tiny legs.

06 Fringed lily

The edges of the leafless fringed lily are like the fine lace used in haute couture. Its delicate purple petals open at dawn and are closed by the afternoon, like a shy beauty.

07 Donkey orchid

Let's be honest, the donkey orchid looks like an ass. As its name suggests, its perky petals resemble a donkey's ears. Its flowers are delightful – and with their bright colours, easy – to spot.

08 Firewood banksire

This woodland species *(Banksia menziesii)* seems dry and scratchy until its intricate details are seen up close.

01 ANNE-TIPODEES/SHUTTERSTOCK, **02** BLICKWINKEL/ALAMY, **03** ROB DAVIS/LONELY PLANET, **04** ROB DAVIS/LONELY PLANET, **05** ROB DAVIS/LONELY PLANET, **06** ROB DAVIS/LONELY PLANET, **07** ROB DAVIS/LONELY PLANET, **08** CHRIS DE BLANK/SHUTTERSTOCK

48 Under-the-Radar Perth BEACHES

BEACHES | OUTDOORS | SHIPWRECK

Once you see a Perth beach, you'll be forever ruined for other city beaches. But it's not only silky white sand and crystal-clear waters you'll find here. Rock pools, dusk swims and fire twirlers are also part of the allure.

MICHAEL WILLIS/ALAMY

How to

Getting here These beaches are most conveniently accessed by car. A bike route also links most destinations along the coast.

When to go Perth beach lovers hit the sand from October to June. Only the truly dedicated make it into the water all the way through the winter months.

Top tip Hit the coast before 10am for the best water clarity and the calmest waters before the 'Fremantle Doctor' blows in.

The privacy-lovers' beach If gazing into rock pools and sheltering in eroded rock caverns sounds like your kind of adventure, make your way to **Bennion Beach** in Perth's north. The tiny stretch is wedged between popular Trigg Beach and Mettams Pool, the latter a much-loved snorkelling and annual abalone-diving spot. Go exploring to find your own private nook facing a soft reef and calm, shallow waters. This beach is open to dogs; it can be great fun watching joyful pooches bound about. Those in the know come here for the tranquillity – it pays to bring a good book.

The hippy haven What **South Beach** lacks in pristine sand (it's a mix of caramel and black grains) it makes up for in eye-catching entertainment. By day there's a grassy park for picnics and a playground shaded by Norfolk pines leading to calm water that seems

STEPHEN DOREY/ALAMY

Top left Bennion Beach
Left South Beach

knee-deep forever – perfect for paddling. As dark approaches, out come fire twirlers, hacky-sack players, buskers and all manner of eccentric visitors. It's busy in a laid-back kind of way. In the warmer months, a floating pontoon just offshore draws swimmers and sun seekers, while just south of the groyne a dedicated dog beach becomes a joyous free-for-all of paws and waves. Adding to the ritual, a **pop-up beach sauna** nearby offers a steamy contrast to ocean dips.

The sunset spot Closest to Perth's centre, **City Beach** is one of few stretches of sand to be floodlit at night, allowing for delightful dusk swims on steamy evenings. It's also a prime sunset-watching spot; join the groups of friends and families sharing hot fish and chips from the nearby **Clancy's Fish Pub** beach cafe as the giant orb plunges below the ruled line of horizon. Seaside sunsets are something of a WA speciality.

CY O'Connor Beach

Mix beauty with history with a visit to CY O'Connor Beach in North Coogee. The vast ruins of the 1950s South Fremantle Power Station loom in the sand dunes, providing a dramatic backdrop. Look out for the statue of CY by WA artist Tony Jones out in the ocean. Most visible at low tide, it marks the site where the state's hugely impactful chief civil engineer rode his horse into the ocean and shot himself in 1902, in despair that his Goldfields water pipeline wasn't going to work. In fact the pipeline did work, and it's celebrated today as one of the great engineering feats of the early 20th century.

Marcus Canning, *artist and explorer*

ALISA HR/SHUTTERSTOCK

Beach Etiquette

Perth beachgoers are accustomed to having plenty of sand to themselves, so be careful not to sit too close or set up directly in front of your fellow sun worshippers – it won't be appreciated. Beach thefts are rare; be relaxed about your belongings, but keep them within sight.

The submerged shipwreck The newly developed coastal suburb of **Coogee** is in Perth's far south, and when you see its glass-clear waters and blindingly white sand, you'll wonder why it took so long for the estate builders to come. Off a nondescript street, look for a steel staircase that descends over a rock groyne into the shallow ocean. Just beyond it is the **wreck of the Omeo**, a cargo steamer that ran aground here in 1905 and has since become a snorkeller's exploration site. If you have kids or aren't a confident swimmer, check the tides before you come and arrive at low tide, when part of the wreck is accessible by wading in on foot, in just over a metre or so of water. Otherwise, splash in and consider following the **Coogee Maritime Trail**, an underwater snorkelling route that runs from 2m to 7m deep. Look out for the golden sea lion sculpture – its nose peeks above the waterline.

RIGHT: DYLAN ALCOCK/SHUTTERSTOCK, LEFT: EA GIVEN/SHUTTERSTOCK

Left CY O'Connor sculpture by Tony Jones
Above top *Omeo* shipwreck
Above City Beach

49 Overnighting on ROTTNEST

ISLAND | WILDLIFE | BEACH

Keen to understand the living creature behind the thousands of grinning selfies with celebrities? Rottnest Island's quokkas are known for their photogenic poses, but a simple snap sells them short. Experience the transformative nature of spending a night – or three – in Perth's holiday haven, surrounded by curious wildlife, peaceful coves and oodles of natural beauty.

BENNY MARTY/SHUTTERSTOCK

How to

Getting here Rottnest-bound ferries depart from Perth's city centre, Fremantle and Hillarys Boat Harbour. There are also light plane and helicopter options.

Getting around Most people hire bicycles. You can also get about on foot or by e-bike, take the shuttle, or buy a ticket for the hop-on, hop-off bus that loops around the 11km-long island.

When to go The days are warm and skies are blue from September to May.

GRAKHANTSEV NIKOLAI/SHUTTERSTOCK

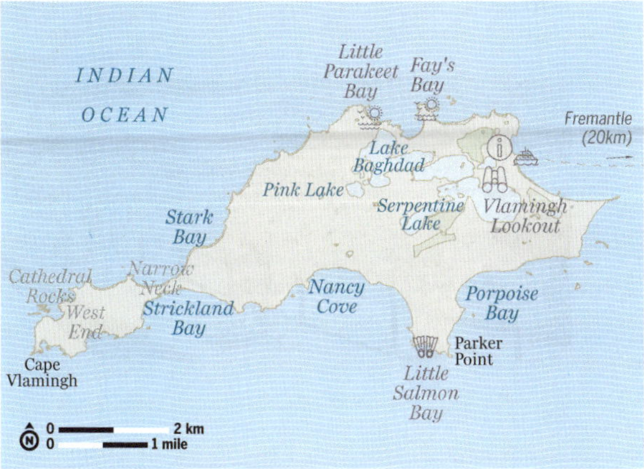

Top left Little Salmon Bay
Bottom left Quokka

Gone are the crowds With many day trippers departing on the 6pm ferry, tens of thousands of visitors to Rottnest Island never see it at its best – as the sun softens, the bustle calms and the marsupials emerge. They leave with quokka selfies, a slick of sunscreen and the crunch of salt in their hair. It's fun, sure, but you can do better. Those who stay overnight have an entirely different experience. As night nears, quokkas – which are nocturnal – come out in droves. In the dark they're most active, bouncing across walking paths and around anyone wandering by. They scramble up trees, tussle with one another and nibble on grasses. It's a significant contrast from daytime, when they barely move, appear stunned or lazily scavenge. These quokkas are only there because of people – and that's why feeding them is a no-no. If you see a quokka sleeping during the day – they curl up while seated and rest their heads on their tails – don't bother them; they need their shut-eye.

Relax into 'Rotto' pace While you're here, explore beyond the main settlement to follow little-used hiking trails and boardwalks and have enchanting beaches all to yourself. Paradisiacal **Little Parakeet Bay** is flanked by eroded limestone formations and faces an ocean pool. At **Fay's Bay**, a curving, flat beach gives way to craggy rocks with leafy seagrasses and rock pools at their base; it's an ideal spot for children to explore and amateur fishers to drop a line. At sheltered **Little Salmon Bay**, an excellent snorkel trail is dotted with underwater panels.

Fun Quokka Facts

When 17th-century Dutch sailors explored the craggy limestone island, they mistook its resident fur balls for large rats. The quokkas' presence resulted in the island's name, Rottnest, which means 'rats nest' in Dutch.

Quokkas get most of the hydration they need from eating native greenery, such as grasses, succulents and seedlings, so they rarely drink water.

Quokka joeys poke their little heads out of their mothers' pouches each September, and the island holds a public, weekend-long Quokka birthday party for all the newborns. They're ultra-cute but should never be touched.

Beyond the Quokkas

ROTTNEST ISLAND'S LAYERED AND COMPLEX BACKSTORY

Rottnest Island – called Wadjemup by the Whadjuk Noongar people – is outshone by its famous quokkas. But look beyond the cuteness and you'll find an isle of living history, where heritage buildings tell stories of lonely colonial settlement, world-war efforts and hard-knocks farming.

Left Thomson Bay
Centre Path from Vlamingh Lookout
Right Old Salt Store

JON ARNOLD IMAGES LTD/ALAMY

Early Origins

Perth's playground, winking 19km across the Indian Ocean, wasn't always an island. Some 7000 years ago, Rottnest Island formed part of the WA mainland. Artefacts found, such as a 27,000-year-old cutting tool made of chert, suggest Rottnest's Traditional Custodians, the Whadjuk Noongar people, walked across the land bridge well before sea levels rose, using it as a meeting place and ceremonial site.

It was far more recently, in 1831, that Rottnest's first European residents set up here. Robert Thomson and his wife and children are believed to be the first people to have lived on Rottnest Island in modern times. Along with other colonists, they farmed everything from livestock to grains, tobacco and fruit, as well as harvesting salt from central saline lakes. Rottnest's main settlement, Thomson Bay, is named after the family.

Parts of the Thomson homestead and water well – possibly the oldest human-made structures on Rottnest – can still be viewed. A 4km walking trail weaves through the area that the Thomsons farmed. Follow it from hilltop Vlamingh Lookout down to a boardwalk with pink-hued salt lakes and samphire carpets on either side that leads to Little Parakeet Bay (p251).

A Hidden History

The Thomson family was the last to privately own land on Rottnest – in 1839 private ownership was prohibited. The island became an Aboriginal penal colony, and over the next century nearly 4000 men and boys were imprisoned here.

EA GIVEN/SHUTTERSTOCK

FRITZ16/SHUTTERSTOCK

Prisoners undertook brutally hard labour, quarrying stone and constructing most of the colonial buildings still standing in Thomson Bay. Tragically, at least 373 Aboriginal men and boys are believed to have died and been buried here, making this the largest known site of Aboriginal deaths in custody in Australia. The burial ground remained unknown to the public until the 1980s. The prison, known as the Quod, was closed in 1904; the last inmates left in the 1930s. The many Aboriginal lives lost on Wadjemup mean the island holds special significance for WA's Aboriginal peoples.

A New Era Dawns

In the decades that followed, Wadjemup was steadily repurposed for holidaymaking. Once washed with white lime that reflected harshly in the lucid light, its small workers' cottages were slapped with a peach ochre that remains synonymous with the island today. The two world wars pressed pause on tourism, with Rottnest used as a prisoner-of-war camp and military defence base. After the wars, the canons and army barracks became tourist attractions, the Boys' Reformatory was turned into accommodation, and the governor's summer residence was converted into a pub.

Private ownership remains banned, with only long-serving staff allowed to live on the island. While the settlement's holiday houses have been gently upgraded over time, they retain a deliberately simple feel. More recently, rising visitor numbers have brought new accommodation, including Samphire Rottnest, the Lodge Wadjemup and Pinky's Rottnest Island. While these additions have prompted debate, Rottnest's sandy-footed, car-free simplicity remains central to its appeal, with a careful balance continually struck between old and new.

The Wadjemup Project

Launched in 2022, the Wadjemup Project is an Aboriginal-led initiative reshaping how Rottnest Island is understood and experienced today. Developed with Whadjuk Noongar Elders and communities across WA, it focuses on truth-telling, ceremony and memorialisation. Conservation works are underway at the Quod, the island's former prison and most visible symbol of this history, following major state funding announced in 2023. As part of the project, Traditional Custodians have led Wadjemup Wirin Bidi, a spirit trail ceremony that acknowledges the spirits of Aboriginal men and boys imprisoned on the island. Planning is also underway for a permanent memorial at the Wadjemup Aboriginal Burial Ground.

50 A Margaret River TASTER

FOOD | WINERIES | TOURS

As a leading Australian winegrowing region, here you'll taste some exquisite wines, from cabernet sauvignon to chardonnay, and gourmet food while in the Margaret River/Wooditchup area. But don't miss out on getting your hands dirty – learn how food is grown and made, follow an organic wine trail or join an innovative tour to get up to date on lo-fi winemaking.

MICHELLE MORRISON PHOTOGRAPHY

How to

Getting around Pick a designated driver when visiting the wineries and breweries, and if no one's willing to put their hand up, join a bus tour.

Farm-gate food Roadside stalls around Manjimup offer the freshest produce – look out for seasonal stone fruit, berries, apples, asparagus and avocados.

Top tip Buy directly from the farmers themselves every Saturday morning at the **Margaret River Farmers Market**. Fresh and delish!

PHIL HILL/ALAMY

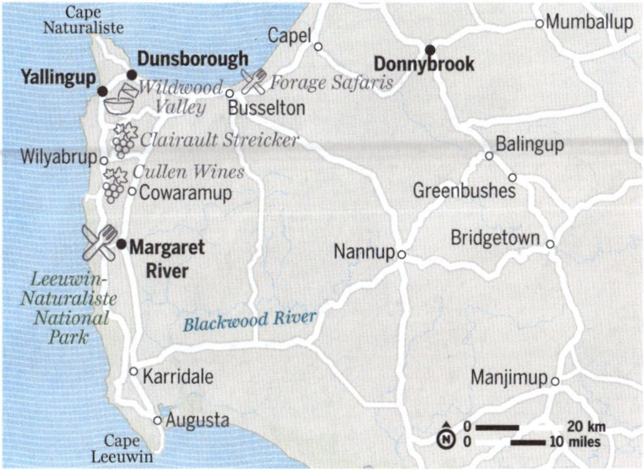

Get hands on with local produce Forage your way through quality farms of the South West, including avocado, apple and chestnut, with **Forage Safaris**. Customisable tours delve into the intricacies of farming with tastings of the unbeatable produce this region has to offer. In the quiet serenity of Yallingup, the **Wildwood Valley** cooking school, run by a trained chef, offers classes that highlight fresh, local produce inspired by an interesting mix of Tuscan and Thai flavours.

Wineries With over 200 wineries in the region, there's certainly a lot of choice. **Cullen Wines** in Wilyabrup is known for impeccable organic and biodynamic wines, including the cabernet-based red Diana Madeline and chardonnay Kevin John wines. At **Clairault Streicker**, create your own cabernet sauvignon or shiraz blend using real-deal equipment and under the expert guidance of a winemaker; you'll expand your knowledge of wine blending, learn what makes your palate zing and then take your creation home. You even get to name your own drop.

Foodie festival The hugely popular **Western Australia Gourmet Escape** (gourmetescape.com.au), held in late November, combines the Margaret River region's pristine landscapes with an extravaganza of fresh, innovative food. It's considered the premium showcase of Western Australia's food and wine, and the star-studded guest list usually includes some of the biggest international and Australian names in the foodie world. It's not just for the elite gastronome but for people who simply love great food.

Top left Wildwood Valley
Bottom left Cullen Wines

Best Winery & Cultural Tours

Koomal Dreaming Learn about the native ingredients used by many chefs in the Margaret River region on a tour led by Wadandi man Josh Whiteland. You'll forage for native bush foods, discover their cultural uses and then gather around the campfire for a seasonal lunch – dishes might include kangaroo, emu, abalone, coastal herbs or quandong.

Margaret River Discovery Tour A handpicked winery and gourmet experience, plus exciting 4WD and canoeing adventures, led by tour guide Sean Blocksidge – and all in a day.

Walk Talk Taste Meet locals working in the food and beverage scene and hear about the produce that inspires them on an intimate evening tour of Margaret River town.

51 An Almighty COAST

BEACHES | SURFING | MARINE LIFE

From incredible rock formations to natural spas, unique wines and ocean creatures of all kinds, it's impossible to visit this region without spending time on the coast. While the area is known for its world-class surf and famous championships, there's plenty to experience if surfing isn't your style.

SARA BIANCARDI/SHUTTERSTOCK

How to

Getting around All the places listed here are accessible with 2WD, but be aware that these are narrow and winding country roads, so watch out for wildlife. Always drive to the conditions.

When to visit Between June and December whales pass along this coast during their annual migration north to warmer waters.

Swim safe The ocean here is powerful and dangerous; observe the warnings and be careful at all times, especially on rocky coastal areas. If a sign says 'No Swimming', then this is what it means.

Rockin' Rocks & Natural Havens

The unique rock formations of the Leeuwin-Naturaliste coast are the result of granite gneiss rocks being weathered over eons by the powerful movement of the waves. Some of the more notable are **Canal Rocks** near Yallingup and **Sugarloaf Rock** at Cape Naturaliste (also an incredible spot to watch the sunset).

A short drive from Sugarloaf Rock, to the other side of the cape, is **Meelup Beach**, with clear aquamarine waters and pure white sand – it's perfect for a tranquil swim. If a bit more froth has you bubbling, then **Injidup Natural Spa** is a hidden rock pool where waves crash over the rocks to create a spa-like sensation. For protected snorkelling, head to the **Aquarium** near Smiths Beach.

AGENT WOLF/SHUTTERSTOCK

Top left Injidup Natural Spa
Left Canal Rocks

Short Coastal Walks

There's nothing more invigorating than short walks to appreciate this coast. An easy and fully accessible option is the 4km walk from Cape Naturaliste Lighthouse (p262) to Sugarloaf Rock, while the 4km return hike to **Quinninup Falls** from Moses Rock car park takes you along part of the Cape to Cape Track for a true wilderness experience.

Hiking is best from September through November when wildflowers dot the coastal heath and you might spot the thrilling sprays of whales as they migrate northward. Also, it shouldn't be too hot, though keep a lookout for snakes.

Spotting Graceful Rays

Beautiful **Hamelin Bay**, to the south of Margaret River, is another beachside getaway.

Whale Highway

Flinders Bay in Augusta is where humpback, southern right and blue whales first reach land after crossing the ocean from Antarctica. Between June and August, whale-watching cruises here enable you to get a close, though respectful, look.

From September to November you can also take whale-watching trips from Dunsborough as the whales and calves make their way back south after the calves are born in the warmer waters of the north.

The **lighthouses** at Cape Naturaliste and Cape Leeuwin both provide great vantage points for whale watchers, as does Sugarloaf Rock.

Seaside Winery

Home to the state's most unique winery, the coast of Augusta offers the chance to sip wines that have been aged in an underwater process at **Subsea Estate**. Utilising the natural sway, low light, and consistent temperature and pressure of the Southern Ocean gives the wines a distinctive flavour profile.

WENDY JOHNSON/ALAMY

It's best known for its frequent visitors, three species of wild sea creature: smooth stingrays, black stingrays and eagle rays. On calm mornings these locals can be seen around the picturesque old Hamelin Bay jetty and along the shallows of the beach. Remember that these are wild creatures – keep a safe distance, don't touch them and definitely don't feed them.

4WD Adventures

The pristine **Yeagarup Dunes** form one of the largest land-locked dune systems in the world. Driving along the top of the dunes, with karri forest on one side and pure sand on the other, is awe-inspiring. Equally incredible are the towering hexagonal basalt columns of **Black Point**, formed 135 million years ago, as is nearby **Lake Jasper**, the largest natural freshwater lake in WA. These are true adventures for experienced 4WDers. Alternatively, contact **Pemberton Discovery Tours** for their unique options.

RIGHT: RANDOM LIGHTS PHOTOGRAPHY/ALAMY; LEFT: NATHAN STAFFORD/SHUTTERSTOCK

Left Humpback whale
Above top Yeagarup Dunes
Above Black Point

52 Fun for All Ages in BUSSELTON

FAMILY FRIENDLY | ADVENTURE | PLAYGROUNDS

With family-oriented resorts and a lively foreshore, Busselton/Undalup is a solid option for your first visit to the South West. In fact, the whole region is extremely child-friendly – plan on making day trips along the coast, including to Dunsborough or Margaret River, and be confident that everyone will be happy.

ARIANA SVENSON/LONELY PLANET

How to

Getting around Set yourself up in Busselton and then make day trips with a car.

Where to stay Busselton is the quintessential family resort town; accommodation options feature waterslides, bouncing pillows and endless pools. Alternatively, farmstays and forest retreats often include playgrounds and animal feeding.

Make lots of stops In Myalup, the **Crooked Carrot** has a fun playground and restored vintage Melbourne trams, while the **Old Coast Road Brewery** has a WA-themed mini-golf course.

KAI EGAN/SHUTTERSTOCK

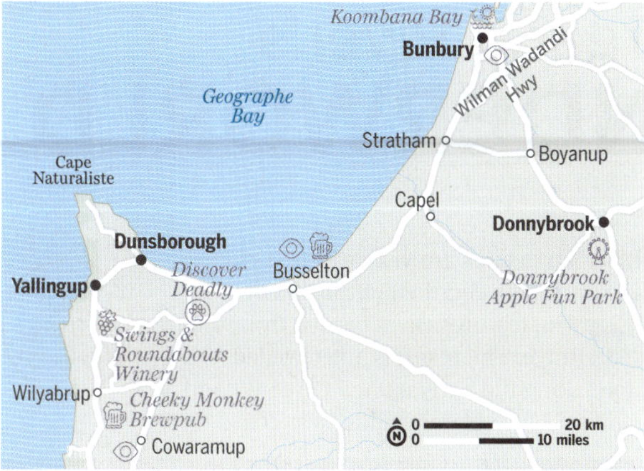

Top left Donnybrook Apple Fun Park
Bottom left Old Wife fish, Busselton jetty

Busselton jetty and foreshore Kids of all ages will love taking the cute solar-powered train out to the end of the 1.8km-long Busselton jetty, where the underwater observatory enraptures with a glimpse of what lies below. Back on land, there's an awesome playground, a seasonal fairground and the **Shelter Brewery Company** on the foreshore. At sunset, take an easy walk, salt in your hair, ice cream in your hand, and there's really nothing quite like it. This place is pure family fun.

Kid-friendly wineries and breweries At most dining establishments you'll find children's menus and kid-friendly playgrounds. A good choice is **Swings & Roundabouts Winery** in Yallingup, a 30-minute drive west of Busselton; everyone loves the yummy pizzas and, yes, swings here. Just 10 minutes further south along Caves Rd, the **Cheeky Monkey Brewpub** in Wilyabrup has an awesome family atmosphere and pours top brews with lake views.

The biggest there is Around 60km east of Busselton is the revamped **Donnybrook Apple Fun Park**, the long-time holder of 'the biggest free fun park in Australia' title. Combine your trip here with some fruit picking in season and Donnybrook makes a great day out.

Detour to Cowtown Cowaramup gets its name from the Aboriginal word *cowara*, meaning purple-crowned lorikeet – but at some point it was dubbed 'Cowtown' due to the area's thriving dairy industry. The town's main street features 42 life-size black-and-white Friesian cows. Get your sweet fix at the **Candy Cow** lolly shop or grab a scoop or two at **Millers Ice Creamery**.

Fun & Adrenaline in the Southwest

A Maze'n (Margaret River) One of the largest hedge mazes in Australia.

Discover Deadly (Carbunup River) An interesting introduction to snakes and other reptiles.

Koombana Bay (Bunbury) Extremely cool foreshore playground. Next door, the **Bunbury Dolphin Discovery Centre** has a state-of-the-art interpretation centre and tours that get you up close to the dolphins that come to the bay most mornings in the warmer months (October to April).

Manjimup Timber Park Rad adventure playground with a mega slide that can be combined with the interactive **Power Up Electricity Museum**.

53 Margaret River's UNDERWORLD

CAVES | HISTORY | LIGHTHOUSES

Not all of Margaret River's treasures are visible at first glance. In fact the entire cape-to-cape area, between the lighthouses of Cape Naturaliste and Cape Leeuwin, features caves eroded from the sandstone Leeuwin-Naturaliste Ridge. The result is a bejewelled network of 150 caves to explore along the aptly named Caves Rd and breathtaking lighthouses standing sentinel on a wilderness coast.

MATT DEAKIN/SHUTTERSTOCK

How to

Getting around It's around a 1½-hour drive from cape to cape on Caves Rd, along which is a wealth of caves, tranquil forest and places to eat and drink. Reduce driving time by focusing on the northern or southern cape – don't try to do them all in one day.

When to go The caves all share the same slightly humid atmosphere, which makes them great to visit year-round.

Some fitness required Both lighthouses and all of the caves have a lot of steps; you'll need reasonable physical fitness.

The Cape Lighthouses

The **Cape Naturaliste Lighthouse** and **Cape Leeuwin Lighthouse** (pictured), both still operational, are a perfect juxtaposition with the darkness of the caves. Soak up wild views, turbulent oceans and the feel of the salty wind in your hair. Cape Leeuwin Lighthouse, the tallest mainland lighthouse in Australia, stands at the most southwesterly tip of the country.

01 After a short guided tour through **Ngilgi Cave**, the most northerly of the caves, near Yallingup, take in the bright colours, stalagmites and stalactites in your own time.

02 The self-guided **Mammoth Cave**, near Margaret River town, provides universal access for the first section and is a good choice if you have little kids.

03 The remarkable **Lake Cave** (pictured below) is named for its beautiful lake and reflections, but it's just as memorable for its karri-framed entry (and lots of steps).

04 For a more adventurous caving experience, head to the 86m-deep **Giants Cave**. Get in contact with Margaret River Climbing Co for caving and abseiling tours.

05 The most southerly cave is considered by many to be the most beautiful: **Jewel Cave**, 8km northwest of Augusta, has three massive, crystal-encrusted chambers.

FROM LEFT: NATALIA VOSTRIKOVA/SHUTTERSTOCK, MICHAEL HERITAGE/SHUTTERSTOCK

54 For Beach LOVERS

WHITE SAND | SWIMMING | SOLITUDE

The South Coast juxtaposes a wild and powerful coastline with turquoise water, long expanses of white sand and, quite often, blissful seclusion. Whether you're tempted by the remote white swathes found in national parks or the gentle kid-friendly city beaches with waterfront cafes in sight, getting your toes in the sand should be a top priority.

ARIANA SVENSON/LONELY PLANET

How to

Swim safe Don't underestimate the water on the South Coast. Follow the signs and look out for rips, even at popular swimming beaches.

Avoid the crowds Most beaches see few people, except on school and public holidays. To explore off the beaten track, hire a 4WD.

Water sports SUP or snorkel at spots like Peaceful Bay, Twilight Beach in Esperance and Greens Pool. The water can be very cold year-round; consider wearing a wetsuit.

ARIANA SVENSON/LONELY PLANET

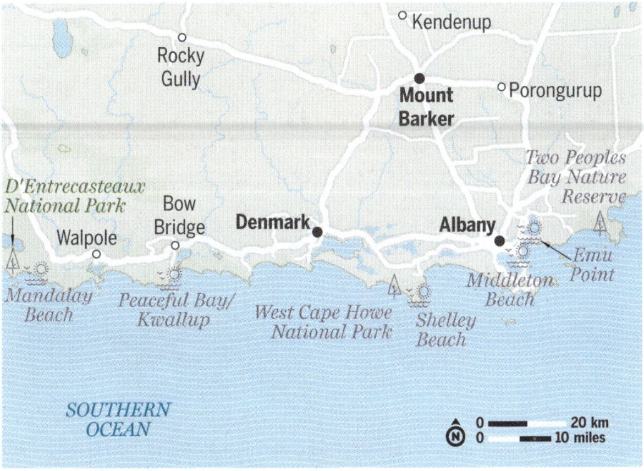

Family-friendly Picturesque **Middleton Beach** and **Emu Point**, both within Albany city, offer the quintessential day at the seaside, with safe swimming enclosures, playgrounds for the kids and excellent cafes such as Three Anchors at Middleton Beach and Emu Point Cafe. Both beaches get bonus points for the excellent walking trails and photo ops.

Easy access The only 2WD-accessible spot in West Cape Howe National Park is **Shelley Beach** – and what a spot! This pristine beach is perfect for swimming, camping and fishing, and it's the best place on the South Coast for paragliding – watch as these graceful crafts flip and float on the breeze from a cliff above you.

A peaceful option Between Walpole and Denmark, **Peaceful Bay/Kwallup** is a less popular option than nearby Greens Pool in William Bay National Park, but this pretty turquoise bay has a sheltered swimming area and a busy boat launch. It's home to a small settlement and caravan park, and families have been holidaying here for generations. There's a real 'step back in time' vibe. Don't miss the delish fish and chips.

True wilderness In remote D'Entrecasteaux National Park, just 20km west of Walpole, the sublimely beautiful **Mandalay Beach** has views out to Chatham Island. The beach is named for the shipwrecked *Barque Mandalay*, which emerges every few years from the shifting sands and wild surf – you never know, you might just see it! This is a spot for contemplation, not swimming.

Top left Middleton Beach
Bottom left Mandalay Beach

Two Peoples Bay Nature Reserve

Popular for its white sand, aquamarine waters and granite rock outcrops, **Two Peoples Bay** and **Little Beach**, both located within the Two Peoples Bay Nature Reserve around 35km east of Albany, have been ranked among the 'best beaches in Australia' – yet their real treasures lie deeper.

Take the 4.6km Heritage Trail from the Two Peoples Bay Visitor Centre to the beach, and you are in a truly extraordinary landscape of animal diversity. Both quendas and quokkas can be seen on the trail. Keep your ear attuned to the call of the noisy scrub bird, which was rediscovered here after it was thought to be extinct. You might also see a seal basking on the rocks or whales in the bay.

Sarah Comer, *Regional Ecologist, Department of Biodiversity, Parks & Attractions, @exploreparkswa*

55 More than Whale SHARKS

MARINE LIFE | REEF | UNDERWATER

Most people come to Ningaloo Reef to swim with the whale sharks – and you should too. Stretching almost 300km, Ningaloo is the world's longest fringing reef, home to some of the richest marine life in the southern hemisphere. You can also plan your visit around humpback whales, manta rays and turtles.

WATERFRAME/ALAMY

How to

Getting there and around Exmouth is the main base for Ningaloo; it's connected by air to Perth and to just about anywhere by road. Coral Bay is also good.

When to go Whale sharks visit from mid-March to September and even later. For humpbacks it's June to October.

Tours Try Kings Ningaloo Reef Tours, Ningaloo Whale Shark-N-Dive or Three Islands Whale Shark Dive for whale shark and interactive whale tours.

FROZYGRAPHIE/SHUTTERSTOCK

Swimming with Whale Sharks

UNESCO World Heritage-listed Ningaloo is one of the few places in the world where solitary speckled whale sharks *(Rhincodon typus)* arrive like clockwork each year to feed on plankton and small fish. The largest fish in the world, whale sharks can reach up to 18m long and are believed to live 70 to 100 years. Those encountered at Ningaloo are mostly between 3m and 12m; a 12m whale shark may weigh as much as 11 tonnes and have a mouth more than a metre wide.

From March to August (and sometimes even as late as October), you can join a tour to snorkel alongside these extraordinary creatures.

EMPPICTURES/SHUTTERSTOCK

Humpback-Whale Sightings

And you thought whale sharks were big! From May to October around 35,000 humpback

Citizen Science

Once you're back on dry land, upload your whale-shark pics to **Wildbook for Whale Sharks** (sharkbook.ai), which will identify and track your whale shark. Similarly, happywhale.com will take your humpback images. Snorkellers and divers can add new meaning to saltwater adventures by collecting marine data for reefcheckaustralia.org.

Top left Whale shark
Left Vlamingh Head Lighthouse (p268)
Above Newborn green turtle

whales *(Megaptera novaeangliae)* migrate along the WA coastline, heading north to warm Kimberley calving grounds before returning south to feed on krill in the Antarctic summer.

Whale-watching tours from Exmouth go out to sea in hopes of sighting a classic breach. Your other option is to drive up to **Vlamingh Head Lighthouse** with a pair of binoculars.

Nesting Marine Turtles

Between December and March you can join a two-hour guided tour run by the **Jurabi Turtle Centre** (exploreparks.dbca.wa.gov.au/site/jurabi-turtle-centre) to see green and loggerhead turtles nesting on the beach; tours depart a few evenings each week, and advance bookings are essential. If you have five weeks to spare and a passion for conservation, consider volunteering with the **Ningaloo Turtle Program** (ningalooturtles.org.au).

Above & Below

Over 220 species of hard coral have been recorded in Ningaloo. While they're less colourful than soft corals (normally found in deeper water on the outer reef), hard corals

Drift Snorkelling at Turquoise Bay

If you're a strong swimmer (a necessary precondition), there's nothing quite like drift snorkelling at gorgeous Turquoise Bay, off Yardie Creek Rd on the western shore of Cape Range National Park, 63km from Exmouth. As the current carries you over coral bommies, watch for everything from bulbous brain corals to delicate branching staghorns. Avoid swimming when currents are strong, and don't miss the exit point or you'll be swept out to sea. From the Drift car park, head 300m south along the beach, then wade 40m into the water. Sadly, you'll see strong evidence here of the 2024–25 bleaching event.

FAR LEFT: JACOBLOYACANO/SHUTTERSTOCK
LEFT: EMILY HAMLEY/SHUTTERSTOCK

Far left Coral, Ningaloo Reef
Near left Turtle, Ningaloo Reef
Below Kayaking, Ningaloo Reef

are all about shape, with formations including bommies, plate corals, brains, fingers, bubbles and staghorns.

Spawning, where branches of hermaphroditic coral simultaneously eject eggs and sperm into the water, occurs en masse at neap tides after the March and April full moons. This underwater blizzard attracts krill and plankton, and in turn whale sharks, in addition to an already astonishing diversity of fish, rays, turtles and other marine life.

Snorkelling is the easiest way to see this wonderland. Because Ningaloo is a fringing reef, you can launch directly from shore at places like **Bundegi Beach**, **Lakeside** and **Turquoise Bay**; the latter offers both bay and drift snorkelling. Hire snorkel gear from any of the dive shops in town.

From a kayak you might see turtles, dolphins and manta rays. Ningaloo has several dedicated moorings in the sanctuary zones of **Osprey**, **Tantabiddi**, **Bundegi** and **Maud** (Coral Bay) that allow you to tether your craft while you explore below, enjoying the best of both worlds.

In 2024–25 Ningaloo experienced its worst ever coral bleaching event. The underwater heatwave was particularly devastating to the shallower corals.

SUZANNE LONG/ALAMY

56 Oddities & Curiosities of KATTER KICH

OUTBACK | ADVENTURE | ROCKS

Imagine a monster wave poised just as it's about to crash. That's the scene that greets you at Katter Kich (Wave Rock), a 15m-high, 2.7-billion-year-old slab of granite that stretches 110m long. Here's how best to visit it.

MARTIN HELGEMEIR/SHUTTERSTOCK

How to

Getting here Katter Kich is a four-hour drive inland from Perth. Coach tours are possible, but for ease of exploration it's best to drive.

Stop-offs Visit historic York, the quirky Tin Horse Hwy, the 182m-long community water slide at Kulin and Corrigin's poignant dog cemetery.

When to go Avoid summer, when temperatures soar.

Top tip Park by Wave Rock village to avoid pricey parking in bays closer to the rock.

JAMESTEOHART/SHUTTERSTOCK

Some 300km east of Perth, surrounded by scrub and dry, sunbaked earth flushed the shade of sienna, is **Katter Kich (Wave Rock)**. The formation, naturally eroded by wind and water that has hollowed out its softer underside, achieved global fame in the 1960s when *National Geographic* magazine published a photograph of it. It's vertically striped in a rainbow of earthy stains, the result of rain flushing iron oxide and carbonates down its curved surface.

Most visitors come during the day, when piercing light mutes the rock's colours. Instead, go at sunset. As the bruising sunlight softens, the wave's scale becomes more apparent and it's vastly more enjoyable to walk around. Edge along the base (be sure to snap a playful pic of you 'surfing' the wave) and carefully across the peak, where you're gifted endless views of bush and farmland.

MINO SURKALA/SHUTTERSTOCK

Tin Horse Highway

Detour 15 minutes from the main road to take in the Tin Horse Hwy. With their tongues in their cheeks, local farmers have welded and painted more than 70 characterful horses from bits of tin and metal, dotting them along a 15km stretch. Most are on the Gorge Rock–Lake Grace Rd.

Top left Katter Kich (Wave Rock)
Left Tin Horse Hwy
Above View from the top of Katter Kich

Float like an Astronaut

Only 800m away is the **Lake Magic Swimming Pool**, with water so saline you bob about weightlessly, as though you have zero gravity. Take the steps gingerly – they can be slippery – and expect squishiness underfoot. Limestone cabanas with hammocks and showers have been built around the perimeter, adding a desert day-spa vibe. It's part of the Wave Rock Resort site, but the pool is open to anyone. The water comes from **Lake Magic**, a gypsum-rich expanse next door that provides beautiful reflections at dusk.

Hippo's Yawn

Another rock formation, **Hippo's Yawn** stands almost 13m tall and is reached via a 1.7km loop walking trail from the Katter Kich car park. You can crawl to the back of the gaping 'jaw' and scramble up a tumble of boulders. It really does look like a hippo yawning. Kids bound through the gaps, whereas for adults it's more of a twist and slide.

WA's Most Inland Winery

About an hour's drive south of Katter Kich (a small distance in these parts) is **Walkers Hill Vineyard**. Any wine buff knows it shouldn't be possible to grow grapevines this far east, but the owners of this establishment are not wine people. The former truckie and hairdresser were desperate to buy land; this piece came with a vineyard. The wine tastes of its terroir – flinty, dusty ironstone – but they do the best food for miles (bookings essential).

Tip: the owners hold a community grape pick each February/March. Anyone can join in. Exact dates are announced on Facebook, with about a week's notice.

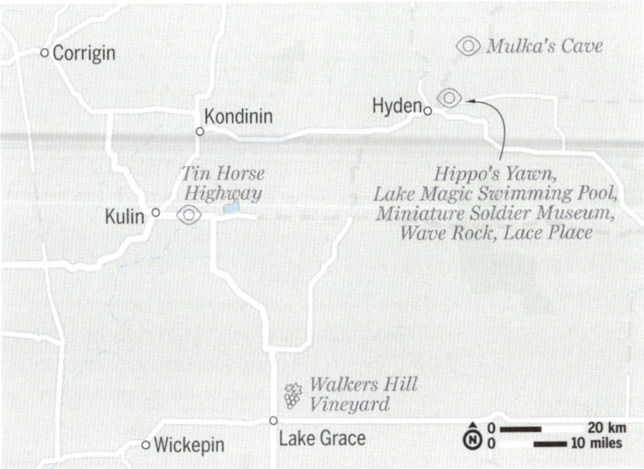

Left Hippo's Yawn
Below Mulka's Cave

Mulka's Cave

This site holds the largest collection of Noongar paintings in southwestern WA, yet few have even heard of it. While most other sites have fewer than 20 works, **Mulka's Cave** is home to more than 450 pieces on its cool, dark walls. Look carefully and you'll see hundreds of Aboriginal handprints captured with ochre spray, plus other art motifs depicted in seven colours. It's worth taking the 18km graded dirt road out – drive carefully.

Niche Collections

Now for a few things you'd never expect to find in the outback. The **Miniature Soldier Museum**, only metres from Katter Kich, features at least 10,000 army characters assembled in detailed war scenes, alongside large ships made from sardine tins, Spam cans and bottle tops. Both world wars are represented, along with others including the Napoleonic and American Civil Wars. Under the same roof, the **Lace Place** houses a vast collection of delicate creations under protective low light. Each inch of lace represents an hour of embroidery. As you exit into the adjoining cafe, gaze upwards or you'll miss the huge, butterfly-shaped dried-flower creations the owner made in the 1980s to act as insulation.

Listings

BEST OF THE REST

Best Sunset Drinks

Rooftop at QT

The city stretches out around you in all directions from the roof of the QT Perth hotel. Best seen at night when the lights are glittering, with a cocktail in hand.

Old Man & the Sea

Geraldton's only rooftop bar is perfect for sunset viewing, and not only because the cocktails come by the jug.

Shark Bay Hotel

Known locally in Denham as the 'Old Pub', Australia's most westerly boozer has the perfect sunset beer garden and all your pub favourites.

Carnarvon Hotel

When the sun's going down in Carnarvon, its namesake Fascine-front pub is the place to enjoy the show over a cool drink and a solid feed.

The Last Sunset

Overnight tours to Dirk Hartog include sundowners on the island's western tip, where you'll truly be the last people in WA watching the sunset.

First Nations Tours

Go Cultural

Walk through Perth's waterfront precinct, Elizabeth Quay, with a Noongar guide and feel as though the pavement and buildings have been stripped away, revealing the cultural use of this land before European colonisation.

Nyungar Tours

Perth's Kings Park has deep cultural significance for Noongar people. A Noongar woman will guide you over the park's treetop bridge and through its bush gardens while telling rarely heard Whadjuk Yorga (women-focused) stories.

Djurandi Dreaming

Explore Perth's southern lakes by torchlight with Noongar man Justin Martin as he shares how these freshwater sources were once vital connections to the ocean, along with other stories.

In Culture Tours

Offers immersive walking tours through sites including Fremantle, Kings Park and Rockingham. Whadjuk Noongar man Steven Jacobs shares stories of the land with heart and humour, often weaving through personal family anecdotes and reflections.

Murujuga Rock Art Tours

Learn the stories behind the world's largest rock-art site, just north of Karratha, with Murujuga Aboriginal Corporation Rangers.

Mabu Buru

The Broome-based operator's experiences include a ceremonial family gathering experience with traditional dancing.

Bundy's Cultural Tours

Bush tucker, bush medicine, spear-making and night fishing: they're all possible under the guidance of Bundy, a Bardi man who runs tours along the Dampier Peninsula.

Mimbi Caves

Gooniyandi-owned Girloorloo Tours run cultural tours through the subterranean labyrinth of Mimbi Caves, part of the ancient Devonian Reef.

Luridgii Tours

Get a personal guide through the gorges, thermal pools and Dreaming stories of Miriuwung Country by Traditional Custodians on these 4WD cultural tag-alongs, starting from Doon Doon Roadhouse. Also offers cultural awareness tours.

Southern Cross Cultural Tours

Take an inspiring journey through Bardi Jawi culture and the mangroves, paperbark forests, salt plains, creeks and springs of the Dampier Peninsula.

Uptuyu Adventures

In Nyikina Country on the Fitzroy River, 50km from the Great Northern Hwy, Neville runs 'designer' cultural tours taking in wetlands, rock art, fishing and Aboriginal communities.

Kimberley Dreamtime Adventure Tours

The Jarlmadangah Burru Aboriginal Community runs cultural tours based in Nyikina Mangala Country on Mt Anderson Station, 126km southeast of Derby. Camp under the stars, ride camels, fish, hunt, walk and learn about Aboriginal culture.

Waringarri Art & Culture Tours

Receive a traditional Welcome, explore bush foods and meet local artists at Waringarri in Kununurra on these informative 90-minute gallery tours. Their 2½-hour art and culture tours around Mirima National Park are exceptional.

Just Over the Hills

These Balanggarra family-run 4WD tag-along tours showcase local culture and rock art in the remote northeast Kimberley. Your 4WD needs to be in top condition for these tours.

More Beautiful Beaches

Elephant Rocks

Towering granite boulders look like herds of elephants standing in the water at this glorious beach near Denmark. Around the headland is similarly scenic Greens Pool.

PHILIP SCHUBERT/SHUTTERSTOCK

Mimbi Caves

Misery Beach

There's no reason to be sad at this gorgeous bay, south of Albany.

Lucky Bay

This azure bay with a campground near Esperance is so beautiful that even the local kangaroos choose to hang out here.

Bill's Bay

Coral Bay's perfectly positioned town beach. Easy access and sheltered ultramarine waters make this a favourite with everyone from snorkellers (keep to the southern end) to families.

Monkey Mia

'Beautiful with a chance of dolphins' is the forecast at Shark Bay's main beach, anchored by the RAC Monkey Mia Dolphin Resort.

80 Mile Beach

On the road to Broome is one of the most exquisite and most deserted beaches in the country (once you leave the camping area). And it's way longer than 80 miles.

Indigenous Art Centres

East Pilbara Arts Centre

One of WA's most successful art collectives, Martumili Artists has a beautiful gallery and workspace in Newman where you can admire the acclaimed, vibrant art of the Martu people.

Mangkaja Arts

Fitzroy Crossing collective uniting river and desert artists, known for their mix of bright acrylics, dot style and forays into printmaking, textiles and basket weaving.

Nagula Jarndu Women's Resource Centre

This Broome studio gallery, run by Yawuru women, showcases and sells beautiful screen- and block-printed textiles and other crafts.

Bidyadanga Artists

Bringing together inspiration from the desert to the coast, five different language groups create brilliant acrylic artworks in WA's largest Aboriginal community, two hours from Broome.

Warmun Arts

Inspect traditional ochres and learn how each is used at this wonderful arts centre in the Great Northern Hwy community of Warmiun, between Kununurra and Halls Creek.

Waringarri Aboriginal Arts

This excellent Kununurra centre hosts artists from the East Kimberley working in both traditional and contemporary styles, using ochres and acrylics alongside some etchings and lino-prints.

Scenic Flights

Broome Aviation

Half-day flights over Cape Leveque and the Horizontal Falls from Broome. Full-day tours add on Windjana Gorge, Bell Gorge and Mt Hart, Mitchell Falls or even the Bungle Bungles. Wow.

Fly Broome

Flies a loop from Broome out over the Dampier Peninsula and Buccaneer Falls to the Horizontal Falls, then lands at Cygnet Bay for an inclusive meal and pearl-farm tour.

Horizontal Falls Seaplane Adventures

Operating out of Derby, these seaplanes land on Talbot Bay where you'll transfer to high-powered speedboats for an adrenaline-packed ride through both sets of the Horizontal Falls.

HeliSpirit

The Kimberley's largest chopper outfit offers scenic flights over the Bungle Bungles, Mitchell Falls, Kununurra, King George Falls, Lake Argyle and anywhere else in the Kimberley.

Unmissable South Coast Hikes

Bluff Knoll

Hike the highest (1099m) and most well-known peak in the Stirling Ranges, a paradise for hikers and photographers: incredible biodiversity, stark jagged peaks and wildflowers.

LEANNE IRWIN/SHUTTERSTOCK

Bluff Knoll

Nancy Peak

This 5.5km loop walk offers sweeping views out to the Stirling Ranges. Reward yourself after your hike with a pizza and a local craft beer at historic Karribank Tavern.

Destination Dining

Wildflower $$$

Occupying the rooftop space of COMO The Treasury, Perth's best fine diner has a focus on local ingredients attuned to the six seasons of the Noongar calendar.

Lontara $$$

Asian flavours ripple through the menu at the Samphire resort's signature restaurant, overlooking the ocean on Rottnest Island.

Oscar's in the Valley $$

Set above the Avon River, this elegant Swan Valley classic draws diners for refined modern Australian cooking and tranquil water views. Come for a long lunch on the deck.

Luxe Island Seafood Cruise $$$

Savour a good-value seafood tasting menu aboard a private vessel with Rottnest Cruises. Before your white-tablecloth, wine-paired lunch begins, try to catch a coveted Western rock lobster in the boat's pots.

Cheap Eats

Chu Bakery $

After just one bite of the flaky raspberry almond croissant, you'll have forgotten the 15-minute wait in the queue outside. Grab a sourdough loaf while you're there. In Highgate.

Alfred's Kitchen $

Located in Guildford, it's Perth's longest-running roadside burger kitchen, with everything cooked on the grill until late.

EMMYLOU DZUBIEL/LONELY PLANET

Baked goods from Bread Local

Hooked Up Fish & Chips $

Take your blanket and find a spot to watch the sunset over Surfers Point at Prevelly while munching on delicious fish and chips. During the day, watch the surf.

Bread Local $

Esperance's renowned bakery brings ultimate beach-town vibes with bread, sandwiches and pastries of a quality on par with some of Australia's best city bakeries.

Banh Mi Up $

Tiny, hole-in-the-wall Vietnamese takeaway serving up the best banh mi between Perth and Broome right on Geraldton's main street.

The Social Society $

Everything is vegan or vegetarian and made from locally sourced organic ingredients at this Exmouth cafe.

Sampey Meats $

Carnivores can stock up for the Gibb River Rd with homemade jerky, biltong and vacuum-sealed steaks at this excellent Derby butcher.

Wild Mango $

Hip and healthy offerings here in Kununurra include breakfast burritos, salads, pancakes, chai smoothies, strong coffee and homemade gelato.

DARWIN & THE NORTHERN TERRITORY

ABORIGINAL ART | NATIONAL PARKS | OUTBACK LIFE

RESEARCHED BY SARAH REID

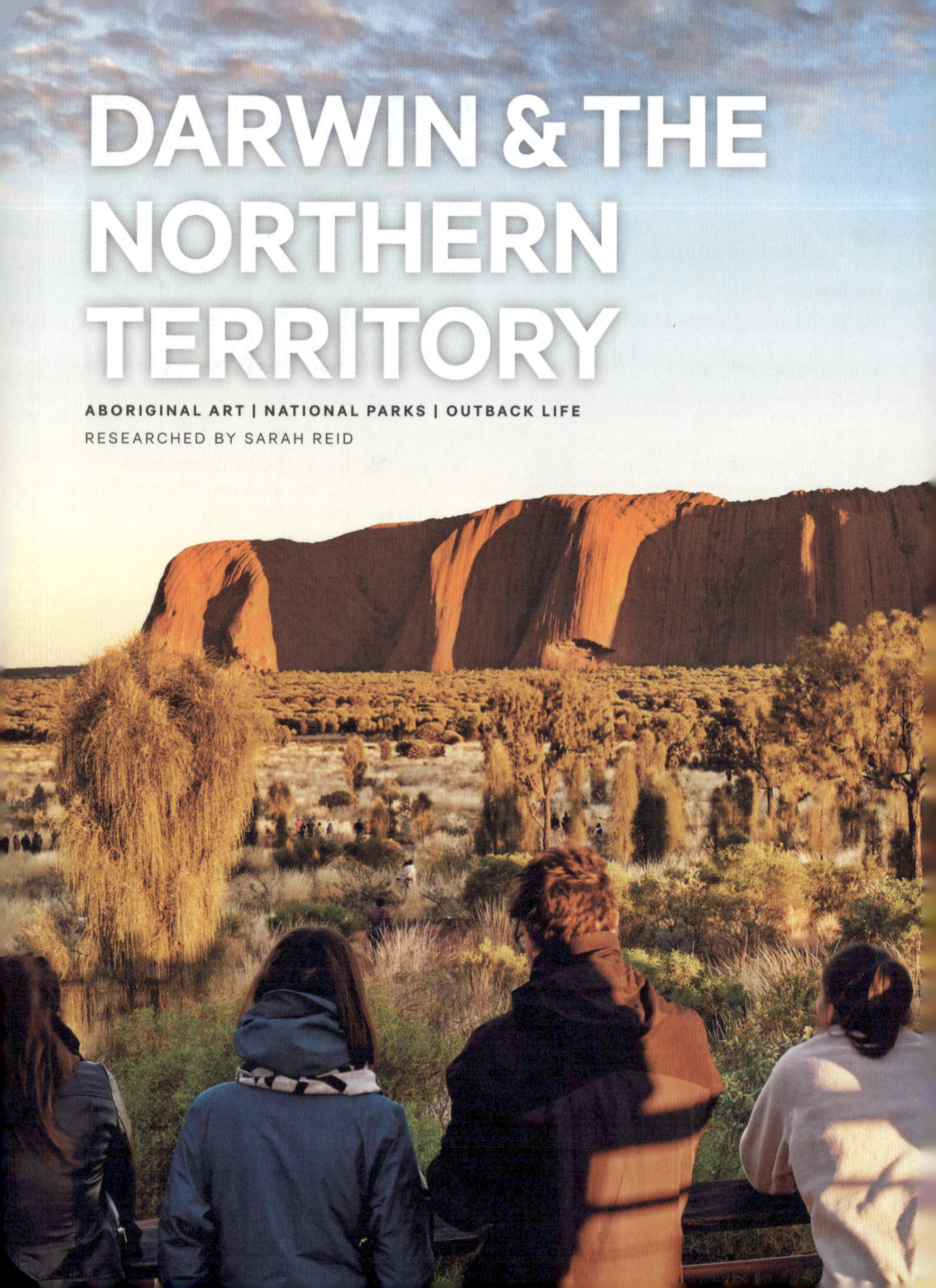

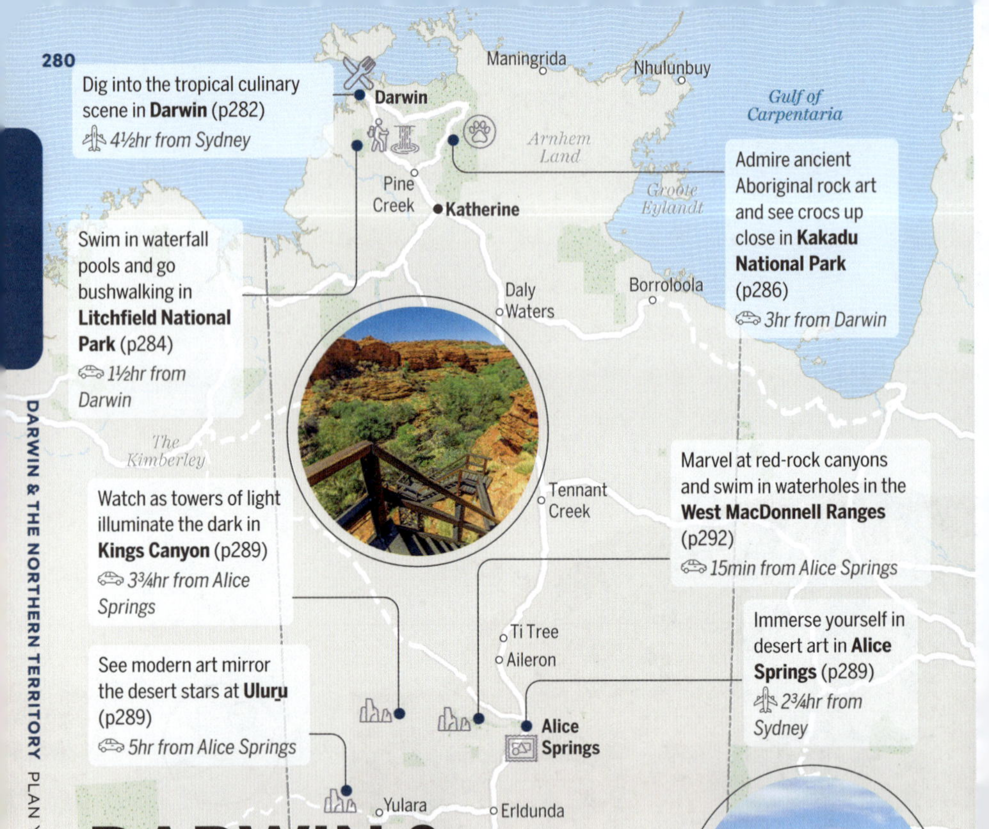

DARWIN & THE NORTHERN TERRITORY

Trip Builder

Australia's sultry northern capital is the gateway to adventures in the Top End (the northernmost part of the NT), from the rock art of Kakadu National Park to the waterfall trails of Litchfield National Park. The otherworldly landscapes and rich cultures of the Red Centre unfold to the south.

Great Australian Bight

0 — 200 km
0 — 100 miles

Practicalities

ARRIVING

Darwin International Airport Only a 15-minute taxi or Uber ride from the city.

Alice Springs Airport Situated 15km south of town. A shuttle to city accommodation meets flights.

CONNECT

Wi-fi is available in hotels and some public areas; mobile phone reception is usually restricted to towns. Telstra has the best coverage.

MONEY

Credit cards are usually accepted, but carry some cash for small purchases, when the power's down or buying art directly from artists.

WHERE TO STAY

Location	Characteristics
Darwin	Hostels, hotels spanning luxury to budget, and a campground in Winnellie.
Kakadu and Litchfield NPs	Both have basic camping. Resorts in Jabiru (Kakadu) and Batchelor (Litchfield) have more facilities.
Alice Springs	Small but good selection of accommodation across all budgets.
Uluṟu	The six hotels and campground in the township of Yulara are managed by Ayers Rock Resort. Or try luxury lodge Longitude 131.

GETTING AROUND

Car and 4WD A 2WD is generally fine for paved roads, but outback trails require a 4WD. Road distances are vast (eg 1496km from Darwin to Alice Springs) and fuel costs are high in outback regions.

Plane With long drives between the NT's main hubs, many travellers opt to fly between them.

TOP: JYK20180915/SHUTTERSTOCK
BOTTOM: MYSTIC STOCK PHOTOGRAPHY/SHUTTERSTOCK

EATING & DRINKING

The NT is a powerhouse of native foods that have sustained local Aboriginal communities for generations. From barramundi to kangaroo, you'll see many of these foods on modern menus across the state. Darwin's food scene is spiked with Southeast Asian flavours, while outback roadhouses serve up steaks and camel burgers. Don't expect anything fancy beyond Darwin, Alice Springs and Uluṟu, with the exception of remote luxury lodges. Pack ample snacks for road trips.

Best Asian food Ella by Minoli (p283), Darwin

Must-try dining Tali Wiru (p297), Uluṟu

DEC–FEB
Hot and sunny in the centre, humid up north.

MAR–MAY
Tail end of Top End rainy season.

JUN–AUG
Milder temperatures and clear skies in the desert and Top End.

SEP–NOV
Good weather but humidity building up north by October.

57 Darwin DELIGHTS

EATING | DRINKING | MARKETS

Closer to Bali than Bondi, Darwin – also known by its Larrakia name, Garramilla – is one of Australia's most multicultural cities, which is reflected in its vibrant food scene. From spicy laksa to kangaroo jerky, you can get it all here, with cracking cocktails to match.

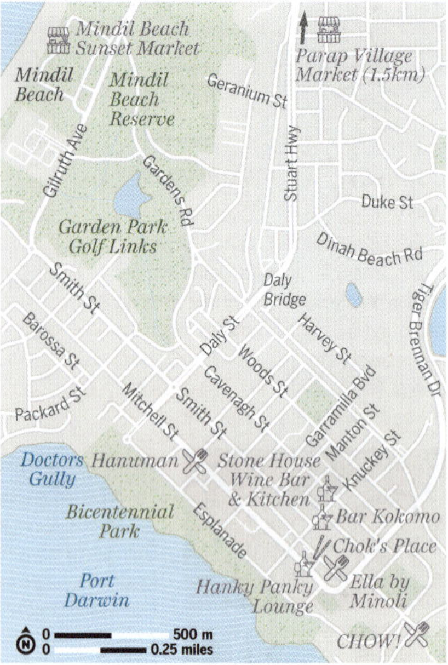

How to

When to go Some venues only open during the Dry (May to October).

Getting around Darwin's compact city centre is walkable. Admire excellent street art between venue hops.

Food tours Taste nine local plates on Darwin Gourmet Tours' signature three-hour walking tour.

Aboriginal dining Get a taste of native ingredients and support an Aboriginal-owned business at the Aboriginal Bush Traders Cafe in the city centre.

Moreish markets Darwin's biggest and most popular market, **Mindil Beach Sunset Market** springs up on the foreshore on Thursday and Sunday from 4pm to 9pm, late April to October. Food – starring indigenous ingredients and Southeast Asian flavours – is the main attraction, but there are also arts and crafts stalls. Other markets run year-round. On Saturday, the compact, food-focused **Parap Village Market** takes over Parap Shopping Village, 4km north of the city centre, from 8am to 2pm. This is the place for a stellar Southeast Asian feed (Mary's Laksa is a local favourite). Held at the Rapid Creek Business Village on Saturday and Sunday (7am to 2pm), the **Rapid Creek Market** is an Asian marketplace where tropical fruit and vegetables mingle with swirls of spices and satay smoke. Also on Sunday is **Nightcliff Market** (8am to 2pm), held

SIMON FURLONG/GETTY IMAGES

Laksa Obsession

If there's one dish that defines Darwin, it's laksa. The spicy Malay noodle soup has such a special place in the hearts of locals that in 2019 the city launched its inaugural **Darwin International Laksa Festival** (darwinlaksafestival.com.au), a month-long event in October. During the celebration, the Laksa Festival Food Tour encourages people to visit the many food venues registered and vote for their favourite dishes via the festival website. On the last Sunday of October, the Laksa Festival Finale is a celebration of all things laksa, culminating in the Laksa Festival Awards. **Chok's Place** (Smith St) and **CHOW!** (Darwin Waterfront) have both won the coveted Golden Bowl several times.

in the Nightcliff Shopping Centre. Grab something to eat and browse clothes, arts and crafts or indulge in a Thai massage.

Hot tables Top dinner choices include **Ella by Minoli** for fiery modern Sri Lankan and **Hanuman** for Southeast Asian gastronomy. **Pee Wee's at the Point** serves classic Darwin dining by the water, with dishes like wild-caught barramundi with macadamia, herbs and lemon myrtle.

Cool bars Darwin's sophisticated bar scene may surprise you. Begin your evening with piña coladas at **Bar Kokomo** or a crisp glass of fine wine at **Stone House Wine Bar & Kitchen**, then kick on at clandestine cocktail bar **Hanky Panky Lounge**.

Above Laksa

58 LITCHFIELD Discovery

WILD SWIMS | MESMERISING MOUNDS | BUSHWALKS

Smaller and more manageable than Kakadu, Litchfield National Park is doable in a day trip from Darwin, but the camping's great too. With year-round waterfalls that pour off rugged cliffs into crystal-clear cascading pools you can swim in, the 1500-sq-km national park is simply stunning.

PHILIP SCHUBERT/SHUTTERSTOCK

Pre-Park History

Established around 1906 just north of Walker Creek, the eerie **Bamboo Creek Tin Mine** provides an insight into the hardships of the era's tin miners. Interpretive panels offer insights as you wander its rusting relics, abandoned along with the mine in 1955. It's about 1km return from the car park.

How to

Getting here and around Litchfield is a 90-minute drive south of Darwin. The main attractions are 2WD-accessible; you'll need a 4WD to see the rocky outcrops of the **Lost City**.

When to go The Dry (May to October) is busy, but also the best for swimming and hiking.

Tours Recommended operators include **Northern Territory Indigenous Tours** and **Ethical Adventures**.

Don't miss Paddle in the oasis-like natural pool at Berry Springs on the way to or from Darwin.

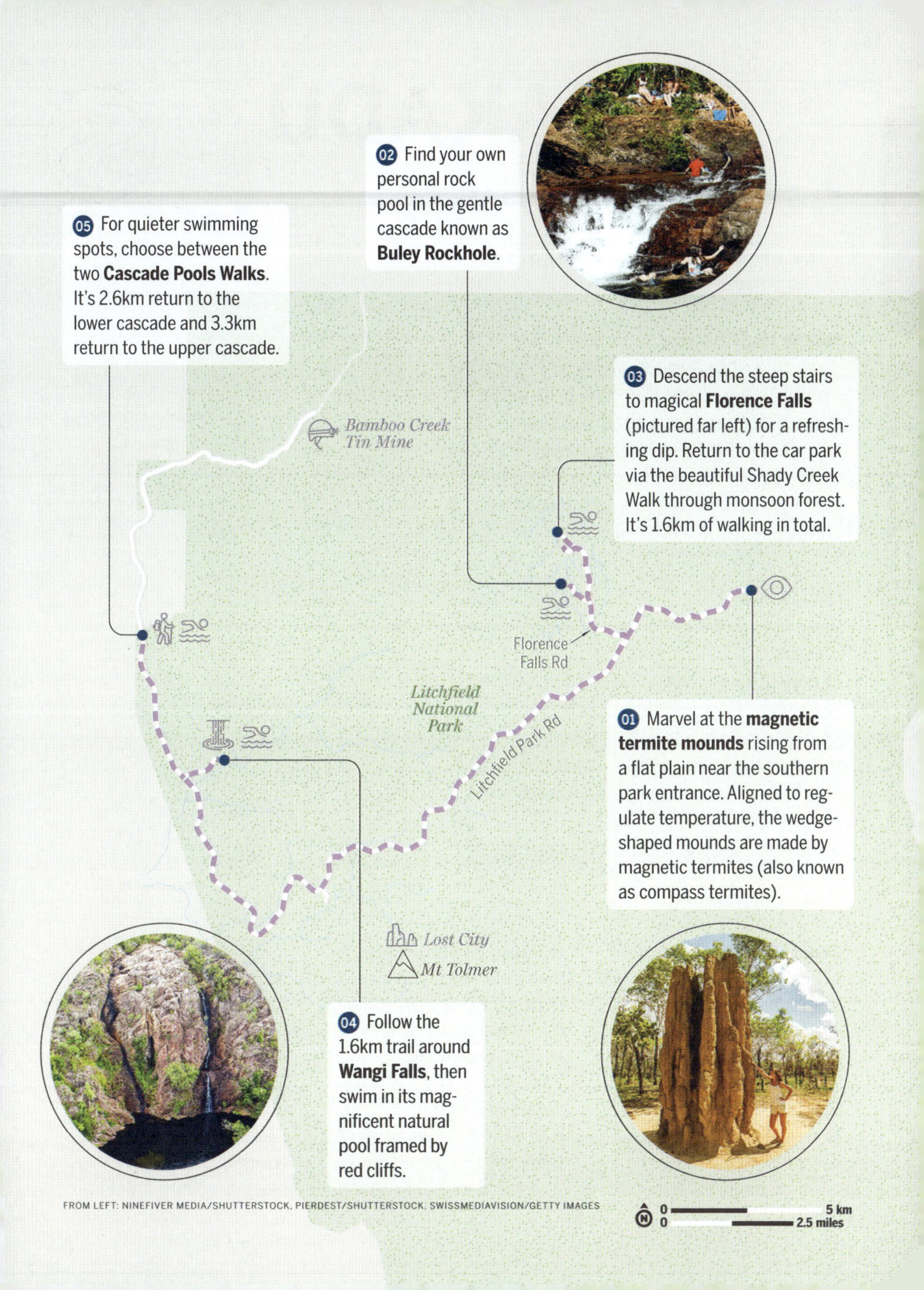

01 Marvel at the **magnetic termite mounds** rising from a flat plain near the southern park entrance. Aligned to regulate temperature, the wedge-shaped mounds are made by magnetic termites (also known as compass termites).

02 Find your own personal rock pool in the gentle cascade known as **Buley Rockhole**.

03 Descend the steep stairs to magical **Florence Falls** (pictured far left) for a refreshing dip. Return to the car park via the beautiful Shady Creek Walk through monsoon forest. It's 1.6km of walking in total.

04 Follow the 1.6km trail around **Wangi Falls**, then swim in its magnificent natural pool framed by red cliffs.

05 For quieter swimming spots, choose between the two **Cascade Pools Walks**. It's 2.6km return to the lower cascade and 3.3km return to the upper cascade.

FROM LEFT: NINEFIVER MEDIA/SHUTTERSTOCK, PIERDEST/SHUTTERSTOCK, SWISSMEDIAVISION/GETTY IMAGES

59 KAKADU Calling

ROCK ART | WILDLIFE | WATERHOLES

How do you see a 20,000-sq-km park in a short space of time? Even if you only have one day to see Kakadu, it's possible to get a thrilling taste of the Top End's showpiece national park, where ancient culture threads through a savagely beautiful slice of the Australian wilderness.

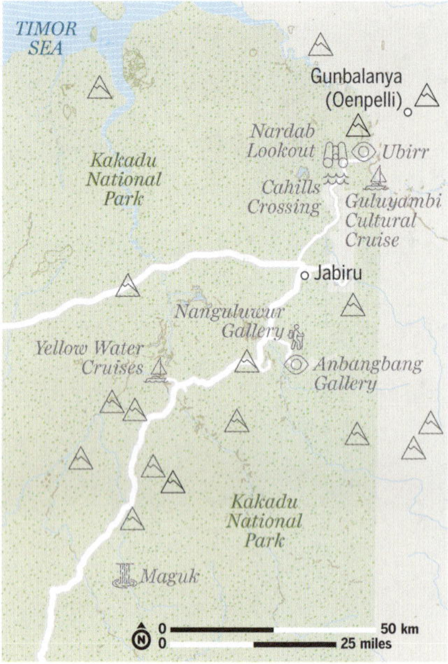

How to

When to go For the best access, go in the Dry (May to October).

Getting there Your own wheels offer more flexibility (major attractions are 2WD-accessible), but tours from Darwin are also available.

Park pass Valid for seven days, park passes (adult/child $40/20; kakadu.gov.au) cost less in the low season (November to mid-May).

Be crocwise Only swim where there are designated safe swimming signs. Visit becrocwise.nt.gov.au for more croc safety advice.

Crocodiles It wouldn't be a trip to Kakadu without a visit to **Cahills Crossing**. Salties (saltwater crocodiles) line up along this concrete causeway on the East Alligator River, 285km east of Darwin, to feast on fish as the tide rushes in. Watch from the bank, or climb aboard a **Guluyambi Cultural Cruise** to learn about crocs in local Aboriginal cultures and see some rock art upriver. Another great way to see Kakadu's crocs (and myriad birdlife) is a Cooinda wetland cruise with **Yellow Water Cruises**.

Rock art The closest major Aboriginal rock-art site to Darwin is **Ubirr**, less than 3km from Cahills Crossing. Above its five main galleries (look for the painting of a Tasmanian tiger, which has been extinct on mainland Australia for over 2000 years), the magnificent **Nardab Lookout** is the best place to enjoy a Kakadu

HEATHER RUTH ROSE/SHUTTERSTOCK

Camping in Kakadu

There are more than 20 campgrounds in Kakadu National Park; some are free, while those with more facilities require fees paid in cash (from $6 to $15 per adult), so don't forget to bring change. With sites available on a first-come, first-served basis, arrive early in the Dry to snag a good spot.

There's a supermarket in Jabiru and a small store in Cooinda, but it's best to bring everything you'll need from Darwin, especially drinking water. Alcohol is permitted only in the Mardukal campground, near Cooinda. You can also camp at several privately run holiday parks in Jabiru, and the Ngurrungurrudjba (Yellow Water) Campground & Caravan Park at Cooinda.

sunset. Deeper inside the park, the **Burrungkuy** (Nourlangie) rock-art site is similarly spectacular. Its main **Anbangbang Gallery**, featuring vivid Dreaming characters, is wheelchair-accessible. Take the 3.5km-return walk (allow 1½ hours) to the **Nanguluwur Gallery** to see a good example of 'contact art', a painting of a two-masted sailing ship towing a dinghy.

Wild swimming About 100km southwest of Burrungkuy, **Maguk** (Barramundi Gorge) is one of Kakadu's prettiest waterfall pools; the 2km-return access trail is framed by lush pandanuses. The gravel access road is best suited to 4WDs.

Above Crocodile, Kakadu National Park

60 Modern Art in the RED CENTRE

INDIGENOUS ART | CONTEMPORARY ART | CULTURAL HISTORY

From Alice Springs (Mparntwe) to Uluṟu, Aboriginal art is central to the Red Centre experience. The installations that light up iconic landscapes rank among the most exciting examples of Australian public art in recent times.

JESSICA LOCKHART/LONELY PLANET

How to

Getting here Fly into **Alice Springs Airport** or **Ayers Rock Airport** near Yulara.

When to go It gets fiercely hot in summer; avoid the months from November to February.

Accommodation Rooms can be eyewateringly expensive; sign up to get updates on cheaper deals from Ayers Rock Resort (ayersrockresort.com.au).

Picnic with a view Pack some goodies and head to the Uluṟu sunset area for dinner.

MIKE GREENSLADE/ALAMY

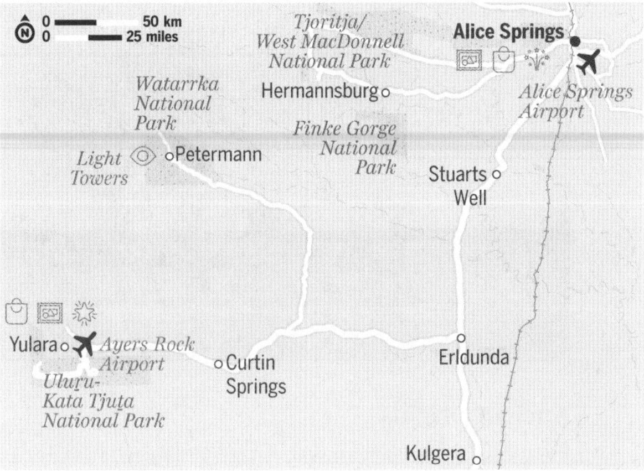

Top left *Field of Light* by Bruce Munro
Bottom left Araluen Arts Centre

Alice Springs Make time for the excellent Aboriginal art galleries in Alice Springs. The **Araluen Arts Centre** is a great first stop, especially if you're a fan of Albert Namatjira's exquisite watercolour landscapes. Visit **Papunya Tula Artists**, with Western Desert canvases that draw on deep traditions but are as fresh as when dot painting first took the world by storm. Then sit with modern desert artists Marie Ryder and Kevin Bird for **Ayeye Atyenhe Art**. They'll take you through painting techniques, cultural meanings and the evolving world of desert art.

Kings Canyon Experience the **Light Towers**, a 2023 installation that brings light and colour to the desert night beneath a spray of stars at Kings Canyon Resort.

Uluṟu Step into the haunting half-light of dusk and fall silent amid the **Field of Light**, an immensely popular 2016 art installation by Bruce Munro extended until at least mid-2027. Then be mesmerised by newer light-and-sound shows, including the sensory dawn experience **Sunrise Journeys** and **Wintjiri Wiṟu**, which sees more than 1100 drones take flight in the evening sky to depict a chapter of the ancient Mala story. In Yulara, Uluṟu's tourism hub, the **Gallery of Central Australia** features revolving exhibitions and champions emerging artists. Near the base of Uluṟu, **Maruku Arts** is a must-visit Aboriginal art centre.

Celebrating Indigenous Art

Alice Springs hosts a rich array of festivals during the cooler months. Aboriginal-run **Parrtjima: A Festival in Light**, held over 10 days in April, sees live performances and sound-and-light shows playing off the West MacDonnell Ranges and sites around town to soulful effect.

Typically running across September and October, **Desert Mob** brings together hundreds of artists to celebrate desert culture in Alice Springs, with exhibitions, markets, artist talks, workshops and more. It's a great opportunity to buy Aboriginal art directly from the artists.

Aboriginal Art in NT: Ancient & Modern

VENERABLE TRADITIONS AND NEW DIRECTIONS

Australia's oldest known rock art is 47,000 years old. By comparison, the Western Desert Art Movement began just half a century ago. And some of what you'll see in the Northern Territory today could have been made as recently as yesterday. It's an exciting blend of ancient and contemporary.

Left Landscape around Papunya
Centre Rock art, Burrungkuy (p287)
Right Yubu Napa Art Gallery, Alice Springs

KASIA PAWLIKOWSKI/SHUTTERSTOCK

Ancient Origins

Over 5000 of Australia's 100,000-odd Aboriginal rock-art sites are found in Kakadu National Park alone. Some of the artworks are 20,000 years old, while the newest significant paintings date from the 1960s.

Rock art takes two main forms: petroglyphs (rock engravings) and pictographs (drawings or paintings). The Northern Territory is famous for its paintings, particularly the detailed X-ray style seen in Kakadu and Arnhem Land depicting skeletons and inner organs – and sometimes even what the subject has eaten. Typically created with ochre, a natural earth pigment, mixed with a natural binder like saliva, blood, animal fat or honey, these paintings aren't just decorative. They are powerful expressions of culture, spirituality and identity still relevant to Aboriginal peoples today. They also serve as a crucial historical record, documenting everything from the historical ranges of extinct wildlife to how humans adapted to rising sea levels.

Some rock art could only be painted by people with the right knowledge. Other paintings were created for educational purposes. The act of repainting or overpainting a site is a vital part of cultural practice for many Aboriginal groups. While it continues in some places, it has ceased in many others, either because of conservation-based restrictions or because nobody with the cultural authority to renew the artworks remains. Combined with other threats including climate change, pollution, vandals, development and animals, there are fears that Australia's rock art may disappear by 2060.

LOUIELEA/SHUTTERSTOCK

ALEXANDRE ROSA/SHUTTERSTOCK

Modern Movement

In 1971, a Sydney schoolteacher named Geoffrey Bardon arrived in Papunya, 240km by road northwest of Alice Springs, to teach at the local primary school. Concerned about low rates of school attendance, he introduced paints and asked students to paint a mural on one of the school building's walls. The children quickly lost interest, but some of the town's Elders took over and began to paint.

The dot-painting style that the Elders used was both new and very old, steeped in the tradition of sand drawings used as visual props for storytelling. After they finished the mural, they began painting on boards, and Bardon took the first few back to Alice Springs. The original paintings sold there for $20 each, but they now fetch hundreds or even thousands of dollars at auction. Australia's Western Desert art movement was born. More than 50 years later, Papunya Tula Artists (p289) in the heart of Alice Springs is the standard-bearer for the movement.

Just like rock art, modern Aboriginal art is as diverse as the artists who create it.

Just like rock art, modern Aboriginal art is as diverse as the artists who create it. Technology, including light and sound, is increasingly being used to deepen our understanding of stories and landscapes.

Buying Aboriginal Art Ethically

Art is a life source for Aboriginal communities, both culturally and economically. Art sales allow Aboriginal people to remain on their traditional homelands – where other employment opportunities tend to be scarce – and share culture through their art.

This is why making an ethical art purchase is so important. A good way to gauge if a sale is ethical is to ask whether the seller is connected to the **Indigenous Art Code** (indigenousartcode.org), especially if it's a city gallery. Ethical dealers will be comfortable discussing how much the artists will receive from the sale. Check too for an authenticity document, which may be a scannable QR code.

61 Rove the RANGES

ROCK FORMATIONS | SWIMMING HOLES | HIKING

Just outside Alice Springs, the rugged ridgelines of the West MacDonnell Ranges seem shaped by otherworldly forces. Indeed, this ancient rocky wilderness is an important cultural landscape sheltering a number of standout stops, from rugged gorges to serene waterholes.

NIAL FULTON/SHUTTERSTOCK

Trip Notes

Getting around Hiring a car offers more flexibility, with major attractions 2WD-accessible. Or take a half- or full-day tour from Alice Springs.

When to go Visit from May to September for the most comfortable daytime temperatures. It gets *very* hot here.

Dining With only a few places to eat in the area, including a kiosk at Standley Chasm, it's a good idea to bring a picnic lunch.

Larapinta Trail

A spectacular long-distance trek through Australia's Red Centre, the 223km **Larapinta Trail** follows the spine of the West MacDonnell Ranges from near Alice Springs to Mt Sonder. Split into 12 sections, the full trail takes 12 to 14 days to complete, with 26 designated campgrounds along the way.

01 Red cliffs tower over a near-permanent waterhole at **Ormiston Gorge** (Kwartatuma), ideal for a dip. The Ghost Gum Walk (2.4km loop, allow one to 1½ hours) offers excellent views from a lookout.

02 An important place and cultural resource for Western Arrernte people for millennia, the vivid cliffs of the **Ochre Pits** (pictured left and below) reveal ancient seams of natural pigments used for ceremonies and rock art.

03 Thousands of years of floods have carved out **Ellery Creek Big Hole** (Udepata), a huge permanent waterhole surrounded by red cliffs that glow crimson at sunset.

04 Owned and managed by the local Western Arrernte community, **Standley Chasm** (Angkerle Atwatye) is a sacred women's site. Its sheer red walls rocket 80m skyward.

05 A level trail traces a dry riverbed lined with river gums and desert grasses at the spectacular natural gorge known as **Simpsons Gap** (Rungutjirpa; pictured above).

CLOCKWISE FROM TOP: JESSICA LOCKHART/LONELY PLANET, BENNY MARTY/SHUTTERSTOCK, FRITZ16/SHUTTERSTOCK

Outback Bush

FOODS & MEDICINE

03

01

02

04

05

01 Kangaroo
This tasty lean meat has fuelled Aboriginal communities for generations, with roo bones used for tools and its skin for clothing.

02 Green tree ant
High in protein and traditionally also used to treat coughs and colds, green tree ants have a unique citrus flavour.

03 Desert quandong
This tart, vitamin C–rich 'bush peach' is delicious in jams, chutneys and sauces. Also used for its antibacterial and anti-inflammatory properties.

04 Witchetty grub
These plump, protein-packed grubs taste like scrambled eggs when cooked. Also traditionally used to treat burns.

05 Crocodile
An important food for some Top End Aboriginal groups, croc meat features on many contemporary local menus; it tastes like a mix of fish and chicken.

06 Emu bush
Eremophila, commonly

known as emu bush, is a sacred medicinal and ceremonial plant with antiseptic and antibacterial properties.

07 Spinifex
Along with wattleseed and native millet, spinifex seeds can be ground into flour to make 'bush bread', also known as damper.

08 Bush tomato
Also known as desert raisins, bush tomatoes are rich in antioxidants, vitamins and minerals. This caramel-y desert snack is also used for immune support.

09 Emu
Emu is prized for its tasty lean meat, while emu oil is known as an anti-inflammatory.

10 Kakadu plum
These small, tart fruits are renowned as the world's richest source of vitamin C. The tree's bark is used to treat skin ailments.

11 Native waterlily
These violet lilies blooming in the wetlands of Kakadu provide nutritious roots, stems, seeds and even bulbs. Crushed leaves repel leeches.

Listings

BEST OF THE REST

Must-Visit Museums

Museum & Art Gallery of the Northern Territory

Top End–centric exhibits include an excellent Aboriginal-art collection and an entire room devoted to Cyclone Tracy. In Darwin.

Darwin Military Museum

At this innovative museum and multimedia experience, you can hear personal accounts of those affected by, and those who participated in, Australia's defence during WWII.

Royal Flying Doctor Service

Don virtual-reality glasses at this Stokes Hill Wharf museum to witness in vivid detail the 1942 Japanese bombing raid on Darwin Harbour, harnessing tech with flying colours.

Araluen Cultural Precinct

Alice Springs' cultural hub is home to the Araluen Arts Centre, Museum of Central Australia and Central Australia Aviation Museum.

Telegraph Station

The old telegraph station in Alice Springs, which used to relay messages between Darwin and Adelaide, offers a glimpse of the town's early days as a European settlement. It's a 4km walk or cycle north from Todd Mall.

Uluṟu-Kata Tjuṯa Cultural Centre

Just 1km from the rock, the centre's displays and exhibits focus on Tjukurpa (the foundation of Aṉangu culture), and on the natural and human history of the park.

Typically Territorian Festivals

Beer Can Regatta

This bonkers one-day Darwin festival in July features races for boats made from beer cans.

Darwin Aboriginal Art Fair

This four-day August festival at the Darwin Convention Centre showcases Indigenous art from communities throughout the NT.

Darwin Fringe Festival

The biggest platform for emerging, independent and experimental artists in the NT runs for 10 days in July.

Darwin Festival

Australia's hottest winter arts festival transforms Darwin for 18 days in August.

Tiwi Cultural Festival & Tiwi Islands Football Grand Final

This combined two-day festival kicks off with a day of cultural festivities, followed by the Australian Rules football final, both in Wurrumiyanga on Bathurst Island. SeaLink ferries shuttle attendees across from Darwin.

Camel Cup

A carnival atmosphere prevails in mid-July during the running of the Camel Cup at Blatherskite Park in Alice Springs.

CYNTHIA A JACKSON/SHUTTERSTOCK

Royal Flying Doctor Service

Henley-on-Todd Regatta

These boat races on the dry bed of Alice Springs' Todd River are a light-hearted denial of reality. The boats are bottomless; the crews' legs stick through and they run the course.

fabAlice Festival

Alice Springs' vibrant LGBTIQ+ scene brings its A-game for this four-day celebration of drag, diversity and cabaret.

Outback Dining Hitlist

Daly Waters Pub $$

Stopping for a beer and a feed at an outback roadhouse is a quintessential experience. Just off the Stuart Hwy, this historic pub (built in 1930) is chock-full of character, and the grub's good, too.

Warung Makan Alice $

Darwin isn't the only place you can find fantastic Southeast Asian food in the NT. The first Indonesian restaurant in Alice Springs serves up authentic, good-value dishes from *mie goreng* (fried noodles) to beef rendang.

The Locals $$

Fuel up with a hearty breakfast at this Alice Springs favourite before a day exploring the West MacDonnell Ranges, or swing by later on for a refreshing gin cocktail.

Kings Creek Station Cafe $$

Do your bit for the desert and order a camel burger. Camel meat is sourced from the outback's vast feral (wild) population.

Tali Wiru $$$

Uluṟu's signature fine-dining experience includes a fabulous four-course dinner served in the desert dunes, with a didgeridoo performance and Indigenous storytelling.

KATACARIX/SHUTTERSTOCK

Daly Waters Pub

Sounds of Silence $$$

A bit easier on the wallet than Tali Wiru, this three-course buffet dinner at Uluṟu is accompanied by a star talk beneath the southern night sky.

Stuart Highway Swim Stops

Leliyn

This impressive series of cascading waterfalls and natural swimming holes (formerly Edith Falls) in Nitmiluk National Park is a worthy detour on a Stuart Hwy road trip.

Bitter Springs

In Mataranka's Elsey National Park, this natural hot spring is perfectly clear and around 34°C all year. It's just 3km from the Stuart Hwy.

Urban Wildlife Encounters

Alice Springs Desert Park

The creatures of central Australia are housed in predominantly open-air exhibits that faithfully recreate the animals' natural habitats: inland river, sand country and woodland.

Crocosaurus Cove

Can't get to Kakadu? Some of the largest crocs in captivity can be seen in aquariums and pools at this Darwin attraction.

Practicalities

Right Blue Mountains (p68), New South Wales

EASY STEPS FROM THE AIRPORT TO THE CITY CENTRE

Located 8km south of central Sydney, Sydney Airport (officially Sydney Kingsford Smith Airport; pictured below) is Australia's busiest air hub. The international (T1) and domestic (T2 and T3) terminals are 4km apart on either side of the runways. Each has a train station. Melbourne, Brisbane and Perth Airports are also major international gateways.

AT THE AIRPORT

SIM CARDS
Available from the Optus and Vodafone stores in the T1 arrivals hall. Major supermarkets like Woolworths often have better-value options, or you can purchase a digital SIM. If you're travelling through rural Australia, Telstra offers the best coverage.

FOREIGN EXCHANGE BOOTHS
Operate in the arrivals hall of Sydney Airport, but airport ATMs offer better rates; choose one belonging to your home bank's global ATM network for lower fees.

STEPAN SKOROBOGADKO/SHUTTERSTOCK

FREE WI-FI Connect to Free SYD Wi-Fi, then follow the prompts. Connectivity is reasonable, with coverage reaching taxi and Uber stands.

ATMS Located in the arrivals hall; stick to ATMs belonging to major banks (ANZ, Commonwealth Bank, Westpac), not exchange bureaus.

CHARGING STATIONS Found throughout T1, including wireless charging stations. Cables are provided for both Android and Apple phones.

ENTRY FORMALITIES

Duty free Limits per incoming passenger include 50 cigarettes and 2.25L of alcohol (for passengers aged 18 and over) and general goods up to the value of $900 ($450 for people aged under 18).

Biosecurity Quarantine regulations are strict, so declare all goods of animal or vegetable origin. Flowers and fresh food (including meats and cheeses) are prohibited.

GETTING TO THE CITY CENTRE

Train Rail services connect the international and domestic terminals to central Sydney (around $22) in 15 minutes. Trains run every six to 22 minutes from 4.22am (4.42pm weekends) to around midnight.

Opal Sydney's public-transport network runs on a ticketing system called Opal (opal.com.au). Rechargeable, 'tap-on, tap-off' Opal cards for adults and children are available from WH Smith (international terminal), NewsLink and Relay (domestic terminal), and both airport train stations. Minimum credit load is $10/5 per adult/child ($35 at airport stations).

HOW MUCH FOR A...

Train
$22
15 mins

Taxi
$60–80
20 mins

Bus + train
from $4.60

Taxi A $60 flat fee ($80 for maxi taxi) and takes around 20 to 40 minutes. Pickup is from the front of the terminals.

Ride-share There is a dedicated Uber pickup zone at the end of the taxi rank at T1. T2/T3 domestic terminals use the priority pickup zones; follow the signs.

Bus Bus 420 connects the terminals to nearby Banksia train station, from where regular trains run to Central. Download the TripView app for planning.

OTHER POINTS OF ENTRY

Melbourne Airport This is Australia's second-busiest international gateway after Sydney. It services daily nonstop flights to destinations in New Zealand, the Pacific, Gulf countries, Asia and the Americas.

Perth Airport International flights to Perth are increasing, and the airport services regular interstate flights.

Other airports Brisbane Airport serves numerous nonstop international flights, as well as an extensive network of flights within Queensland. It also has good ground connections to the Gold Coast and Sunshine Coast. A handful of nonstop international flights also reach Gold Coast, Sunshine Coast and Cairns Airports.

International cruises Cruise ships dock at one of two terminals in Sydney. The Overseas Passenger Terminal in Circular Quay is handily located right in the city centre, but the less convenient White Bay Cruise Terminal is in inner-west Rozelle. The latter is roughly a 5km taxi or Uber ride from central Sydney. In Melbourne, international cruise ships dock at Station Pier, Port Melbourne, a 4km tram, taxi or Uber ride from the city centre. Other major cruise-ship terminals include Brisbane, Cairns, Darwin, Fremantle (Perth), Adelaide and Hobart.

TRANSPORT TIPS TO HELP YOU GET AROUND

Australia is huge, so getting from A to B requires some thought. While driving offers the freedom to travel at your own pace and explore more remote areas poorly serviced by trains and buses, the country's affordable internal flights will save you some long travel days when moving between distant locations.

CAMPERVAN & CAR HIRE

Most car-rental companies in Australia require drivers to be over the age of 21; some add a surcharge for drivers under 25. When booking, check if unlimited kilometres are included – it's almost essential in Australia, as extra kilometres can add to your costs considerably.

DRIVING LICENCES

To drive in Australia you'll need to hold a current driving licence from your home country. If the licence isn't in English, you'll also need to carry an International Driving Permit, issued in your home country.

CAR RENTAL PER DAY

from $120

Petrol approx $1.98 per litre

Sydney Harbour Bridge/Tunnel toll from $2.76

RESPECT THE RULES Road rules are strictly enforced. Speed- and red-light cameras are common, and being just a few kilometres over the limit can land you a hefty fine. High-tech cameras can now also detect motorists handling mobile phones while driving, which is illegal and subject to heavy fines. At roadside tram and light-rail stops, always stop behind the tram until the doors have closed and any disembarking passengers are safely off the road.

AUTOMOBILE ASSOCIATIONS Every state and territory has its own automobile club, among them NSW's NRMA (mynrma.com.au), Victoria's RACV (racv.com.au), Queensland's RACQ (racq.com.au), and WA's RAC (rac.com.au). All are handy resources for road rules and driving tips, as well as insurance and holiday information.

ROOS AHEAD Kangaroos sometimes jump onto country roads, especially at night, dawn and dusk. Avoid driving at these times. If a roo does leap out in front of you, brake in as straight a line as possible to wipe off speed, and only then swerve if safe.

DRIVING ESSENTIALS

- KEEP LEFT — Drive on the left; the steering wheel is on the right.
- 50 — Speed limit is 100km/h or 110km/h; 50km/h in urban areas unless otherwise posted.
- 0.05% — Blood-alcohol limit is 0.05% (0% for drivers on a learner's or provisional licence).
- Seatbelts are mandatory for all passengers; small children must be belted into an approved safety seat.
- Give way to the right at intersections and roundabouts.

FLYING Time pressure, combined with the scale of the Australian continent, can make air travel a very convenient option. The country's flight network is extensive, safe and generally competitive. Qantas (qantas.com) is the flag carrier, with Virgin Australia (virginaustralia.com) the nation's other full-service airline. Other carriers include Rex (rex.com.au) and low-cost carrier Jetstar (jetstar.com).

BUS & TRAIN Greyhound Australia operates an extensive network along the east coast, and charter buses run along the main coast road between Perth and Broome, and between Perth and Kununurra or Wyndham. Long-distance train travel on the east coast is comfortable and affordable but slow.

BICYCLE Cycling around Australia is possible, but distances can be gruelling, so considerable fitness and excellent planning are essential. In the major cities, kerbside bike lanes and off-road trails are increasingly common; invest in a heavy-duty lock to avoid theft. Bike helmets are compulsory nationwide.

KNOW YOUR CARBON FOOTPRINT A domestic flight from Sydney to Melbourne would emit about 196kg of carbon dioxide per passenger. A car carrying four people would emit around 75kg of carbon dioxide per person, while a train would emit about 76kg of carbon dioxide. There are numerous carbon calculators online. Try MyClimate: co2.myclimate.org/en/calculate_emissions

ROAD DISTANCE CHART (KM)

MAINLAND AUSTRALIA

	Adelaide	Brisbane	Broome	Byron Bay	Cairns	Melbourne	Perth	Sydney
Brisbane	2000							
Broome	4000	4700						
Byron Bay	1900	160	4800					
Cairns	3000	1700	3950	1900				
Melbourne	725	1800	4700	1600	2800			
Perth	2700	4400	2000	4300	5300	3400		
Sydney	1375	900	5200	750	2400	900	3900	
Uluru	1600	3300	3200	3200	2700	2300	2000	2800

TASMANIA

	Bicheno	Cradle Mountain	Devonport	Hobart	Launceston
Cradle Mountain	280				
Devonport	240	85			
Hobart	180	320	250		
Launceston	180	150	100	200	
Queenstown	380	120	190	260	240

SAFE TRAVEL

Australia is one of the safest travel destinations in the world. That said, it pays to use common sense and to be aware of the few but real risks you may encounter by the water, in the bush and on city streets.

SWIMMING Hazards include rips, sharks, jellyfish and, in northern Queensland, crocodiles; heed safety signs and swim between the flags where surf lifesavers are on beach patrol. There's also sunburn: wear SPF50+ sunscreen, a broad hat and sunglasses, particularly in the warmer months.

BUSHFIRES Bushfires can be fast-moving and unpredictable, especially in spring and summer. Check the fire danger rating, which ranges from Low-Moderate to Catastrophic, for the district you're in. If fires are in your area, pay attention to the news and follow any orders to evacuate. One of the best apps for monitoring wildfires is Fires Near Me.

URBAN SAFETY While crime rates are relatively low, avoid walking alone late at night and never leave valuables in a parked car, especially within sight. Keep an eye on your belongings in public places and be cautious if someone offers you a drink in a bar; drink spiking is not unheard of, especially for women.

Bushwalking Always choose a trail within your realm of fitness and experience, and check with local authorities for weather and track updates. Also, tell someone where you are going and when you will be back.

DAVIDF/GETTY IMAGES

KEN GRIFFITHS/SHUTTERSTOCK

Snakes You're very unlikely to encounter snakes in the city. In bushland, urban or rural, stick to trails and avoid long grass. If you see a snake, leave it alone. If bitten, call an ambulance.

INSURANCE
Essential for all travellers. Some policies specifically exclude activities such as scuba diving, skiing and even bushwalking. Make sure the policy you choose fully covers you for your planned activities and interests.

HITCHHIKING
Despite the general friendliness of Australians, hitching a ride is dangerous and never recommended, whether you're in the country or the city. This applies to both solo travellers and those travelling in pairs.

QUICK TIPS TO HELP YOU MANAGE YOUR MONEY

CREDIT CARDS Visa and MasterCard are widely accepted for accommodation, activities, meals and drinks, and are essential when renting a car. Contactless payment is the norm, and Apple Pay and Google Pay are increasingly popular. Credit cards can be used for cash advances at ATMs and banks, but charges apply. Diners Club and American Express (Amex) aren't as widely accepted in Australia and may incur surcharges.

CHEAPER TRAVEL
In big cities, using a rechargeable transport card is often cheaper than buying single tickets; check your destination's transport website for fares.

PAYING THE BILL
While most cafes have table service, it's common to pay at the counter when you leave. You may also need to order at the counter.

CURRENCY

Australian dollar

HOW MUCH FOR A...

Flat white
$6

Pint of craft beer
$14

Cafe lunch for 2
$55

MONEY-CHANGERS Foreign currency can be changed at most Australian banks and licensed money-changers including Travelex, but the exchange rate for cash withdrawals from an ATM will always be superior.

ATMS & EFTPOS
ATMs are widespread throughout Australia, including in smaller towns. Eftpos terminals – usually offering contactless transactions – are ubiquitous at retailers and hospitality venues and used for even very small transactions.

BARGAINING
Gentle haggling is OK at some weekend markets, but it's generally not done in Australia. It's acceptable to ask for a small discount on expensive items when paying cash or buying more than one item.

TAXES & REFUNDS A flat 10% goods and services tax (GST) is applied to most items and experiences for sale and is included in the price quoted. If you purchase goods with a total minimum value of $300 from any one supplier no more than 60 days before you leave Australia, you are entitled to a refund of any GST paid under the Tourist Refund Scheme (TRS). For details, search TRS on the Australian Border Force (abf.gov.au) website.

TIPPING
While tipping is not obligatory in Australia, many locals leave a modest tip (usually around 10% of the total bill) at restaurants where service has been exceptional. At cafes with great table service, leave the change or tip a dollar or two. In taxis, round up the fare to the nearest dollar.

POSITIVE-IMPACT TRAVEL

Tips to leave a lighter footprint, support local and have a positive impact on local communities.

ON THE ROAD

Report injured wildlife If you come across an injured native animal, contact the relevant state's wildlife-rescue organisation. For more information, see wires.org.au (NSW), wildlife.vic.gov.au (Victoria) or wrq.org.au (Queensland).

Consider renting an electric vehicle Most of the big hire companies at least have hybrids available.

Grey water If you're travelling in a campervan or caravan, make your grey water more environmentally friendly by choosing natural, plant-based soaps and detergents, dry-wiping plates and cutlery with paper towels before washing up, and pouring vinegar and baking soda down drains to clean them. Empty your grey-water tanks regularly.

Choose reusable bags, cups and cutlery These make a handy ecofriendly travel kit.

GEKKO GALLERY/SHUTTERSTOCK

GIVE BACK

You can help save koalas affected by fires, deforestation and disease by donating to the Australia Koala Foundation (savethekoala.com) or the World Wildlife Fund (wwf.org.au).

Volunteer a few hours of your time to an Australian Conservation Foundation (acf.org.au) or Conservation Volunteers Australia (conservationvolunteers.com.au) project. These range from planting and weeding to beach-litter clean-ups.

Broome volunteer opportunities are offered by Roebuck Bay Working Group, Broome Bird Observatory and Environs Kimberley.

Eat and shop at places that support and empower local communities and the disadvantaged, such as Streat (streat.com.au) and the Social Studio (thesocialstudio.org) in Melbourne, and Kyiv Social (plateitforward.org.au/kyiv-social) and Song Kitchen (songkitchen.com.au) in Sydney.

DOS & DON'TS

Do experience an Indigenous perspective by seeking out Aboriginal-owned tours and cultural experiences.

Don't photograph Aboriginal ceremonies and sites of significance without permission.

Don't throw cigarette butts onto the street or in the landscape; it's illegal and can cause bushfires.

Don't cuddle koalas; it's stressful for the animals and has been banned in most states.

LEAVE A SMALL FOOTPRINT

Spend more time in fewer destinations. Not only will you shrink your footprint, you'll form deeper connections and memories in the place you're in.

Research neighbourhoods in large cities and base yourself in one with good transport links and/or within walking distance of places that interest you.

Do not use plastic bottles – tap water is safe to drink almost everywhere; bring a reusable bottle.

Book tour operators known for their green credentials. Many are listed at Eco Tourism Australia (ecotourism.org.au).

GLEN BERLIN/SHUTTERSTOCK

SUPPORT LOCAL

Support businesses that are small and independent over large chains, whether Australian or international.

Feast sustainably by visiting local farmers markets (farmersmarkets.org.au), organic and biodynamic wineries (grenum.com), and eateries that champion local, seasonal produce and sustainably sourced coffee.

Buy souvenirs made by local artisans. When buying Aboriginal art, ensure that you are buying authentic items that support the artist and Indigenous communities (indigenousartcode.org).

CLIMATE CHANGE & TRAVEL

Lonely Planet urges all travellers to engage with their travel carbon footprint, which will mainly come from air travel. While there often isn't an alternative, travellers can look to minimise the number of flights they take, opt for newer aircrafts and use cleaner ground transport, such as trains.

One proposed solution—purchasing carbon offsets—unfortunately does not cancel out the impact of individual flights. While most destinations will depend on air travel for the foreseeable future, for now, pursuing ground-based travel where possible is the best course of action.

The UN Carbon Offset Calculator shows how flying impacts a household's emissions:

The ICAO's carbon emissions calculator allows visitors to analyse the CO2 generated by point-to-point journeys:

RESOURCES

ecotourism.org.au
indigenousartcode.org
parksaustralia.gov.au
australiangeographic.com.au

UNIQUE & LOCAL WAYS TO STAY

From basic camping by wild ocean beaches to living it up in art-crammed, inner-city boutique hotels, Australia's slumber options offer a gamut of experiences. Disconnect from the world in a designer eco-cabin, realign your chakras at a holistic spa retreat, or hire a campervan and hit the highway for an epic road trip along Australia's dazzling shores.

HOW MUCH FOR A...

Dorm bed **$27**

Unpowered campsite **$7–35+**

Tiny house **$300**

TARAS VYSHNYA/SHUTTERSTOCK

CAMPERVAN CRUISING

Spectacular scenery and well-maintained roads make Australia prime road-trip territory. If time is on your side, hiring a campervan offers maximum independence. Private holiday-park chains including G'day Parks (gdayparks.com.au) and Big4 (big4.com.au) have locations across Australia, and most are equipped with family-friendly perks such as pools, water parks, playgrounds and laundry facilities. If you plan on numerous stops, consider joining one of the chains, which offer member discounts. Bookings for popular national-park camping spots are often handled online by state departments, so plan ahead.

ART HOTELS

The closest thing to a gallery sleepover, art hotels lure with their caches of striking contemporary art. Among them are the Art Series (artserieshotels.com.au) suite of properties: midrange hotels in Melbourne, Brisbane and Adelaide named for (and featuring the work of) a particular modern Australian artist. Free collection tours are offered to guests.

SPA RETREATS

If the budget allows, retreat to a seductive spa resort, where luxurious digs and holistic treatments are set in lush surrounds. Top choices include Gaia (gaiaretreat.com.au) near Byron Bay and Daintree Eco Lodge (daintree-ecolodge.com.au; pictured) in Far North Queensland. The latter offers Aboriginal-inspired spa treatments.

ELISE HASSEY

TINY HOUSES

To unplug sustainably and fully immerse yourself in Australia's natural beauty, consider spending a few nights in a 'tiny house'. Also known as wilderness or eco-cabins, these pocket-size holiday abodes are often set in a secluded corner of a farm or other private land. Depending on the cabin, you might find yourself based beside a gurgling river, overlooking mountain ranges or the ocean, or within a stone's throw of a photogenic vineyard.

While these tiny houses may be off the grid, there's nothing rudimentary about many of them. Several are inspired by minimalist Scandinavian or Japanese design, with clean lines, contemporary finishes and panoramic floor-to-ceiling windows made for snug observation of passing wildlife and shifting light. Queen- or king-size beds and kitchen facilities are standard, along with higher-end compostable toilets and bathrooms with (hot) showers. Many also come with a fire pit, perfect for evening chats under star-soaked southern skies. Some crank up the luxe factor with a sauna, an outdoor bath or edibles from local artisan producers and winemakers.

For standout options, check out Unyoked (unyoked.co), Cabn (cabn.life), Shacky (shacky.com), Into the Wild Escapes (intothewildescapes.com) and Salty Cabins (saltycabins.com), which together cover destinations across eastern and southern Australia. Just remember to book well ahead: word is out and these petite sanctuaries are a big hit.

BOOKING

Booking accommodation in advance is highly recommended, especially for beach destinations during the Australian summer (December to February), at Easter and over long weekends. Booking ahead is also recommended during winter (June to August) in popular Queensland destinations including the Gold Coast, the Sunshine Coast, the Whitsundays and Port Douglas, when holidaymakers from the chillier southern states head north.

Airbnb (airbnb.com) Wide range of options, from city apartments to beach houses.

Green Getaways (greengetaways.com.au) Beautifully curated selection of stylish, eco-friendly accommodation across Australia.

Stayz (stayz.com.au) Holiday rentals and apartments, with many beachfront options.

Wotif (wotif.com) Hotels, resorts, serviced apartments, motels and more.

Great Small Hotels (greatsmallhotels.com) Boutique hotels, inns and resorts.

Luxury Lodges of Australia (luxurylodgesofaustralia.com.au) High-end accommodation, often with a focus on gourmet dining and natural beauty.

Hostelworld (hostelworldgroup.com) Find and book hostels across the country.

G'day Parks (gdayparks.com.au) Caravan and holiday parks throughout Australia.

CAMPING APPS

The free Campermate app is great for finding campsites and facilities around Australia. Other resources for campers include Camps Australia Wide (campsaustraliawide.com), and Hipcamp (hipcamp.com).

ESSENTIAL NUTS & BOLTS

SHOUTING

Shouting (buying a round of drinks) is common when out drinking with friends. If someone shouts you, it's considered polite to shout them back.

PUBLIC TOILETS

The National Public Toilet Map (toiletmap.gov.au) shows public-toilet locations, including disabled-access toilets.

BYO

Bring your own (BYO) drinks to a barbecue, and ask whether you should bring a plate (a dish or salad) to share.

FAST FACTS

Time Zone
GMT+8–10

Country Code
61

Electricity
230V/50Hz

GOOD TO KNOW

All visitors to Australia need a valid visa to enter the country (immi.homeaffairs.gov.au).

The legal drinking age in Australia is 18; public drinking laws vary between states.

Stand on the left on escalators and overtake on the right. Also, stay on the left when using stairs and footpaths (sidewalks).

If there's a queue, respect it, and apologise if you unintentionally cut in line.

In case of emergency, dial 000 (police, fire and ambulance).

ACCESSIBLE TRAVEL

Hotels commonly have lifts, ramps and rooms with accessible bathrooms, as do some serviced apartments and hostels. Accessible Accommodation (accessibleaccommodation.com) has a database.

Public transport in major cities and towns is usually wheelchair accessible, though some stations and stops are not; check official local transport websites.

Taxi companies offer WAV (wheelchair-accessible vehicles), which need to be requested ahead. Uber also has WAVs in some locations.

Tour operators with vehicles catering to travellers with limited mobility operate from most capital cities.

Parking bays for people with disabilities are generally available at shopping centres and other attractions.

Key attractions commonly provide access for those with limited mobility. Numerous places also address visual or aural impairments. WheelEasy (wheeleasy.org) has lists of accessible sights and activities.

Accessible dining can vary. It's always best to call the restaurant, cafe or pub in advance to make sure.

PUNCTUALITY
If you're running more than 10 minutes late to an appointment, text or call ahead to apologise.

ALCOHOL
Check whether restrictions apply when visiting remote communities. It may be illegal to have booze in your vehicle.

SMOKING
Smoking is banned in all indoor public spaces, and in some outdoor spaces where crowds congregate.

GOOD MANNERS
Australians are relatively casual and not especially big on formalities. Moderate swearing is common among friends and not always considered rude. Not saying 'please' and 'thank you' *is* considered rude, however. So too are intrusive questions about a person's age, weight or income.

PHOTOGRAPHY
For Indigenous Australians, photography can be highly intrusive, especially when camera-toting travellers arrive in remote communities. Photographing cultural places, practices and images, sites of significance and ceremonies may not be welcomed. Respect is essential. If in doubt, ask permission before taking any pictures.

FAMILY TRAVEL

Public transport is usually free for children aged under four or five. Older children usually pay half the adult fare.

Admission to some museums and galleries is free. Most paid attractions offer reduced-price tickets for kids and families.

Hotels can usually provide cots, with notice. Some boutique B&Bs and resorts do not welcome children.

Cafes, pizzerias and casual restaurants are child-friendly. Fine-dining restaurants usually discourage bringing babies or small kids.

Breastfeeding in public is widely accepted.

FILEDIMAGE/GETTY IMAGES

LGBTIQ+ TRAVELLERS

Same-sex marriages are legally recognised in Australia, and it's against the law to discriminate against someone on the basis of their sexual orientation.

Australians are generally open-minded, but you may experience some suspicion or hostility in more conservative neighbourhoods or regions. Inner Sydney and Melbourne have especially vibrant gay scenes.

Major events include the Sydney Gay and Lesbian Mardi Gras (mardigras.org.au), Melbourne's Midsumma Festival (midsumma.org.au) and Perth's PrideFEST (pridewa.com.au).

Online resources include Visit Gay Australia (visitgayaustralia.com.au), which lists LGBTIQ+ businesses across the country.

Index

F

000 Map pages

G

H

I

K

L

M

O

P

Q

T

U

V

W

Y

Z

000 Map pages

'Paying $31 for a half-dozen fresh Pacific oysters in Adelaide, then $9 en route to Turrakana/Tasman Peninsula (p210) a week later. Priceless.'

CHARLES RAWLINGS-WAY

'Having Litchfield National Park's Wangi Falls (p285) all to myself as the surrounding cliffs glowed scarlet at sunset was a trip highlight.'

SARAH REID

'I love meeting friends for a sunset picnic at Kings Park among the eucalypts, or catching a gig in the botanical gardens. A quintessential Perth experience.'

ROSAMUND BRENNAN

'That time when the driver-side door on my King Island rental car stopped opening and I spent three days climbing in and out of the window.'

ANDREW BAIN

'Exchanging tips in a dusty camp kitchen on the edge of a desert at night is what travelling's all about.'

STEVE WATERS

FROM LEFT: IAN CROCKER/SHUTTERSTOCK, ANASTAS STYLES/SHUTTERSTOCK

THIS BOOK

This 2nd edition of Lonely Planet's *Experience Australia* guidebook was researched and written by Andrew Bain, Rosamund Brennan, Emmylou Dzubiel, Charles Rawlings-Way, Sarah Reid and Steve Waters. Previous edition writers include Brett Atkinson, Fleur Bainger, Cristian Bonetto, Anthony Ham, Caoimhe Hanrahan-Lawrence, Trent Holden, Jessica Lockhart, Craig McLachlan, Mwende Mutuli Musau, Ariana Svenson, Phillip Tang and Josh West.

Destination Editor
Jessica Lockhart

Coordinating & Production Editor
James Appleton

Cartographer
Dorothy Davidson

Image Researcher
Carol Farrell

Assisting Editor
Helen Koehne

Cover Researcher
Sam Ubinas

Thanks Alison Killilea, Kellie Langdon, Jenna Myers, Darren O'Connell, Charlotte Orr, Gary Quinn, Saralinda Turner